Ecotourism

Since the first edition of the title, ecotourism has become a major phenomenon in tourism and society in many countries and regions throughout the world. The profusion of experiences has generated a variety of means of theorising, analysing and marketing ecotourism, all that have yet to be encompassed in one book.

Ecotourism fills the gap by synthesising the changes in thinking and society over the last decade. This third edition has been fully revised and updated to include:

- updated chapters addressing modern thought and discourse, including neoliberalism, consumer culture and quality management in the ecotourism industry;
- critical analysis drawn from a range of theoretical frameworks, which models and advances the thinking in ecotourism towards a socio-geographical analysis;
- new and international case studies from emerging markets such as China and Brazil.

Providing a critical introduction to the analysis of tourism from a sociological and geographical perspective, the title is essential reading for higher-level and graduate students and researchers in tourism, sociology and geography. It will also be of interest to environmental groups and practitioners.

Stephen Wearing is an Honorary Adjunct at the UTS Business School Sydney, Australia.

Stephen Schweinsberg is a Senior Lecturer in sustainable management at UTS Business School Sydney, Australia.

Ecotourism

Transitioning to the 22nd Century

Third Edition

Stephen Wearing and
Stephen Schweinsberg

Routledge
Taylor & Francis Group

LONDON AND NEW YORK

Third edition published 2019
by Routledge
2 Park Square, Milton Park, Abingdon, Oxon, OX14 4RN

and by Routledge
711 Third Avenue, New York, NY 10017

Routledge is an imprint of the Taylor & Francis Group, an informa business

First edition published by Butterworth-Heinemann 1999
Second edition published by Routledge 2009

British Library Cataloguing-in-Publication Data
A catalogue record for this book is available from the British Library

Library of Congress Cataloging-in-Publication Data
A catalog record has been requested for this book

ISBN: 978-1-138-20204-7 (hbk)
ISBN: 978-1-138-20210-8 (pbk)
ISBN: 978-1-315-47493-9 (ebk)

Typeset in Iowan Old Style
by Servis Filmsetting Ltd, Stockport, Cheshire

Contents

Preface to the Third Edition   vi

1   Sustainable ecotourism futures in a corporatised consumer society   1
2   If ecotourism is not just an activity but a philosophy, which philosophy?   13
3   Tourism development: government, industry, policy and planning   25
4   Ecotourism and natural resource management   43
5   Professionalisation and quality assurance   81
6   Interpretation as provocation   93
7   The community perspective   104
8   Marketing ecotourism: shaping expectations for a sustainable future   122
9   Could the presidential ecotourist please stand up?   136
10   Ecotourism's educational futures   146

Glossary   157
A guide to ecotourism agencies and other sustainable tourism resources   167
Index   169

Preface to the Third Edition

It has now been twenty years since the first edition of *Ecotourism: Impacts, potentials and possibilities* was published and ten years since the second edition. In that time ecotourism has become synonymous, for many in industry, academia and society, with ideas around environmental and social best practice in tourism management – a developmental pathway, if you will, to the nirvana of sustainable tourism.

Over the last decade or so, there has been a proliferation in academic texts and journals on ecotourism, works that have sought to articulate aspects of its management and operation in different localities throughout the world. The increasingly sophisticated nature of this academic dialogue is reflective of a realisation that ecotourism must be actively responsible for its own future. It is not possible to uncritically hold ecotourism up as the antithesis of unsustainable mass tourism; however, we equally cannot ignore the potential opportunities ecotourism may afford for the education of society around pressing environmental and social issues like climate change.

Ecotourism is, in the end, an industry grounded in neoliberal principles. As more and more remote areas of the world are in effect privatised and turned into the playgrounds of wealthy consumers, ecotourism is presented with opportunities for almost infinite growth. But is this a good thing? As recent commentary over the killing of a polar bear by cruise ship workers on the Svalbard Archipelago attests – ecotourism, when practiced correctly, can be a mechanism for environmental and social good. To understand, however, what correct practice means requires that we throw off the rose-coloured glasses that commonly characterise ecotourism commentary. We must be prepared to critically assess the sustainability merits of ecotourism and to ask the hard questions about ecotourism's future in the context of its past and present.

It is in this context that the third edition of *Ecotourism* is subtitled *Transitioning to the 22nd Century*. In the pages that follow, we will seek to explore aspects of the interplay between the neoliberal market-based expectations of the ecotourism industry and its traditional conservation and community focus. We will argue that the ecotourism industry has the opportunity, through alternative labels such as Community Based Ecotourism (CBET), to further refine its practices to achieve more sustainable outcomes. The third edition sees the addition of a new author, Stephen Schweinsberg. John Neil has moved on from his academic post to pursue a career with an ethics centre. There is a slight change in structure of this edition in that it provides fewer case studies and more references to the now-extensive work available online and in journals. This work is now more instantly accessible via the Internet and can provide readers with access to material on the ideas formulated or discovered on reading this book. Given the breadth and depth of new knowledge published in ecotourism since the first and second editions, it is believed this is a much more effective way of providing the basis for the readers learning in the 21st century and preparing for ecotourism's future in the 22nd century.

With warm (but not too warm, we hope) regards,
Stephen Wearing and Stephen Schweinsberg

Chapter 1

Sustainable ecotourism futures in a corporatised consumer society

Introduction

All tourism is situated in an environmental, social and economic world. Its development is both a product of that world as well as a major determinant of the future of the world. On a global scale there were over a billion international tourist arrivals in 2012 (Wood, 2017). Although ecotourism is still a fairly minor component of total global travel demand (Sharpley, 2006), it is nonetheless one of the fastest-growing tourism subsectors and is also often intrinsically aligned (or perhaps misaligned) to notions of sustainability and sustainable development. Since the 1990s there has been evidence of a greater level of academic and professional attention being afforded to the sustainability potential of tourism in its various forms. The International Year of Ecotourism in 2002 (Butcher, 2006; Global Development Research Centre, 2002; MacLaren, 2002), for example, afforded academics the opportunity to critically reflect on how ecotourism can be a mechanism for conservation and development, with a focus on the developing world in the early 21st century.

What will constitute ecotourism in the 22nd century is essentially unknowable. When Urry and Larsen (2011) included a discussion of tourism futures in the final chapter of *The Tourist Gaze 3.0*, they did so on the basis of a series of hypotheticals. Competing futures were identified as having consequences for the global tourism industry, and Urry and Larsen (2011) noted that different futures might lead to a fundamental realignment of what the tourist gaze can and indeed should be. Urry and Larsen (2011) argued that the tourist gaze in the future stands to be influenced by a range of stakeholder forces. In their second scenario for instance they identify a future that "is what many environmentalists argue for, namely a worldwide reconfiguration of economy and society around the idea of local sustainability" (Urry and Larsen, 2011, p. 234). In such a future, "values of community and eco responsibility could come to be viewed as more valuable than those of consumerism and unconstrained tourism mobility" (Urry and Larsen, 2011, p. 235). What does this mean for ecotourism?

The essential paradox of ecotourism is, and remains, its supposedly non--consumptive nature. Is it really possible to practice a form of consumption where one's goals extend beyond the simple relationship between the producers and consumers of products and services? Can ecotourism continue to grow in importance as part of a wider neoliberal setting, whilst instilling in its participants a reverence for the active preservation of the environment in its various forms? Fennell (2014) has recently written of the evolution of ecotourism since the 1980s. Ecotourism, Fennell (2014) notes, used to be defined

> by a rather restricted range of opportunities in a few charismatic destinations ... The market, typically bird watchers and scientists, was much more predictable ... [such] ecotourists were affiliated with conservation organisations; they invested heavily in the gear that would allow them to better capture these travel experiences; they travelled as ecotourists frequently; and they were long-staying, well educated, financially well off and allocentric in their travel desires.

Fennell (2014) goes on to note that

> the allure of this type of travel, no doubt stemming from the onset of [wider community discussions around sustainability and] sustainable development (see Diamantis & Ladkin, 1999; Hunter, 1995; Hunter, 1997) ... and the media hype generated from its coverage, gave way to an expanding market clamouring to take advantage of new alternative tourism activities in places that were virtually terra incognita.

The effect of this growth in consumer interest in so-called alternative tourism activities is that it is getting harder and harder to find truly unique places in the world. Whilst changing climactic conditions mean that, in a sense, the tourism environment is always evolving and opening up regions of the world to new forms of tourism endeavours (see for example Eijgelaar, Thaper, & Peeters, 2010; Lemelin, Dawson, & Stewart, 2013; Piggott-McKellar & McNamara, 2017 for a discussion of last chance tourism), the fact remains that tourism is now a truly global industry. Greenwood once described modern tourism as "the largest scale movement of goods, services and people that perhaps humanity has ever seen" (1989, p. 171 in Fletcher, 2011, p. 443).

One of the fastest-growing industry subsectors over the latter half of the twentieth century, and one that is closely connected to ecotourism, is marine or ocean tourism (Orams & Lück, 2015). Orams has defined marine tourism as "those recreational activities that involve travel away from one's place of residence and which have as their host or focus the marine environment (where the marine environment is defined as those waters which are saline and tide affected)" (1999, p. 9). In viewing this definition, it is important to acknowledge the breadth of marine environments that it implicitly encompasses. Additionally, we must keep in mind that marine tourism exists in the shadow of a range of other marine activities, which depending on one's circumstance and cultural perspective can perhaps lay equal claim to being sustainable uses of the world's common marine environments.

In this opening chapter we will seek to consider aspects of the place-based circumstance of ecotourism, with a particular focus on whale watching (and whale swimming). This discussion will draw on the work of Henri Lefebvre, who once argued that traditional understandings of "space have emerged from a traditional western, Cartesian logic to produce an abstract space – a scientific space" (Watkins, 2005,

p. 210). In contrast to these traditional positivist conceptualisations, Lefebvre argued that space should actually be conceptualised as lived. Space, as he noted in his influential work *The Production of Space*, is an amalgam of three interrelated forces: representations of space, spatial practices and spaces of representation (Lefebvre, 1991[1947]). This triadic conceptualisation of space does not seek to deny space's physical underpinning. Instead it seeks to lay a human stratum over the top of the physical.

By seeing space as lived we are able to conceptualise ecotourism's future in the 22nd century not in terms of some abstract future projection, but rather in the context of a constantly evolving network of stakeholder influences. In doing so we will suggest that discussions of tourism, and indeed sustainability more broadly, must be careful not to uncritically valorise principles such as intergenerational equity. To quote Butler, "what do we really know of the needs of future generations?" (Butler, 2015, p. 236). The work of Lee and Moscardo (2005) has demonstrated high levels of tacit agreement amongst ecotourists in intergenerational equity principles, whilst at the same time acknowledging scepticism amongst these same people as to the degree that their own travel behaviour impacted the environment. In the present work we will not argue against intergenerational, or indeed intragenerational, equity in tourism. Instead, we will suggest that greater attention needs to be given to the evolving networks of values-based complexities underpinning the situational linking of sustainability's economic, environmental and social forces.

Dredge has defined stakeholder networks in a destination management context as "sets of formal and informal social relationships that shape collaborative action between government, industry and civil society" (Dredge, 2006b, p. 270). The socially constructed nature of sustainable development necessitates that policy planners and industry engage with the "peculiarities of place and time" (Dredge, 2006a, p. 562). Whale tourism and commercial whaling are industries that are framed in relation to cultural and ethical norms (Cunningham, Huijbens, & Wearing, 2012). Ever since commercial whaling began in the 1800s, it has been subject to concerted debate at a national and international level as to its merits as a sustainable form of capitalism. Today many whale species, including the fin whale, sei whale, humpback whale and sperm whale, are recognised as being endangered by the Endangered Species Act or the IUCN (Sea World Parks and Entertainment, 2018). The near extinction of many whale species has led to whale watching being associated with so-called disaster capitalism in the second half of the twentieth century (Klein, 2007). In 1993 the International Whaling Commission recognised whale tourism as "a legitimate tourism industry which provided for the sustainable use of these animals" (Higham & Neves, 2015, p. 115).

The rapid escalation in the size of the global whale tourism industry has led academics to consider a range of management issues relating to tourist behaviour and education, community involvement in whale-based ecotourism development, tourist expenditure patterns and whale tourism's sustainability potential (e.g., Cunningham et al., 2012; Orams, 2000; Rowat & Engelhardt, 2007; Silva, 2015; Valentine et al., 2004). Cunningham et al. (2012) have argued that the sustainability of whale tourism is connected to the unviable long-term nature of commercial whale harvesting. However, with the rapid escalation in the number of sites around the world that allow closer and closer tourist contact with whales (including swimming with them), the sustainable future of whale watching is itself in doubt. Whether it is Tonga, Australia, Norway or Tahiti, the decision to permit whale watching and sometimes

3

whale swimming is made on the basis of the social construction of place. Massey (1995) has argued that place as a local (and unique) construct exists both in the context of larger geographical forces as well as in relation to societal perspective of an idealised past. It is through the past that we can see illustrated the place as lived.

Ecotourism as sustainable and situational capitalism

Dean MacCannell (1976, p. 1), in his pioneering work *The Tourist: A New Theory of the Leisure Class*, defined the tourist in two ways. In the first instance, the tourist "designates actual tourists: sightseers, mainly middle class, who are at this moment deployed throughout the entire world in search of experience". But at the same time for MacCannell, the tourist is perhaps "one of the best models available for modern-man-in-general"; the tourist becomes a metaphor for modern society's quest for meaning (1976, p. 1). McDonald and Wearing (2013) have described the act of consumption as something of a ubiquitous part of modern society. Telfer and Sharpley (2015) have identified how, in addition to providing for basic needs, the act of tourist travel fills a wider role in society, helping to position travellers within often complex and evolving sociological hierarchies.

Ecotourists, as we will show throughout this volume, have tended to be framed historically by academics around a series of simple and often binary demographic metrics (e.g., gender, level of education, relative wealth and length of stay) (Fennell, 2008). While such metrics were useful in early attempts to match particular ecotourist groupings with particular tourism activities, we must also recognise that the act of travel is to implicitly position one's self in a 'place-based' setting (Ryan, 2002). Wheeller (1993) and others have written on the way that eco-travellers have often been seduced into believing they are part of a new golden age of travel, and that by their engagement in such travel, their motivations and behaviours are in some way a cut above those of the standard traveller and the societies they are visiting.

The British sociologist Anthony Giddens has argued with respect to modernity that people are more reflexive, able to respond to evolving traditions of nature and reassess information to continue "to make life of it all" (Giddens, 1998, p. 119). The capacity for critical self-reflection has implications for ecotourists and ecotourism in the sense that the act of ethical purchasing can be said to be a form of life politics, one where "actions at the level of everyday life … connects to a wider social agenda, be it environmentalism, development or human rights" (Butcher, 2008, p. 315). While ecotourism offers opportunities for local conservation outcomes, what will complicate the industry's ability to achieve conservation outcomes is the heterogeneous and socially constructed nature of place.

The idea that place is perceivable as a sociological construct was a product of the late twentieth century. The influential human geographer Yi-Fu Tuan described the limitations of traditional positivist thinking around place in the following terms:

What we cannot say in an acceptable scientific language we tend to deny or forget. A geographer speaks as though his knowledge of space and place were derived exclusively from books, maps, aerial photographs, and structured surveys. He writes as though people were endowed with mind and vision but no other sense with which to apprehend the world and find meaning in it. He and the architect-planner tend to assume familiarity – the fact that we are oriented in space and home in place – rather than understand what "being in the world" is truly like. (Tuan, 1977, pp. 200–201)

For Tuan (1977) place goes far beyond the physical spatial realm to also encompass the personal and subjective realities of an individual's everyday life. It was the idea of place as lived that laid the conceptual foundation for Lefebvre's work to develop a threefold triad of conceptual space. Lefebvre argued that our lived experience of place is made up of three interrelated aspects – "representations of space (conceived space), spatial practices (perceived space), and spaces of representation (lived space)" (Watkins, 2005, p. 209). Capitalist interests, including tourism, often have the effect of creating a form of abstract space, one where the representations of space that Lefebvre proposed can create an assumed and commonly accepted reality (Lefebvre, 1991[1947]).

Tourism has been recognised as a form of global capitalism; in the case of ecotourism, it is one that has developed in the shadow of the environmental movement out of the need to create economic value out of something that otherwise would be left *in situ* (Fletcher, 2011). Through a range of marketing and other planning mechanisms, ecotourism has the potential to generate considerable economic value at a local and regional level. Figures cited by Cunningham et al. (2012) show that in 2008 "there were over 13 million [whale-watching] participants in over 119 countries, generating approximately US$2.1 billion" (p. 143). As Massey (1995) shows through the following example, however, the ability to generate financial returns does not guarantee by itself the sustainability of capitalism at the local level:

In 1993 there was a flurry of dispute over a proposed development in a small area in the Wye Valley on the borders of England and Wales. The proposal was to turn an existing set of buildings into 'a traditional farm' where local products, including crafts, would be sold, and where there would be a restaurant and car park. This scheme would, it was argued by its proponents, serve as a tourist attraction and bring in a source of income. The proposal aroused considerable, high profile opposition. The opposition, perhaps unusually in such cases, came in major part from newcomers to the area: professional people in the arts, the media, and suchlike who, presumably, had emigrated here from other parts of the country. Their opposition to the development centred on the argument that it was 'inappropriate', a term that implied agreement on the nature of the place. Their view of place, conditioned and manifested in their decision to move there, was clothed in quotations from Wordsworth. For them the place offered a romantic association with nature and what was termed 'seclusion' … This view of the place was [in turn] greeted with a mixture of anger and wry amusement by those locals who supported the scheme. For them, the place was where they had always lived and, crucially, where they had made their living, largely from farming. 'Nature' was the physical basis for agricultural activity. 'Seclusion' probably just meant long distances to suppliers and markets. (p. 185)

This idea of a perceived disconnect between tourists and sections of a society in a destination region causes challenges for the industry's sustainable management. Throughout the latter half of the twentieth century, Wearing et al. (2010) have observed an increased sophistication in academic understanding of the nature of tourism. Tourism has long been recognised as a mechanism for economic development, and early studies of the tourist experience sought to understand the nature of consumption as a discrete set of activities in some way separate from the world of work. Nonetheless, there is increasing evidence of the application of sociological theories to the study of tourism – research that aims to shed light on the "question of the relationship between Western modernity … and particularly [on] the issue of authenticity as a cultural motive" (Cohen & Cohen, 2012, p. 2179).

Cohen and Cohen (2012) draw on the work of Anderson (2012) to argue that from a sociological perspective a tourism place needs to be problematized and viewed relationally, not only as a "simple connection of parts, but as a convergence or merger of constituent parts that blur together for a moment in time" (Cohen & Cohen, 2012, pp. 2183–2184). Lefebvre's idea of place as a conceptual triad, one made up of three interrelated forces (representations of space, spatial practices and spaces of representation), has been proposed as a way of viewing the totality of place (Halfacree, 2006). For Lefebvre, space must be seen as lived if we are to avoid limiting our understanding of space as simply the "physical container for our lives rather than the structures we helped create" (Ross, 1998 in Watkins, 2005, p. 211).

In the present work we will promote the idea that tourists and other stakeholders are active agents in the creation of tourism space. Fletcher (2014, p. 3) has argued that whilst most people tend to view ecotourism "as a material process, a means by which economies and physical environments are transformed with the industry's expectations", it is at the same time possible to view ecotourism as a "cultural or discursive process, embodying a particular constellation of beliefs, norms and values that inform the industry's practice".

A constellation of beliefs and the evolving formulation of place – the case of whale tourism

Perhaps more than any other form of ecotourism, whale tourism transcends traditional geographical and place-based boundaries. Drawing on the influential work of the American ecologist and philosopher Garrett Hardin (Hardin, 1983), common pool resources have been defined as "indivisible local or global resources whose boundaries are difficult to delineate" (Briassoulis, 2002, p. 1066). Whether they be forests, wildlife or oceans, common pool resources "are used on the one hand by tourists in common with other tourists and, on the other, for tourists in common with other activities by tourists and locals" (Briassoulis, 2002, p. 1066). As creatures with a truly global migratory reach, whales are held by many to be unique sentient creatures – creatures for whom the very notion of sustainable human use is ethically suspect, and for whom our "ethical responsibility is simply to let whales alone" (Silva, 2015, p. 198). This is, however, often easier said than done.

Whaling has been practiced by many nations for hundreds of years. In Iceland, by way of example, whaling is said to have begun in the 1600s following the arrival of Basque hunters to the region (Bertulli et al., 2016). Modern whaling in Iceland then commenced around 1883; to this day Iceland, along with Japan and Norway, continue to practice so-called scientific whaling in defiance of the 1946 International Whaling Convention (IWC) (Bertulli et al., 2016) and the subsequent ban imposed by the IWC in 1986 (Cunningham et al., 2012). While governments along with nongovernment organizations (e.g., Greenpeace and the International Fund for Animal Welfare) continue to debate the merits of scientific whaling, in the early 1980s, so-called Aboriginal Subsistence Whaling was instigated by the International Whaling Commission in recognition of the important role that whale products play in the nutritional and cultural lives of native peoples (see International Whaling Commission, 2018).

Throughout the rest of this section our focus is not with Aboriginal Subsistence Whaling per se. Rather, we use the example of indigenous whaling simply to emphasise that as much as whales are a global resource, the history of their utilisation is very much tied to the specifics of local place as lived. For example, whaling has a long history with the villagers of the South Pacific island of Tonga, particularly in the northern island group of Vava'u, prior to the banning of whaling by royal decree in 1978 (Orams, 2001). For many years tourism has been recognised as the "star on the horizon" in Tonga (Keller & Swaney, 1998, p. 24 in Orams, 2001, p. 128). Perhaps nowhere has this star power been more evident than in the case of whale tourism. In 2006 there were "more than 9,800 whale-watching participants in Tonga, representing annual average growth of 20% since 1998" (IFAW, 2008, p. 5). Similarly, in Japan we have evidence of a gradual shift away from a sole focus on commercial harvesting and towards a focus on tourism, but one that has its foundation in nationalistic sensibilities and economic recovery post-WW2 (Cunningham et al., 2012). Today, with whale-watching industries based out of Ogasawara, the non-consumptive use of whales as a tourism resource in Japan has an annual economic value in excess of US$22 million.

Higham and Hopkins (2015) have highlighted how the global/local nexus around whaling has seen prevailing ecological modernization discourses applied to the management of whaling at a local level. So-called civic environmentalism has led in many instances to a downplaying of the cumulative impact of whale tourism (and in particular whale swimming), as well as to a popular demonization of extractive whale harvesting. There would doubtless be many readers of the present work who would suggest that this is not necessarily a bad thing. We are all a product of our own histories, and our views on the sustainability (or not) of ecotourism will evolve on the basis of circumstance and the information we receive.

For example, Stephen Wearing has recently retired from full-time academia following more than three decades of work at the University of Technology Sydney, the University of Newcastle and a number of other Australian and overseas institutions. Stephen Wearing's interest in tourism and its sustainability potential developed out of his active involvement in wilderness campaigns in Australia in the 1970s and 80s (see Law, 2001; Wilderness Society, 1983). Works like Edward Abbey's *The Monkey Wrench Gang* (1985) and Peter Stinger's *Animal Liberation* (1995) inspired Stephen to pursue academic and volunteer work to challenge the dominant neoliberal discourses of the time, which focused on short-term extraction of natural resources. Stephen Wearing's interest in ecotourism was in many respects a natural progression from this earlier environmental work, with ecotourism seen as a mechanism to potentially save nature through its utilitarian value. While initially seeing ecotourism as the antithesis of other primarily extractive industries like mining, whaling and hydroelectricity, Stephen's views have recently become more critical. He now holds a view that perhaps what we are observing is a cynical attempt, in many neoliberalist societies, to forge arguments of environmental symbiosis into the encroachment of ecotourism into high-value natural areas that are best left untouched.

The world where Stephen Wearing began to investigate ecotourism is in many respects far removed from the realities of modern business academia, where the present work is positioned. As Boyle (2017) has noted, the integration of sustainability principles into tertiary curriculums frequently suffers on the basis of a range of issues, including lack of educator proficiency, low levels of staff interest, student apathy and clashes with mainstream models of business education. In contrast to Stephen Wearing, Stephen Schweinsberg has come to study ecotourism in a business school context from a background in human geography. Since entering the University of Technology Sydney (UTS) Business School as a PhD student in 2004, Stephen Schweinsberg has become increasingly cynical, not only with the apparently never-ending intractability of sustainability debates, but also with the attempt to simplistically valorise notions of intergenerational and intragenerational equity at the expense of a recognition of place-based complexity.

If sustainability is indeed based on values, then who are we to suggest a universally agreeable outcome to discussions over whale tourism's, or indeed any form of ecotourism's, sustainability potential? Fabien Cousteau recently argued to the World Travel and Tourism Council that "I look forward to the day when there is no sustainable tourism, just tourism" (PATA, 2016, p. 1). This statement, we suggest, was made to draw attention to the apparent disinterest amongst many travellers in pursuing more responsible travel behaviour. The merits of the utopia that Cousteau argues for, where ecotourism sits in harmony with the world around it and thus no longer requires the tag 'sustainable', are certainly attractive. At the same time, however, we would suggest that the nature of tourism's relationship to the environment that surrounds it has not been seen for the complex interaction that it is.

All forms of industry are situated in a place, and we cannot assume the nature of future generations' expectations of their environmental inheritance. The related industries of whaling and whale tourism are subject to the various influences of governments, environmental organizations, whaling enterprises, communities, etc. Together these and other stakeholder groups propagate what Lefebvre referred to as representations of society, "those dominant symbols, codifications and abstract representations" that together define popular understanding of space (Watkins, 2005, p. 212). Each of these stakeholder groups is, itself, the product of complex regional-specific histories. For example, since its initial development as a tourism destination in the 1980s, the Tongan island of Vava'u has been subject to the effects of highly seasonal tourist flows and rapid tourism infrastructure development (see Van der Veeken et al., 2016). In the context of these and other constraints it becomes difficult to criticise the decision to promote whale swimming as a mechanism to differentiate oneself from other destinations; this is in spite of the challenges inherent in providing closer and more intimate tourist encounters with whales, whilst also protecting the very resource on which encounters are based.

Conclusion

As Massey (1995) has suggested, "the claims and counter-claims about the present character of a [future] place depend in almost all cases on particular rival interpretations of its past" (p. 185). We are currently living in a past for a 22nd-century future.

In the present work we will argue for the need for a renewed focus on ecotourism's potential as an environmental management tool. While we hope that a new wave of activism can encourage the development of greater societal awareness of the importance of preserving nature, we equally will be circumspect with respect to aligning the sustainability tag with an industry that in some respects is nothing more than consumption rebadged in a sustainability age.

Further reading

These three journal articles explore various definitions of ecotourism by reviewing stakeholders' perspectives and classic and recent literature.

Conway, T. & Cawley, M. (2016). Defining ecotourism: evidence of provider perspectives from an emerging area. *Journal of Ecotourism, 15*(2), 122–138.

Fennell, D. A. (2001). A content analysis of ecotourism definitions. *Current Issues in Tourism, 4*(5), 403–421.

Donohoe, H. M. & Needham, R. D. (2006). Ecotourism: the evolving contemporary definition. *Journal of Ecotourism, 5*(3), 192–210.

Hector Ceballos-Lascuráin was a pioneer of the ecotourism movement. In this chapter he outlines the emergence of ecotourism, its potential benefits and impacts, and his views on how sustainable development using tourism can be best achieved.

Ceballos-Lascuráin, H. (1993). Ecotourism as a worldwide phenomenon. In K. Lindberg & D. E. Hawkins (Eds.), *Ecotourism: A Guide for Planners and Managers* (pp. 12–14). North Bennington: Ecotourism Society.

Question

If tourism is central in most countries as a form of global capitalism, where does that leave ecotourism?

References

Abbey, E. (1985). *The Monkey Wrench Gang*. Salt Lake City: Dream Garden Press.

Anderson, J. (2012). Relational places: The surfed wave as assemblage and convergence. *Environment and Planning D: Society and Space, 30*(4), 570–587.

Bertulli, C. G., Leeney, R. H., Barreau, T., & Matassa, D. S. (2016). Can whale-watching and whaling co-exist? Tourist perceptions in Iceland. *Journal of the Marine Biological Association of the United Kingdom, 96*(4), 969–977.

Boyle, A. (2017). 26 Integrating sustainability in the tourism curriculum: Dilemmas and directions. In P. Benckendorff & A. Zehrer (Eds.), *Handbook of Teaching and Learning in Tourism* (pp. 389–401). Cheltenham: Edward Elgar.

Briassoulis, H. (2002). Sustainable tourism and the question of the commons. *Annals of Tourism Research, 29*(4), 1065–1085.

Sustainable ecotourism futures

Butcher, J. (2006). The United Nations International Year of Ecotourism: A critical analysis of development implications. *Progress in Development Studies, 6*(2), 146–156.

Butcher, J. (2008). Ecotourism as life politics. *Journal of Sustainable Tourism, 16*(3), 315–326.

Butler, R. (2015). Sustainable tourism: The undefinable and unachievable, pursued by the unrealistic? In T. Singh (Ed.), *Challenges in Tourism Research*. Bristol: Channel View Publications.

Cohen, E. & Cohen, S. A. (2012). Current sociological theories and issues in tourism. *Annals of Tourism Research, 39*(4), 2177–2202.

Creswell, T. (2009). Place. Retrieved from http://booksite.elsevier.com/brochures/hugy/SampleContent/Place.pdf.

Cunningham, P., Huijbens, E., & Wearing, S. (2012). From whaling to whale watching: Examining sustainability and cultural rhetoric. *Journal of Sustainable Tourism, 20*(1), 143–161.

Diamantis, D. & Ladkin, A. (1999). The link between sustainable tourism and ecotourism: A definitional and operational perspective. *The Journal of Tourism Studies, 10*(2), 35–46.

Dredge, D. (2006a). Networks, conflict and collaborative communities. *Journal of Sustainable Tourism, 14*(6), 562–581.

Dredge, D. (2006b). Policy networks and the local organisation of tourism. *Tourism Management, 27*(2), 269–280.

Eijgelaar, E., Thaper, C., & Peeters, P. (2010). Antarctic cruise tourism: The paradoxes of ambassadorship, "last chance tourism" and greenhouse gas emissions. *Journal of Sustainable Tourism, 18*(3), 337–354.

Fennell, D. (2008). *Ecotourism*. London: Routledge.

Fennell, D. (2014). *Ecotourism*. London: Routledge.

Fletcher, R. (2011). Sustaining tourism, sustaining capitalism? The tourism industry's role in global capitalist expansion. *Tourism Geographies, 13*(3), 443–461.

Fletcher, R. (2014). *Romancing the Wild: Cultural Dimensions of Ecotourism*: Duke University Press.

Giddens, A. (1998). An interview with Anthony Giddens (Interviewer S. Loyal). *Irish Journal of Sociology, 8*, 113–123.

Global Development Research Centre. (2002). International Year of Ecotourism 2002. Retrieved from www.gdrc.org/uem/eco-tour/2002/yearecoturism2002.html.

Halfacree, K. (2006). Rural space: Constructing a three-fold architecture. In Cloke, P., Marsden, T., & Mooney, P. (Eds.), *Handbook of Rural Studies* (pp. 44–62). London: SAGE.

Hardin, G. (1983). The tragedy of the commons. In T. O'Riorden & R. Turner (Eds.), *An Annotated Reader in Environmental Planning and Management* (pp. 288–298). Oxford: Pergamon Press.

Higham, J. & Hopkins, D. (2015). Wildlife tourism "call it consumption". In C. Hall, S. Gossling, & D. Scott (Eds.), *The Routledge Handbook of Tourism and Sustainability* (pp. 280–293). London: Routledge.

Higham, J. & Neves, K. (2015). Whales, tourism and manifold capitalist fixes: New relationships with the driving force of capitalism. In K. Markwell (Ed.), *Animals and Tourism: Understanding Diverse Relationships* (Vol. 67, pp. 109–127). Bristol: Channel View.

Hunter, C. (1995). On the need to re-conceptualise sustainable tourism development. *Journal of Sustainable Tourism, 3*(3), 155–165.

Hunter, C. (1997). Sustainable tourism as an adaptive paradigm. *Annals of Tourism Research, 24*(4), 850–867.

IFAW. (2008). Whale Watching Tourism in the Kingdom of Tonga: a report for IFAW and Opérations Cétacés (Prepared by Simon O'Connor). Melbourne: Economists at Large.

International Whaling Commission. (2018). Aboriginal Subsistence Whaling. Retrieved from https://iwc.int/aboriginal.

Klein, N. (2007). *The Shock Doctrine: The Rise of Disaster Capitalism*. London: Allen Lane.

Law, G. (2001). *History of the Franklin River Campaign 1976–83*. Hobart: The Wilderness Society.

Lee, W. H. & Moscardo, G. (2005). Understanding the impact of ecotourism resort experiences on tourists' environmental attitudes and behavioural intentions. *Journal of Sustainable Tourism, 13*(6), 546–565.

Lefebvre, H. (1991[1947]). *The Production of Space* (Vol. 142). Oxford: Blackwell.

Lemelin, H., Dawson, J., & Stewart, E. J. (2013). *Last Chance Tourism: Adapting Tourism Opportunities in a Changing World*. London: Routledge.

MacCannell, D. (1976). *The Tourist: A New Theory of the Leisure Class*. New York: Schocken Books.

McDonald, M. & Wearing, S. (2013). *Social Psychology and Theories of Consumer Culture: A Political Economy Perspective*. London: Routledge.

MacLaren, F. (2002). The international year of ecotourism in review. *Journal of Sustainable Tourism, 10*(5), 443–448.

Massey, D. (1995). *Places and Their Pasts*. Paper presented at the History workshop journal.

Orams, M. (1999). *Marine Tourism: Development, Impacts and Management*. London and New York: Routledge.

Orams, M. (2000). Tourists getting close to whales, is it what whale-watching is all about? *Tourism Management, 21*(6), 561–569.

Orams, M. (2001). From whale hunting to whale watching in Tonga: A sustainable future? *Journal of Sustainable Tourism, 9*(2), 128–146.

Orams, M. & Lück, M. (2015). Marine systems and tourism. In C. M. Hall, S. Gössling, & D. Scott (Eds.), *The Routledge Handbook of Tourism and Sustainability* (pp. 170–182). London: Routledge.

Pacific Asia Travel Association (PATA). (2016) WTTC: Take Part in Shaping Sustainable Tourism Future, www.pata.org/wttc-take-part-in-shaping-sustainable-tourism-future-1-week-left-to-apply-for-the-awards/.

Piggott-McKellar, A. E. & McNamara, K. E. (2017). Last chance tourism and the Great Barrier Reef. *Journal of Sustainable Tourism, 25*(3), 397–415.

Rowat, D. & Engelhardt, U. (2007). Seychelles: A case study of community involvement in the development of whale shark ecotourism and its socio-economic impact. *Fisheries Research, 84*(1), 109–113.

Ryan, C. (2002). *The Tourist Experience*. London: Cassell.

Sea World Parks and Entertainment. (2018). Endangered Whales. Retrieved from https://seaworld.org/Animal-Info/Animal-Bytes/Mammals/Endangered%20Whales.

Sharpley, R. (2006). Ecotourism: A consumption perspective. *Journal of Ecotourism, 5*(1–2), 7–22.

Silva, L. (2015). How ecotourism works at the community-level: The case of whale-watching in the Azores. *Current Issues in Tourism, 18*(3), 196–211.

Singer, P. (1995). *Animal Liberation*. New York: Random House.

Telfer, D. J. & Sharpley, R. (2015). *Tourism and Development in the Developing World*. London: Routledge.

Tuan, Y. F. (1977). *Space and Place: The Perspective of Experience*. Minneapolis: University of Minnesota Press.

Urry, J. & Larsen, J. (2011). *The Tourise Gaze 3.0*. Los Angeles: SAGE.

Valentine, P. S., Birtles, A., Curnock, M., Arnold, P., & Dunstan, A. (2004). Getting closer to whales: Passenger expectations and experiences, and the management of swim with dwarf minke whale interactions in the Great Barrier Reef. *Tourism Management*, *25*(6), 647–655.

Van der Veeken, S., Calgaro, E., Munk Klint, L., Law, A., Jiang, M., de Lacy, T., & Dominey-Howes, D. (2016). Tourism destinations' vulnerability to climate change: Nature-based tourism in Vava'u, the Kingdom of Tonga. *Tourism and Hospitality Research*, *16*(1), 50–71.

Watkins, C. (2005). Representations of space, spatial practices and spaces of representation: An application of Lefebvre's spatial triad. *Culture and Organization*, *11*(3), 209–220.

Wearing, S., Stevenson, D., & Young, T. (2010). *Tourist Cultures: Identity, Place and the Traveller*. Los Angeles: SAGE.

Wheeller, B. (1993). Sustaining the ego. *Journal of Sustainable Tourism*, *1*(2), 121–129.

Wilderness Society. (1983). *Franklin Blockade: By the Blockaders*. Hobart: Wilderness Society.

Wood, M. E. (2017). *Sustainable Tourism on a Finite Planet: Environmental, Business and Policy Solutions*. London: Routledge.

Chapter 2

If ecotourism is not just an activity but a philosophy, which philosophy?

Introduction

Since the publication of *Ecotourism: Impacts, Potentials and Possibilities* (Wearing & Neil, 2009) there has been evidence of an expanding body of scholarship that has sought to consider two fundamental questions. What is the nature of ecotourism as an activity? And what is the philosophical relationship between ecotourism and the broader, natural, sociocultural and economic environment in which it is situated (Cobbinah, 2015; Fennell & Nowaczek, 2010; Weaver, 2005)? Both issues are central to our understanding of the sustainability of an industry like ecotourism. Butler (Butler, 1999) has suggested that ecotourism's sustainability credentials lie in its ability to link conservation and development. In this way the nature of the activity is key; it is more than a holiday – it is also perhaps a philosophy and a model of development (Butler, 1999).

In the present chapter we will explore the evolution of some of the environmental philosophies that lie behind discussions of ecotourism sustainability. Przecławski (1979 in Przecławski 2005) drew attention to the evolutionary nature of tourism space and to the effect of the context in which one's ontological perspectives on tourism are developed. So often the sustainability (or not) of ecotourism is simplified to a series of static binary questions: whether ecotourism is successful in offering opportunities for development within the limits set by conservation and environmental metrics, or whether setting conservation limits on the growth of ecotourism will inadvertently limit the opportunities for economic growth afforded to host communities (Butcher, 2009). These and other similar questions have merit and will likely continue to be debated by scholars into the future. However, we would argue that the trading off of environmental, social, economic and other metrics of sustainability can have the effect of masking much wider temporal, systems-based complexities. McCool (in McCool, Butler, Buckley, Weaver, & Wheeler, 2015) argues that complex tourism systems are underpinned by a range of forces or perturbations emanating from outside and inside the system in question. For this reason, this chapter places ecotourism within its broader historical context in order to chart some of the major philosophical and social currents that have contributed to its development.

The evolving philosophical foundations of ecotourism sustainability

For many, ecotourism is a form of tourism synonymous with the notion of sustainability. Edgell describes ecotourism as a "subset of the larger term 'sustainable tourism' – as are, for example, geotourism, pro-poor tourism, responsible tourism, and ethical tourism" (Edgell, 2016, p. 208). Involving, as Ceballos-Lascuráin (1988, p. 13) once noted, "travelling to relatively undisturbed or uncontaminated natural areas with the specific objective of studying, admiring, and enjoying the scenery with its plants and animals, as well as any existing cultural manifestations (both past and present) found in those areas", ecotourism is a form of tourism that is often perceived to encapsulate all that is good about tourism's interactions with the natural and social world. While the work of Fennell (2012) emphasises the environmental or nature-based setting of most ecotourism operations, it is important to always observe that ecotourism is something more than simply nature based. It is a form of tourism that also ideally encapsulates a range of ethical and educational dimensions. It is a form of tourism that will be sustainable only when it unites a range of different stakeholder interests, including local communities, tourism operators, government and tourists in a symbiotic relationship (Tsaur, Lin, & Lin, 2006). The interaction of these forces is highly context specific. Whilst historically ecotourism has been framed by academia primarily as a Western construct (see for example, Cater, 2006), in recent years there has been greater exploration of what ecotourism is in other settings including China (Cheng, Wong, Wearing, & McDonald, 2017).

Wen and Xue (2008 in Cheng et al., 2017) observe that the ecological values that underpin ecotourism tend to differ between Eastern and Western cultures:

> Western concepts of ecotourism view it as an experience, occurring in the present moment within the natural environment. The Chinese view ecotourism as an experience of the unification between nature and humanity and the opportunity to connect with one's past. (p. 417)

While the embryonic study of ecotourism in China is not the focus of the present chapter, it is nonetheless important to observe the close interaction between ecotourism as an activity and broader environmental philosophies, because they manifest themselves in different cultural settings. Ecotourism owes much of its early success to the rise of the environmental movement and to the urgency in much of society to reassess our relationship to the environment. Historically ecotourism has been demarcated from wider nature-based tourism (see Coghlan & Buckley, 2012) on account of an education agenda that seeks to instil in ecotourists a long-term stewardship mind-set. The environmental education agenda of ecotourism industries still influences the creation of eco-certification and standards programs like those practiced by industry organisations like Ecotourism Australia. Here the aim is to "improve quality and sustainability by practicing minimal impact tourism operations, reducing non-renewable resource consumption, fostering the use of environmental resources and alternative energy, and promoting recycling practices" (Newsome & Moore, 2015, p. 266). In recent years the scope of ethics in relation to ecotourism has expanded, with an increased focus on the maintenance of cultural resources (see Cobbinah, 2015). Social elements of ecotourism are now prominent in the definition presented by the International Ecotourism Society – "responsible travel to natural areas that conserves the environment and improves the well-being of local people" (see Edgell, 2016, p. 208).

The broadening of the scope of what ecotourism does and does not encompass has caused challenges to its sustainable operation. The rapid growth of community-based ecotourism (CBET) (Jones, 2005; Reimer & Walter, 2013) has led to increased scholarship around the development of pro-environmental behaviour amongst residents (Liu et al., 2014). Also in the area of CBET Sakata and Prideaux (2013) have explored industry governance arrangements, noting the way that inequitable power relations between local and external actors can lead to low community participation. More broadly Butcher (2009, p. 254) has observed how the classical circular logic of ecotourism sustainability – "revenue through ecotourism means that conservation is incentivised, and conservation ensures that the ecotourist revenue will keep on coming" – is limited in that it assumes a degree of stasis in human aspiration. What makes ecotourism destinations attractive for the majority of predominantly Western ecotourists is the low level of development in host areas relative to traditional mass tourism alternatives. But what of the development aspirations of the host communities that are reliant on ecotourism for economic growth? Should they in effect be constrained to meet ecotourist expectations?

Wood (2017) provided a fascinating insight into the complexities of juggling often-competing stakeholder interests through a case study of the Huaorani Ecolodge in Ecuador. Founded over twenty years ago through a partnership between industry and local groups, the lodge has helped to preserve more than 135,000 hectares of rainforest. While Wood (2017) acknowledges the way that ecotourism has incentivised conservation in Ecuador, she also notes that the good work is now under threat from moves at a national level to promote oil exploration in the region. The oil companies, Wood (2017) notes, come with a range of material incentives for local villages. At the same time, however, community leaders are forced to make a choice between tradition and progress. It forces ecotourism managers to make a "devil's bargain" (see Wood, 2017, p. 262) and to reconcile their own beliefs and values with an idea from Macnaghten and Urry (1998): that there is no such thing as a single nature, only multiple contested natures that reflect the societal concerns and values of their proponents.

Exchanging value(s)

Questions of value are therefore central to considerations of the (often competing) conceptions and practices of ecotourism towards the natural world. The values we as human beings attach to the environment are not homogenous, nor are they necessarily static with respect to changing normative standards in society. Godfrey-Smith (1980) identifies two primary ways in which value is assessed in Western society. If the value that something is said to hold is a means to a valued end then it is designated as being of 'instrumental' value. 'Intrinsic value' on the other hand is value that exists in its own right, for its own sake.

What is central here is the ethic that such ideas and values underpin.

- An ethic of 'use': this is the normative or dominant mode of how human beings relate to nature, where nature is viewed predominantly as a set of resources that humanity is free to employ for its own distinct ends. It is an instrumental and anthropocentric view.

- An ethic of 'nature': this holds that nonhuman entities are of equal value to the human species. It is broadly intrinsic and ecocentric.

An ethic of use begins from a human locus, and it is this univocal perspective that is often described as anthropocentrism. Such a view allows nature no intrinsic value, in itself and for itself, as its value lies only in satisfying human needs and desires (Hay, 2002). Depending on its context, ecotourism is certainly not immune to the effect of anthropocentric forces. Ryan et al. (2000) for instance observes how ecotourists visiting the Fogg Dam Conservation Reserve in the Northern Territory (Australia) are motivated primarily by affective rather than cognitive learning experience. The primarily ocular nature of the Fogg Dam experience means that the maximisation of spectacle is vital, and the choice of what to observe (or not observe) is made by the tourist in the context of the tourism infrastructure on-site. The idea expressed by Ryan et al. (2000) that tourists visiting Fogg Dam might be characterised as flâneur (see also Wearing & Wearing, 1996; Wearing, Stevenson, & Young, 2009) makes it easy to see how complicated it often is to equate nature as having intrinsic value in its own right. A flâneur is someone characterisable as being static in their interpretation; "his lens and thus his understanding are unchanging" (Wearing et al., 2009, p. 8). For tourists, according to Ryan et al. (2000), there is primarily an instrumental justification that is used to argue for the preservation and conservation of nature. Godfrey-Smith (1980) places such justifications in four main categories:

- the aesthetic/spiritual (the 'cathedral' argument) – where nature is valued for providing spiritual revival and aesthetic delight;
- the biological/biodiversity (the 'silo' argument) – where nature is valued for its stockpile of genetic diversity;
- the scientific (the 'laboratory' argument) – where nature is valued for scientific inquiry;
- and the athletic (the 'gymnasium' argument) – where nature is valued for tourism and recreation (pp. 56–71).

Each of these and other conceptualisations of nature are framed according to the desires and needs of the tourists in question. Slavson (p. 20 in Rojek, 1993, p. 47) has noted that a tourist's desires must be "regulated by society or [it] becomes a menace". Each form of tourism will accordingly have its foundation in a "system of social activities and signs which locate the particular tourist practices" (Urry & Larsen, 2011, p. 3). Over the last thirty or so years the practices of ecotourists, including nature-based educational activities, have come to define a particular form of touristic practice. Przecławski (2005) identifies that human beings exist in a multifaceted physical, social and cultural space. How this space functions is a product of the dialogue that exists between stakeholders. A dialogue is framed on the basis of the interplay of five elements: people, subject, condition, form and phases (Przecławski, 2005). In this way ecotourism will always, it is suggested, have a focus on utilitarian outcomes and the elicitation of certain emotional and other outcomes for participants. At the same time, however, the subject of the dialogue between ecotourists and other stakeholders must be seen in the context of the conditions and context in which the dialogue occurs (Przecławski, 2005).

Over the last thirty to forty years the growth in the global ecotourism industry has been paralleled in a sense by the rise of ecocentric philosophies and other manifestations of the so-called green movement (for a detailed critical analysis of the historical formulation of green environmental philosophies, see Hay, 2002). The broad philosophical foundation of ecocentrism can be said to encompass the following elements:

- a belief in humanities and harmony with nature;
- attempts to alleviate (or eliminate) negative human impacts on the environment – atmospheric pollution, land degradation, etc.;
- arguments for all life having its own specific intrinsic value;
- arguments against economic growth and consumerism;
- embracing of alternative technology, such as solar power, passive energy systems and recycling;
- the devolution of political and institutional structures;
- the promotion of minority, oppressed and marginalised groups into the political process.

Ecocentrism is therefore a broad philosophical position that attempts to give validity to intrinsic value in nature and that is holistic, is strongly grounded in the biology and ecology of nature and rejects the view that the world is divided into mutually exclusive parts. Pepper (1996) cites four eras in recent history when the public voiced its deep-felt concerns for the quality of the environment – the 1890s, 1920s, late 1950s and the early 1970s. To these years we could also add the Chernobyl disaster (1985), the Exxon Valdez oil spill (1989), the global warming concerns of recent decades and the systematic land clearing practices that reached their peak in the late 1980s and 1990s and continue unabated to the present day.

Many existing works have sought to link popular interest in ecotourism to the birth of the environmental movement in the 1960s and 1970s (Holden, 2008; Weaver, 2011). The environmental movement and popular works including Rachel Carson's (1962/2002) *Silent Spring* posed a fundamental challenge to the priority of a solely human-centred value system. By advocating for increased attention to the idea of an ecosphere-centred view of the world, the tourism industry was in effect tasked to develop new forms of activity that would be commensurate with this new way of thinking. The type of behaviours, or ethics, appropriate to such a view can be interpreted in varied ways and continue to be debated to the present day. In recent years, the fundamental question of what or who is deserving of moral consideration in an ecotourism context has received widespread coverage in a range of areas including animal ethics (Burns, Macbeth, & Moore, 2011; Fennell, 2013; Fennell & Nowaczek, 2010) and tourist-host relations (Hinch, 1998). While such topics have become the bread and butter of academia, Wearing and Wearing (2016) debate whether ecotourism, as an industry, is actually changing the way society interacts with nature. They find that ecotourism is perhaps best "viewed as an eco-utilitarian activity that is enabling for a population that is seeking to do something for the environment; it is not an overall solution [for all environmental problems] but a mechanism that provides a link for an increasingly neoliberalised society, to one supportive of nature" (Wearing & Wearing, 2016, p. 218).

While at its core eco-development is about the harmonisation of economic, social and environmental concern (Fennell, 2002), finding the correct balance has seen the industry aligned to a myriad of ideological positions – ecocentrism, technocentrism, shallow and deep ecology, etc. (Acott, Trobe, & Howard, 1998). Our principal thesis in this chapter is that the sustainability of ecotourism must be conceptualised as a wicked problem, one devoid of simple framings and one where traditional ideological philosophies can be limiting in their scope. Therefore, while we do not dispute Wearing et al.'s (2009, pp. 82–83) assertion that the use of philosophies like the idea that "ecocentrism to prolong the integrity of natural ecosystems would be in sharp conflict with the predominantly instrumental uses of nature and the overpowering Western utilitarian ideology", we would also argue that when one moves away from extreme ecocentric ideologies like deep ecology, there exists substantial opportunity for grey space. As a case in point, let us briefly consider the case of the American economist Robert Solow who in December 1987 was awarded the Nobel Prize for Economics. Over the ensuing thirty years, Robert Solow has often been tagged along with other economic luminaries as the enemy of the environmental movement. The growth mantra in neoliberalism, which Solow and others often advocated, combined with misinterpreted observations, such as "the world can, in effect, get along without natural resources, so exhaustion is just an event, not a catastrophe" (Solow, 1974, p. 11) led to a perfect storm of stakeholder conflict. If one, however, delves into Solow's work in more detail, it becomes apparent that the earlier quoted idea forms part of a much more complex argument around the substitutability of resources. Solow observes that

> As you would expect, the degree of substitutability is also a key factor. If it is very easy to substitute other factors for natural resources, then there is in principle 'no problem'. **The world can, in effect get along without natural resources, so exhaustion is just an event, not a catastrophe** ... If on the other hand, real output per unit of resources is effectively bounded – cannot exceed some upper limit of productivity, which in turn is not too far from where we are now – then catastrophe is unavoidable. (Solow, 1974, p. 11)

At the heart of all ecotourism and other sustainable tourism management debates is the question of how we use our resources. The resources of the world are limited, however up to a point, they are potentially substitutable through the pursuit of more efficient business processes. Technological fixes, however, will not be palatable to all. Sustainable growth as a concept is for many an oxymoron on the basis of an argument that there is "no evidence of a decoupling between GDP [gross domestic product] growth in the aggregate and the absolute material throughput of the economic system" (Capital Institute, 2010). At the same time, however, we must acknowledge the inherently values-driven nature of all sustainability debates. Shields et al. (2002) have defined sustainability as being based on the interplay of complex systems, which sections of society will interpret on the basis of circumstance. Sustainability, they note, should not be considered a science, but rather as an ethical precept in which values will help an individual determine their own normative position on the circumstances they are presented with.

A values-based perspective on ecotourism sustainability

Ecocentrism and other environmental philosophies present different interpretations of the ideas of 'balance' and 'wise use' of resources that are at the heart of all sustainability debates. Since coming into vogue in tourism studies in the 1980s and 1990s, the concept of sustainability has become a mediating term in bridging the ideological and political differences between the environmental and development lobbies, bridging the fundamentally opposed paradigms of eco- and anthropocentrism. Sustainable tourism represents one of the most common topics of academic inquiry in the tourism field and one of the great success stories in academic knowledge transfer (Hall, 2010). As such, people who are interested in general backgrounds on the formulation of the term 'sustainable tourism' are directed to a number of excellent works already in existence (Edgell, 2016; Hall, Gössling, & Scott, 2015; Weaver, 2008).

We have chosen to frame this discussion specifically around the notion of sustainability for whom? We wish to draw attention to the way that tourism sustainability debates are framed according to multiple perspectives, each with its basis in a different environmental philosophy that was referred to in the previous section. The practical impacts of these different perspectives on the sustainable management of tourism enterprises manifest themselves in a range of often-intractable issues: How can we ever determine accurately the needs of a future generation that is essentially unknowable? Does that future generation expect what we expect today? Can we talk about the needs of individuals within a tourism system, particularly when seen in the context of wider social issues in tourism destination regions? While these often-called wicked problems (Camillus, 2008; Churchman, 1967; Hall et al., 2015; Rittel & Webber, 1973) may on the one hand be devoid of a universally perfect solution or answer, we must engage with them for, as Przecławski (2005) notes, the act of travel is essentially a social action.

While tourists are now recognised as being intrinsically part of the tourism environment, as Hall et al. (2015) notes, there has been a historical tendency to position tourists ontologically outside the system under analysis. It was not until critical reflection of tourism impacts first came into vogue, in the 1970s and 1980s in the era of the cautionary platform (see Jafari, 1990), that we began to see the first real concerted questioning of whose sustainability should be the underlying driver of tourism development. Academics have had an important role to play in the development of a more questioning mind-set with respect to the sustainability of ecotourism. McKercher (2010) notes that in many respects, ecotourism as an identifiable tourism form would not exist separate from the development of academic scholarship. McKercher (2010) observes how over the last few decades, academic understanding of ecotourism has evolved from what was initially characterised as idealism, through a crisis of legitimacy, to eventually settle at a more nuanced understanding of the sector's sustainability potential. In doing so, the gradations of what ecotourism is and isn't and what this means for its sustainability have begun to be explored. Over the last few decades, debates have centred on a range of topics, including the connection between the size of an ecotourism operation and its sustainability potential (Butler, 1999; Weaver, 2002), the tendency for ecotourism to open up fragile areas of the world to inadvisable levels of development (Wall, 1997), and the merits of aligning the sustainability tag to ecotourists (Beaumont, 2011). Therefore whilst ecotourism has gained a certain moral authority for many on account of its perceived link to conservation, Goodwin (2000) has argued that the link between conservation and ecotourism is not always as simple as finding a mechanism to balance two competing priorities.

Conservation has been defined as a "term that implies the keeping or preservation of something for future use and human benefit" (Adams, 2009, p. 108). While certain stakeholder groups that align more towards deep ecologist positions (see McManus, 2009) believe that natural areas should be conserved by nonintervention, which means little or no human involvement (thus impacts) whatsoever, we must ask whether the 'preservation' or nonintervention position is excessively utopian in an ecotourism context. Whilst laudable in its aims, does a narrow conservationist perspective have the effect of masking more complex values and social relations between ecotourism industries and, for example, host populations? As Stronza (2007) has noted, the links between the conservation benefits of ecotourism and the local populations cannot always be viewed solely in terms of economic equations. Wider changes to the environment (e.g., population pressures) along with a range of ethnic, cultural and historical influences will also play a role.

It is important that we recognise these broader contextual influences because the environmental theme, which is so important to the study of ecotourism, is often viewed as a dichotomy between technocentrism and ecocentrism. Earlier in this chapter we defined ecocentrism as a philosophy that aims to prioritise the wonderment of nature. Technocentrism, in contrast, is said to be more "values-free, scientific, control-oriented, arrogant, manipulative, and with a focus on means instead of the ends" (Hayes, 1959, in Fennell, 2002, p. 1). Whilst technocentrism and ecocentrism present polar opposite approaches to planning, they are more accurately polar opposites on a continuum. The sustainability of an industry like ecotourism is a question of social justice and a "process of seeking a balance between resource preservation and development" (Tsaur et al., 2006, pp. 640–641). This is often easier said than done. Bricker and Kerstetter (2017) recently noted in the context of ecotourism futures that "positive change cannot take place without [first] recognising that ecotourism is dependent upon and a contributor to the ecosystems in which we operate". Similarly, Thompson et al. (2017) have demonstrated, with respect to tourism planning at the Kilim Karst Geoforest Park in Langkawi, Malaysia, how contestation between stakeholders (entrepreneurs, tour companies, government, etc.) exists on the basis of the interplay of normative dogma and the "diverse understandings, motivations, and capacities" of those on the ground (Thompson et al., 2017, p. 257).

Conclusion

Hall (2013, p. 7) has defined an ontology as a "way of seeing, creating and understanding not only different forms of knowledge but also their acceptability" (see also Ayikoru, 2009). The sustainability of an industry like ecotourism is a wicked problem, principally because there is no set of activities that are subject to "unmediated access to the natural world free from frameworks of understanding" (Castree, 2005, p. 16). It is not possible to separate the activity of ecotourism from the philosophy of ecotourism, for as Holden (2012, p. 196) notes, "without an acceptance that tourism is a causal factor of environmental problems, there is an absence of rationale for actions towards addressing them through environmental mitigation or conservation". The plurality of stakeholder positions that are in evidence in any ecotourism setting makes achieving consensus on what constitutes an impact difficult to achieve. In the next chapter we will move on to look at ecotourism planning in the context of government and industry policy. As we do so it is important to always remember that "ecotourism policy does not occur in a vacuum. ... policies are the outcome of a policy-making process which reflects the interaction of actors' interests and values" (Holden, 2008, p. 237). It is these various stakeholder frames that we have sought to explore in this chapter.

Further reading

Carson's book has become one of the most influential environmental texts of the twentieth century. It succeeded in raising environmental awareness, which led to changes in government policy and inspired the rise of the ecological movement.

Carson, R. (1962) *Silent Spring*. London: Penguin.

Like Carson's work, both Leopold's and Hardin's writings have become classics in environmental thinking.

Leopold, A. (1966) *A Sand Country Almanac*. New York: Ballantine.
Hardin, G. (1968) Tragedy of the commons. *Science, 162,* 1243–1248.

Belshaw's and Hay's work provide a good introduction to the various strands of environmental philosophy.

Belshaw, C. (2001) *Environmental Philosophy*. Stocksfield: Acumen.
Hay, P. (2002). *Main Currents in Western Environmental Thought*. Bloomington: Indiana University Press.

Question

What is the philosophical relationship between ecotourism and the broader, natural, sociocultural and economic environment in which it is situated?

References

Acott, T. G., Trobe, H. L., & Howard, S. (1998). An evaluation of deep ecotourism and shallow ecotourism. *Journal of Sustainable Tourism, 6*(3), 238–253.

Adams, W. (2009). Conservation. In R. J. Johnston, D. Gregory, G. Pratt, M. Watts, & S. Whatmore (Eds.), *The Dictionary of Human Geography* (5th ed., pp. 107–108). Oxford: Blackwell Publishers.

Ayikoru, M. (2009). Epistemology, ontology and tourism. In J. Tribe (Ed.), *Philosophical Issues in Tourism* (pp. 62–80). Bristol: Channel View Publications.

Beaumont, N. (2011). The third criterion of ecotourism: Are ecotourists more concerned about sustainability than other tourists? *Journal of Ecotourism, 10*(2), 135–148.

Bricker, K. & Kerstetter, D. (2017). Effecting positive change: An introduction. *Journal of Ecotourism, 16*(3), 201–202.

Burns, G. L., Macbeth, J., & Moore, S. (2011). Should dingoes die? Principles for engaging ecocentric ethics in wildlife tourism management. *Journal of Ecotourism, 10*(3), 179–196.

Butcher, J. (2009). Against ethical tourism. In J. Tribe (Ed.), *Philosophical Issues in Tourism* (pp. 244–260). Bristol: Channel View Publications.

Butler, R. W. (1999). Sustainable tourism: A state?of?the?art review. *Tourism Geographies*, *1*(1), 7–25.

Camillus, J. C. (2008). Strategy as a wicked problem. *Harvard Business Review*, *86*(5), 98.

Capital Institute. (2010). *Is Sustainable Growth an Oxymoron?* Retrieved from http://capital institute.org/blog/sustainable-growth-oxymoron/.

Carson, R. (2002). *Silent Spring*. Boston: Houghton Mifflin Harcourt.

Castree, N. (2005). *Nature: Key Ideas in Geography*. Hoboken: Routledge.

Cater, E. (2006). Ecotourism as a western construct. *Journal of Ecotourism*, *5*(1–2), 23–39.

Ceballos-Lascuráin, H. (1988). The future of ecotourism. *Mexico Journal, January*, 27, 13–14.

Cheng, M., Wong, I. A., Wearing, S., & McDonald, M. (2017). Ecotourism social media initiatives in China. *Journal of Sustainable Tourism*, *25*(3), 416–432.

Churchman, C. (1967). Wicked problems. *Management Science*, *14*(4), B141–B146.

Cobbinah, P. B. (2015). Contextualising the meaning of ecotourism. *Tourism Management Perspectives*, *16*, 179–189.

Coghlan, A., & Buckley, R. (2012). Nature-based tourism. In A. Holden & D. Fennell (Eds.), *The Routledge Handbook of Tourism and the Environment* (pp. 334–344). London: Routledge.

Edgell, D. (2016). *Managing Sustainable Tourism: A Legacy for the Future*. New York: Haworth Hospitality Press.

Fennell, D. (2002). *Ecotourism: Where We've Been; Where We're Going*. Abingdon: Taylor & Francis.

Fennell, D. (2012). Ecotourism. In A. Holden & D. Fennell (Eds.), *The Routledge Handbook of Tourism and the Environment* (pp. 323–333). London: Routledge.

Fennell, D. (2013). Ecotourism, animals and ecocentrism: A re-examination of the billfish debate. *Tourism Recreation Research*, *38*(2), 189–202.

Fennell, D. & Nowaczek, A. (2010). Moral and empirical dimensions of human-animal interactions in ecotourism: Deepening an otherwise shallow pool of debate. *Journal of Ecotourism*, *9*(3), 239–255.

Godfrey-Smith, W. (Ed.) (1980). *The Value of Wilderness: A Philosophical Approach*. Canberra: Canberra College of Advanced Education.

Goodwin, H. (2000). Tourism and natural heritage, a symbiotic relationship. In H. Goodwin (Ed.), *Environmental Management and Pathways to Sustainable Development* (pp. 97–112). Sunderland: Centre for Tourism in association with Business Education Publishers.

Hall, C. (2010). Academic capitalism, academic responsibility and tourism academics: Or, the silence of the lambs? *Tourism Recreation Research*, *35*(3), 298–301.

Hall, C. (2013). The natural science ontology of environment. In A. Holden & D. Fennell (Eds.), *The Routledge Handbook of Tourism and the Environment*, Abingdon: Routledge (pp. 6–18). London: Routledge.

Hall, C., Gössling, S., & Scott, D. (2015). Tourism and sustainability: An introduction. In C. M. Hall, S. Gössling, & D. Scott (Eds.), *The Routledge Handbook of Tourism and Sustainability* (pp. 1–12). London: Routledge.

Hay, P. (2002). *Main Currents in Western Environmental Thought*. Bloomington: Indiana University Press.

Hinch, T. (1998). Ecotourists and indigenous hosts: Diverging views on their relationship with nature. *Current Issues in Tourism*, *1*(1), 120–124.

Holden, A. (2008). *Environment and Tourism* (2nd ed.). London: Routledge.

Holden, A. (2012). Environmental discourses and tourism. In J. Wilson (Ed.), *The Routledge Handbook of Tourism Geographies* (pp. 194–200). London: Routledge.

Jafari, J. (1990). Research and scholarship: The basis of tourism education. *Journal of Tourism Studies, 1*(1), 33–41.

Jones, S. (2005). Community-based ecotourism: The significance of social capital. *Annals of Tourism Research, 32*(2), 303–324.

Liu, J., Qu, H., Huang, D., Chen, G., Yue, X., Zhao, X., & Liang, Z. (2014). The role of social capital in encouraging residents' pro-environmental behaviors in community-based ecotourism. *Tourism Management, 41*, 190–201.

Macnaghten, P. & Urry, J. (1998). *Contested Natures* (Vol. 54). London: SAGE.

McCool, S., Butler, R., Buckley, R., Weaver, D., & Wheeler, B. (2015). Is the concept of sustainability utopian? Ideally perfect but hard to practice. In T. Singh (Ed.), *Challenges in Tourism Research*. Bristol: Channel View Publications.

McKercher, B. (2010). Academia and the evolution of ecotourism. *Tourism Recreation Research, 35*(1), 15–26.

McManus, P. (2009). Deep ecology. In R. J. Johnston, D. Gregory, G. Pratt, M. Watts, & S. Whatmore (Eds.), *The Dictionary of Human Geography* (5th ed., p. 149). Oxford: Blackwell Publishers.

Newsome, D. & Moore, S. (2015). Managing visitors to the natural environment. In C. Hall, S. Gössling, & D. Scott (Eds.), *The Routledge Handbook of Tourism and Sustainability* (pp. 261–269). London: Routledge.

Pepper. D. (1996). *Modern Environmentalism: An Introduction*. London: Routledge.

Przecławski, K. (2005). The philosophical foundations of tourism. In W. Alejziak & R. Winiarski (Eds.), *Tourism in Scientific Research* (pp. 47–62). Academy of Physical Education in Kraków – University of Information Technology and Management in Rzeszów.

Reimer, J. K. & Walter, P. (2013). How do you know it when you see it? Community-based ecotourism in the Cardamom Mountains of southwestern Cambodia. *Tourism Management, 34*, 122–132.

Rittel, H. & Webber, M. M. (1973). 2.3 planning problems are wicked. *Polity, 4*, 155–169.

Rojek, C. (1993). *Ways of Escape: Modern Transformations in Leisure and Travel*. New York: Springer.

Ryan, C., Hughes, K., & Chirgwin, S. (2000). The gaze, spectacle and ecotourism. *Annals of Tourism Research, 27*(1), 148–163.

Sakata, H. & Prideaux, B. (2013). An alternative approach to community-based ecotourism: A bottom-up locally initiated non-monetised project in Papua New Guinea. *Journal of Sustainable Tourism, 21*(6), 880–899. doi:10.1080/09669582.2012.756493.

Shields, D. J., Šolar, S. V., & Martin, W. E. (2002). The role of values and objectives in communicating indicators of sustainability. *Ecological Indicators, 2*(1), 149–160.

Solow, R. M. (1974). The economics of resources or the resources of economics. *Classic Papers in Natural Resource Economics* (pp. 257–276). New York: Springer.

Stronza, A. (2007). The economic promise of ecotourism for conservation. *Journal of Ecotourism, 6*(3), 210–230.

Thompson, B. S., Gillen, J., & Friess, D. A. (2017). Challenging the principles of ecotourism: Insights from entrepreneurs on environmental and economic sustainability in Langkawi, Malaysia. *Journal of Sustainable Tourism*, 1–20.

Tomazos, K. & Butler, R. (2009). Volunteer tourism: The new ecotourism? *Anatolia, 20*(1), 196–211.

Tsaur, S.-H., Lin, Y.-C., & Lin, J.-H. (2006). Evaluating ecotourism sustainability from the integrated perspective of resource, community and tourism. *Tourism Management, 27*(4), 640–653.

Ecotourism as a philosophy

Urry, J. & Larsen, J. (2011). *The Tourist Gaze 3.0*. London: SAGE.

Wall, G. (1997). Forum: Is ecotourism sustainable? *Environmental Management, 21*(4), 481–493.

Wearing, B. & Wearing, S. (1996). Refocussing the tourist experience: The flaneur and the choraster. *Leisure Studies, 15*(4), 229–243.

Wearing, S. & Neil, J. (2009). *Ecotourism Impacts Potentials and Possibilities* (2nd ed.). Oxford: Butterworth-Heinemann.

Wearing, S., Stevenson, D., & Young, T. (2009). *Tourist Cultures: Identity, Place and the Traveller*: Sage.

Wearing, S. & Wearing, M. (2016). Ecotourism or eco-utilitarianism. In M. Mostafanezhad, R. Norum, E. J. Shelton, & A. Thompson-Carr (Eds.), *Political Ecology of Tourism: Community, Power and the Environment* (pp. 188–206). London: Routledge.

Weaver, D. (2002). The evolving concept of ecotourism and its potential impacts. *International Journal of Sustainable Development, 5*(3), 251–264.

Weaver, D. (2008). *Sustainable Tourism*. Amsterdam: Elsevier.

Weaver, D. (2011). *Ecotourism* (2nd ed.). Milton: Wiley.

Weaver, D. (2005). Comprehensive and minimalist dimensions of ecotourism. *Annals of Tourism Research, 32*(2), 439–455.

Wood, M. (2017). *Sustainable Tourism on a Finite Planet: Environmental, Business and Policy Solutions*. London: Taylor & Francis.

Tourism development

Government, industry, policy and planning

Introduction

In Chapter 3 we seek to articulate the way that the sustainability of ecotourism is embedded in evolving environmental paradigms. Since the World Commission on Environment and Development and other international conventions of the late twentieth century, the sustainability of tourism has come to dominate academic and industry discourse. However, whilst the meta-concept of sustainability is now well accepted in tourism, the operation of sustainability and the development of policy and planning approaches that are acceptable to industry and host communities have proven more complicated (Moyle, McLennan, Ruhanen, & Weiler, 2014). In the present chapter we will consider aspects of ecotourism policy and its enactment through tourism planning instruments.

Duffy (2006) has observed how the nature of ecotourism dictates its politics – "can it [ecotourism] be provided by global tour operators, luxury nature based resorts or is genuine ecotourism found in small scale local community run projects and campsites?" (p. 2). Dowling and Fennell (2003, pp. 5–6) have defined policies as the "plan of action adopted or pursued by governments or businesses … [and] plans embrace the strategies with which policies are implemented". In the present chapter we will therefore examine not only the theory of ecotourism planning, but also the mechanisms whereby it can be enacted through strategies like land-use zoning.

Throughout the chapter we will weave an in-depth case study of tourism development in the Royal Botanic Gardens (Sydney, Australia). Sutherland (2013) has argued that in spite of their modified nature, botanic gardens should have a role in ecotourism discussions on account of the opportunities they afford for viewing and being educated about a diverse collection of flora and fauna. In addition, the fact that the tourist appeal of botanic gardens will be dictated by "such factors as tourist experience and demand, the cultural context, as well as individual botanic garden design features and how they are perceived" (Sutherland, 2013, p. 482) makes them a useful contemporary illustration of the impediments to implementing a sustainable tourism policy in contested settings. The case study will be discussed in the context of Hall's (1994, p. 50) model of the tourism policy-making process and will draw heavily on the work of Schweinsberg et al. (2017).

Ecotourism and sustainable tourism policy

Thirty years ago the World Commission on Environment and Development (WCED) produced the report *Our Common Future* (World Commission on Environment and Development, 1987). This report represented the culmination of a process begun by the United Nations in 1983 "to create an independent commission to develop a global agenda for change at a time when it was recognised that the development paths of industrialised nations were not sustainable and the environment was in increasing danger" (Telfer, 2012, p. 213). While the work of the WCED contained only one specific mention of tourism, it was to this document that many of the subsequent political initiatives affecting the sustainable management of ecotourism owe their origin. The United Nations (UN) International Year of Ecotourism's Quebec City Summit in 2002, for example, led to the development of the so-called *Quebec Declaration on Ecotourism*, which was presented at the Johannesburg World Summit on Sustainable Development (Rio +8) (MacLaren, 2002).

What the UN International Year of Ecotourism demonstrated was the increasingly politicized nature of the ecotourism planning process (Buckley, 2002). Dredge and Jenkins (2011) have shown that over the latter half of the twentieth century, approaches to tourism policy and planning evolved from a largely neoliberal and economic growth focus to a more discerning sustainability argument that sought a balance between a range of competing economic, environmental and social planning considerations (see also Cobbinah, 2015). With this shift, Dredge and Jenkins (2011) observed the devolution of responsibility for planning away from central authorities. Management, they noted, would increasingly "place emphasis on facilitating and enabling tourism development by mobilizing the resources of others rather than direct government action and physical planning" (2011, p. 4). Recent work into the concept of community-based ecotourism is emblematic of this trend (see Sakata & Prideaux, 2013).

Ensuring that the economic imperatives of an industry are managed in conjunction with its broader environmental and social obligations is, however, often easier said than done. Das and Chatterjee (2015) have observed that the practical benefits of ecotourism are often hard to see at the local level, because this level is where most of the industry's costs are incurred. In peripheral regions where so much of the world's ecotourism can be found, Hall and Boyd (2005) have noted, policy makers often fail to see ecotourism as being situated within a broader environmental context. At the time of writing, the implementation of Myanmar's Ecotourism Policy and Management Strategy for the period 2015–2025 (see Myanmar Ministry of Environmental Conservation and Forestry & Myanmar Ministry of Hotels and Tourism, 2015) had been hindered on account of the challenges in balancing ecotourism's conservation imperative with the development of strategies to ensure the livelihoods of local farmers (Wai, 2017). As Harvey (2007) once asked, in whose particular interests is it that the state take a neoliberal stance and how have those interests used neoliberalism to benefit themselves rather than, as is claimed, everyone, everywhere?

Ecotourism is (in theory at least) said to value "ethical approaches to management, local people, the protection of natural heritage, and so on" (Dowling and Fennell, 2003, p. 10). Whether this is true or not in practice has in recent years been debated in the context of the planned development of ecotourism attractions in the Australian state of Tasmania. Tasmania is home to some of the world's most pristine and remote natural wonders, including the southwestern World Heritage Area. However, it also has been the birthplace of the modern Australian environmental movement and the site of some of the most iconic environmental protests, including the protest of the damming of the Franklin River in the 1980s (Buckman, 2008; Law, 2001). While the Franklin River lays claim to being one of the best white-water rafting sites in the world, and while environments like Lake Pedder have long been of interest to bushwalkers (Kirkpatrick, 2001), since 2014 the growth of ecotourism in Tasmania has come under sustained questioning. In 2014 the Tasmanian state government sought expressions of interest from developers to foster a greater ecotourism presence inside the World Heritage zones. Arguments in favor of such a move included the opportunity to revitalize a state economy that was struggling. Arguments against included the perception that commercial ecotourism developments are diametrically at odds with the principles of World Heritage designation – to protect nature in perpetuity (Atkin, 2014).

As we will argue later in this chapter, the institutional apparatus of ecotourism policy and planning sits within the context of a series of societal influences. This is important in the sense that whilst there is often the argument that ecotourism offers a win-win for conservation and development, as Holden (2013) has noted with respect to tourism development in world heritage areas:

Although there is an inherent emphasis on the relationship between economic benefits, conservation and community involvement, as would be expected in any strategy of plan purporting to sustainability principles, the problem of community support for a WHS [World Heritage Site] may extend beyond purely its involvement or economic benefit. It can often be a question of how their heritage is being presented to tourists and who controls it. Alongside the problematic issue of how to define and identify a community … Issues of politics, power, representation and authenticity mean that how culture is presented is sometimes contentious. (p. 284)

The contentious nature of ecotourism means that policy must be seen as something more than the "identification of a series of goals and objectives, which help an agency – usually a government one – in the process of planning the tourism industry" (Fennell, 2008, p. 134). Instead policy formation can be seen as

a strategy for the development of the tourism sector … that establishes objectives and guidelines as basis for what needs to be done. This means identifying and agreeing objectives; establishing priorities; placing in a Community context the roles of national governments, national tourist organizations, local governments and private sector businesses; establishing possible coordination and implementation of agreed programs to solve identified problems, with monitoring and evaluation of these programs. (Akehurst, 2008, p. 134)

Pal (1992, p. 3 in C. M. Hall, 2003, p. 21) has defined public policy as that which "stem[s] from government or public authorities … A policy is deemed a public policy not by virtue of its impact on the public, but by virtue of its source". Policy flows from the people and therein lies one of the principal challenges for ecotourism management. Parker (2001) has demonstrated that not only are ecotourism policies formed by the efforts of a diverse range of government entities, many of whom are not principally concerned with the economic viability of the industry, so too are all of these diverse departments and agencies merely cogs in the machinery of pluralistic society. Hall (1994) has gone as far as to argue that the politics of tourism are less about the political machinations of elections and more about the perhaps outwardly irrational juxtaposition of different stakeholder viewpoints and power relations.

Later in the current chapter we will look in detail at the idea of land-use zoning. On one level, zoning represents a rational process of determining the appropriateness of different land uses and managing the intersection of different land uses in heterogeneous spatial settings. However, zoning also represents part of a wider shift towards physical and spatial tourism planning. Planning frameworks including limits of acceptable change (McCool & Cole, 1997; Stankey, McCool, & Stokes, 1984) and the recreation opportunity spectrum (Clark & Stankey, 1979) serve as the foundation for many zoning strategies (King & Pearlman, 2009).

Fennel et al. (2004) have argued that ideas like carrying capacity include an inbuilt social framing. What this means for the present chapter is that discussions of policy and planning in a sense will always become a discussion "about power, who gets what, where, how and why" (Hall, 1994, p. 2). Drawing on the work of Bachrach and Baratz, Hall (2006) has argued against the naivety and romantic ideal that there should be no hierarchy of power in tourism development contexts. There will always be a selection of what Bachrach and Baratz (1970, p. 11 in Hall, 2006, p. 254) defined as "the dominant values and the political myths, rituals and institutional practices, which tend to favor the vested interest of one or more groups". It is with this that we make our first foray to consider the case study of this chapter, the Royal Botanic Gardens (Sydney, Australia).

In discussing this case we will draw particular attention to Hall's (1994) model of the tourism policy-making process (see Figure 3.1). Drawing on earlier work from

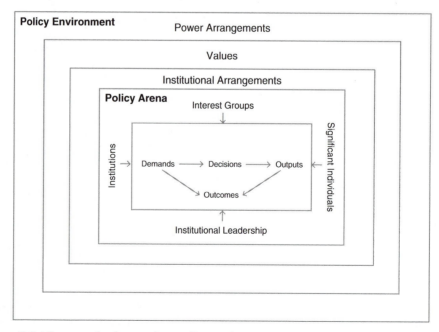

Figure 3.1 Elements in the tourism policy-making process

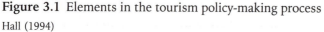
Hall (1994)

Easton, Hall (1994) argued that the policy-making process exists as a system of inputs and outputs operating in a broader policy environment.

As the reader moves into the Royal Botanic Gardens case study it is important to realise that, at the time of writing, the policy process was incomplete and, if anything, in a state of limbo. The Royal Botanic Gardens and Domain Trust (RBGDT), who are responsible for the plan's development, noted on their website that they

CASE STUDY: Royal Botanic Gardens: demands to outcomes

Botanic gardens are a classification of protected areas where management must seek to manage the historically formed interplay of different roles for gardens in society, including scientific discovery, horticulture, conservation, recreation and tourism (Brockway, 1979; Dodd & Jones, 2010; Ginn, 2009; Henty, 1988; Sutherland, 2013). It is against the backdrop of such a mixed land-use history that in 2013–2014 the Royal Botanic Gardens and Domain Trust (RBGDT) began the process of developing a Master Plan for the ongoing management of the Sydney Royal Botanic Gardens – a 30–hectare site on the southern shores of Sydney Harbour, just to the east of the Sydney Opera House and Sydney Harbour Bridge.

The Master Plan was to be the first in the more than 200–year history of the Sydney botanic gardens site. Through a legislative process, which included community consultation in 2013 and 2014, the Master Plan was tasked with providing a "blueprint for the Garden and Domain, setting a direction over the next 20 years" (Royal Botanic Gardens and Domain Trust, 2014a). The RBGDT initially saw the policy process as the development of a "reference document for the next thirty years [and not as a signal of intent] … to start any particular project" (Royal Botanic Gardens and Domain Trust, 2014b). The possible outputs, however, of the initial draft plans, which were developed by the architectural firm Cox Richardson in partnership with Grant and Associates, included a number of initiatives that would have greatly enhanced the viability of the site as a tourism precinct, including hotel construction, visitor information infrastructure and tidal walkways around the section of the site known popularly as Mrs. Macquarie's Chair.

In 2017, the RBGDT Master Plan process has stalled at the community consultation phase. Arguments for and against the proposals (see www.rbgsyd.nsw. gov.au/About-Us/Major-Projects/Draft-Master-Plan) focused on the interplay of sustainable utilization with what was alternatively described as an overtly commercial focus for what are, for many, public lands. Certain stakeholders have gone as far as to suggest that this is an outcome. The so-called third estate (or media) at one point maintained that the shelving of the plan represented a "win for Sydneysiders" (Dumas, 2016). Whilst certain Sydneysiders would doubtless agree with this assessment, Schweinsberg, Darcy and Cheng (2017) have demonstrated the diversity of opinions that exist around the merits of the Master Plan and its objectives. This illustrates the importance of examining the actual policy process in the context of the policy arena.

are currently in the process of reviewing initial community feedback and expect to re-engage the community on the plan in 2017. It is in this context that we open the case study by considering the central section of the model – how the "demands for action arising from inside and outside the political system" (Hall, 1994, p. 49) are managed to eventually achieve policy outputs and outcomes.

The contested nature of the RBGDT Master Plan policy arena is emblematic of the dynamic nature of stakeholder power relations in protected areas (Wegner & Macbeth, 1994) observes that any policy development must be seen in the

> context of the policy arena in which groups (e.g. industry associations, conservation groups and community groups), institutions (e.g. government departments and agencies responsible for tourism), significant individuals (e.g. high-profile industry representatives) and the institutional leadership ... interact and compete in determining tourism policy choices. (pp. 49–50)

In this way, while policy may have its foundation in ideologies (see Chapter 2), strategic planning represents the process whereby policies are achieved. Torres-Delgado and Palomeque (2012) have observed that it is through policy that public institutions across a number of scales take part in tourism planning. Public institutions (or administration) are said to include "all public bodies and organs that are included in the executive branch of government" (Torres-Delgado & Palomeque, 2012, p. 3). While Bramwell (2012) has noted that the ambitious and multi-disciplinary nature of sustainable development often makes public authorities best placed for coordination of efforts, the reality is that active involvement of a range of stakeholders is necessary. On this point, Gunn (1994, p. 244) once noted that sustainable strategy "requires integrated policy, planning, and social learning processes: its political viability depends upon the support of the people it affects through their governments, their social institutions and private activities".

The policy deliberations for the RBGDT case study represents deliberations to formalize the goals and objectives and the setting of priorities (Farsari, Butler, & Prastacos, 2007). Policy and indeed planning seek to manage the relationship between regulation and unfettered growth. Haase et al. (2009) have discussed the challenges of self-regulation around tourism development in environments characterized by common pool resources. Through an Antarctic case study, it is shown how high levels of industry organization and coherence have aided industry self-regulation. For self-regulation to be successful, Ostrom et al. (1999) note that the "benefits perceived by resource users have to be greater than the costs attributed to collective action and any restrictions imposed on resources use" (in Haase et al., 2009, p. 425). In the Antarctic, the rapid diversification of resource users is seen as one of the principal barriers to self-regulation under the Association of Antarctica Tourism Operators. In Sydney, around the site of the Royal Botanic Gardens case study, there is similarly evidence of ever-increasing diversity of commercial users of a site historically focused on the preservation of nationally significant horticulture. The challenges in reconciling the users' views present a wicked policy context. On the one hand, planning represents a rational process composed of sequential steps including study preparation, objective determination, survey, analysis and synthesis, etc. (see Timothy & Boyd, 2015). On the other hand, Stevenson et al. (2008) have observed that it is also an intuitive and human process, one where the achievement of universally acceptable outcomes will be defined in terms of stakeholder communication.

CASE STUDY: Royal Botanic Gardens: the policy arena and the intractability of perspectives on a wicked management problem

Ever since the RBGDT Master Plan was first proposed and a procedure was outlined for community and stakeholder engagement (see www.rbgsyd.nsw. gov.au/about/major-projects/draft-master-plan), the plan has had the effect of dividing the community. Ken Morrison (Director of the Tourism Transport Forum[1]) went on the record at the beginning of the community consultation period arguing that the gardens needed a plan for development, rather than the ad hoc arrangements that had characterized the site over the previous centuries (Morrison, 2014). The director of the RBGDT argued that the Master Plan would "absolutely protect" the core of the gardens, as they had evolved as a public space over the course of Sydney's modern history. Recognizing the need to respond to the demands of changing visitors and locals, Ian Connolly (original Master Plan architect) noted, "Sydney can't rest. You have got to keep looking to improve the experience not only for visitors but for everyone who lives there as well" (Barlass, 2014).

In contrast to the proponents of the plan, various prominent individuals have rushed to lambast the proposals. Chief amongst them was the former Prime Minister of Australia Paul Keating, who passionately suggested that the plan amounted to a selling-out of public land to commercial interests. Noting a personal opinion not only that the gardens represented one of the great horticulture gardens of the world, Keating also said that the gardens represented "the nearest thing to a sacred site in Sydney – held sacred by the non-Aboriginal community as well as the Aboriginal community" (Nicholls, 2014).

When dialogue is achieved among a range of individual and other stakeholder groups, it becomes possible to consider how one might reconcile the ambit of economic, social and environmental factors related to ecotourism in its destination context (see Spenceley & Manning, 2013). The presence of conflicting stakeholder views on the planning process emphasises that tourism planning and policy making is, at its core, a social process (see Dredge & Jenkins, 2011). Hall (2011) has observed that in the second half of the twentieth century, government policy generally was affected by an increasing array of interest groups. Hall notes,

> up until the 1960s, interest groups were primarily business association based. However, since the early 1960s, there has been rapid growth in western nations in the number of citizen and public interest groups, particularly in the area of consumer and environmental concerns. (Hall, 2011, p. 138)

Institutions of policy formation flow from this social nature in the sense that they frame the relationship between individuals or groups of individuals (Hall, 2003). Scrutton (1982, p. 225 in Hall, 2003, pp. 22–23) defines an institution as "an established law, custom, usage, practice, organization, or other element in the political or social life of a people; a regulative principle or convention subservient to the needs of an organized community or the general needs of a civilization".

CASE STUDY: Royal Botanic Gardens: policy institutions as situated in a web of values and power relations

At the time of writing, the Royal Botanic Gardens is governed by the Royal Botanic Gardens and Domain Trust (RBGDT). This statutory authority also has responsibilities for the management and stewardship of the Australian Botanic Garden Mount Annan and the Blue Mountains Botanic Mount Tomah. At an administrative level the Trust staff is integrated with the administrative staff of the Centennial and Moore Park Trust. The New South Wales (NSW) Government Office of Environment and Heritage employs trust staff.

Reinmuth (2014) drew attention to the considerable challenges faced by policy bodies like the RBGDT as they look to fulfill their principal responsibilities under the *Royal Botanic Gardens and Domain Trust Act*. Responsibilities under the act include:

- maintaining and improving the Trust lands, the National Herbarium and the collections of living and preserved plant life owned by the Trust;
- increasing and disseminating knowledge with respect to the plant life of Australia, and of New South Wales in particular;
- encouraging the use and enjoyment of the Trust lands by promoting and increasing the educational, historical, cultural and recreational values of those lands.

As with most categories of protected areas, the preservation of the natural features of the site is recognised by the Trust as being its dominant focus (Rettie, Clevenger, & Ford, 2009). This does not devalue the Trust's other priorities, but it does mean that recognition needs to be given to the nature of the democratic process and the manner in which decision makers wield both hard and soft power. Hall (2011) has observed how the presence of checks and balances in the policy-making process increases the necessity of stakeholder engagement. The Barangaroo headland development[2], which is located only a few kilometers from the Botanic Gardens and encompasses the state government–sponsored redevelopment of prominent areas relating to Sydney's maritime history, was described by Johnston and Clegg (2012, p. 294) as an example of how "competing narratives ... are one of the most important influencing instruments of public management".

In the case of the Botanic Gardens, Reinmuth (2014) has observed how the sensitive nature of the site necessitates that any move to redevelopment must be undertaken on the basis of a pragmatic consideration of the full spectrum of public views. These views must be considered transparently. We must also move beyond seeing policy debates as situated along the fault lines of banner headlines, media-driven debates (see Schweinsberg et al., 2017) and the dominant influences of significant individuals and interest groups. Instead we need to educate the public, not just on the site-specific characteristics of a tourism policy initiative, but how that initiative sits within a locale that is inherently contestable and evolving. Values represent "ends, goals, interests, beliefs, ethics, biases, attitudes, traditions, morals and objectives that change with human perception and with time" (Henning, 1974, p. 15 in Hall, 1994, p. 51). These values represent normative positions of society. They have emerged as part of a living and evolving history. Over the last two hundred years the Royal Botanic Gardens have played host to events as part of the Sydney 2000 Olympics; they have also, for a brief period, been the site of the Sydney Garden Palace, which was built to house the Sydney International Exhibition in 1879. Today both of these tourism events still impact the public's perception of the site. Any move to redevelop tourism policies for the Garden precinct must avoid seeing tourism uses as in some way separate from the area's primary focus as a horticulture enclave. The values Sydneysiders ascribe to the Royal Botanic Gardens as an ecotourism site today are a product of the sum of the area's total history.

Enactment of policy through planning

In this section we will argue that the sustainable development credentials of ecotourism are supported by robust planning approaches. Planning involves anticipating and regulating change to encourage appropriate development so as to increase the social, economic and environmental benefits of the actual process (Murphy, 1985). In this section we will consider planning processes that can assist with achieving sustainable ecotourism. There is a commonly held idea that the only way that sustainability can ultimately be achieved in tourism is through the minimization of visitor numbers. In this way ecotourism management is often looked at in supply-focused terms – how can the industry control or be controlled in terms of the spread of its activities and the behaviour of its constituents? Can we ever achieve sustainability of an industry like ecotourism if the industry continues to be one of the fastest-growing sectors in the wider tourism economy? Whilst sustainable tourism planning is a recognised focus of traditional mass tourism industries in localities like Calvià, Spain (see Dodds, 2007), the close relationship between ecotourism and the natural and social features of the destination means that active attention must be given to understanding the mechanisms through which the tourism/ destination relationship can be managed.

Over the last decade or so a considerable body of academic scholarship has considered the applicability of different planning tools (e.g., zoning, codes of practice, certification, etc.) to the sustainable management of ecotourism (Ballantyne & Packer, 2013; Font, 2007; Font & Harris, 2004; Font, Sanabria, & Skinner, 2003; Goodwin, 1996; Honey, 2002; Jamal, Borges, & Stronza, 2006; Karlsson & Dolnicar, 2016; Medina, 2005; Sharpley, 2006; Wearing & Neil, 2009; Weaver, 2011). Rather than simply revise this material, we wish in this chapter to examine in-depth one approach to planning – land-use zoning – and in particular to consider the way in which a range of cultural framings articulate the appropriateness or inoperability of different land uses.

CASE STUDY: Royal Botanic Gardens: configuration and zoning

The Royal Botanic Gardens is a 29–hectare site bordered by 51 hectares of parklands that comprise the Sydney Domain. The following description of the layout of the Gardens is taken from a description of the NSW Office of Environment and Heritage (ND-b):

> Traditionally designated as four areas reflecting its development – the Middle Garden, the Upper Garden, the Lower Garden and the Garden Palace Grounds...
>
> The layout of the Gardens is exceptionally important, each area (the Middle Garden, the Lower Garden, the Palace Lawn etc.) reflecting an important stage in the development of the gardens and the current fashion in landscape design almost from the founding of the colony. The squared beds of the Middle Garden are traditionally believed to reflect the first furrows and shortly thereafter the first garden plots of the new settlement.
>
> The old Garden Palace grounds are the area bordering Macquarie Street and the Conservatorium of Music (former Government House stables). The Middle Garden is the first farm site. The Upper Garden comprises of the southern section housing administrative offices and National Herbarium on Mrs. Macquarie's road as well as the nursery and depot area bordering the Cahill Expressway. The Lower Garden comprises the rest of the area extending north of the Middle Garden to Farm Cove.
>
> The Garden Palace grounds being the highest point have excellent views and are maintained as lawn areas, garden beds, Australian shrubs and turf species. A paling fence for grazing the Governor's stock originally enclosed the area. An ornamental fence was constructed along Macquarie Street and in the grounds stood the Garden Palace built 1879, which was destroyed by fire in 1882.
>
> The Middle Garden is now the most closely cultivated section of the gardens where both native and exotic species are well labelled. It included the spring walk famous for its azalea display (currently (2003) undergoing renovation), one of the finest collections of outdoor palms in the world and a 1970s succulent garden...

The Middle Garden

The long rectangular beds have evolved from the rectangular beds of the earliest garden. The land before the first Government House and Bennelong Point was laid out in the manner of an English park; the Botanic Garden was treated in a purely functional way. The gate in the wall, which Macquarie had completed in 1816 to protect the garden from the harbour, and which now, separates the Middle and Lower Gardens...

Lower Gardens

Charles Moore directed the reclamation of and expansion of the 'Lower Garden' into Farm Cove, extending the gardens' pleasure grounds with curving pleasure walks, tree and shrubbery plantings. This work took place over 30 years, resulting in a gardenesque parkland which retains much of its original layout and composition today. Within this layout there are collections of plants of note, including from the Canary Islands, New Zealand and the Pacific Islands...

Domain

The Tarpeian Rock is a prominent, dramatic and significant sandstone cliff landscape feature on the northwest boundary of the Domain facing Bennelong Point and the Sydney Opera House, cut for the extension of Macquarie Street. It derives its name from the famous rock on the Capitoline Hill in Rome from where prisoners were hurled to their deaths in ancient times. A stairway gives access from close to the Sydney Opera House to the top of the rock and Domain. An early carving in the sandstone cliff is located about 3 meters above the fifth step from the base of the cliff. The carving reads "The Tarpeian Way". It possibly dates from the time of construction in the 1880s.

Inskeep (1991, p. 432) defined zoning as the "regulations that demarcate specific areas for different types of land use and the development [of] standards to be applied within each land use zone". Extensively applied in Marine Park and terrestrial protected area contexts (e.g., Day, 2002; Shafer, 1999; Shani, Polak, & Shashar, 2012; Wu et al., 2015; Yochim, 2007), land-use zoning forms part of the wider planning framework. Examples of planning frameworks include the recreation opportunity spectrum, limits of acceptable change (LAC), protected area visitor management, etc. Buckley and Pannell (1990, p. 29) have observed that at a pragmatic level, the principal aim of land-use zoning is to ensure that "activities in one zone do not impinge on the planned functions of another". In spite of this, however, it has been suggested that the employment of zoning strategies in an ecotourism context has been limited to date on account of ecotourists requiring few facilities and causing minimal disruption to the environment (Diamantis, 2011). In one of the few works to specifically canvass the role of botanic gardens as ecotourism sites, Sutherland (2013) observes that gardens were deemed by most visitors to offer opportunities for learning about plants, wildlife and nature. By appealing to a softer class of ecotourists, botanic gardens are able to leverage existing approaches to zoning within their grounds (see Benfield, 2013) to provide targeted tourist experiences. Below we have provided a NSW government description of some of the different zones that exist in the Sydney Royal Botanic Gardens.

The description of the general layout of the Royal Botanic Gardens emphasises how the horticulture of the site has evolved over a long period of time. Similarly in the context of tourism, Mason (2013) has shown how the historical evolution of a site can make it difficult to establish one predominant land use. What this means for the impacts of zoning on the place of ecotourism in the RBGDT Master Plan is that the policy must be seen in the context of the history of the site. As case in point, let us consider the area of the Domain (just outside the boundaries of the Gardens proper) that includes Mrs. Macquarie's Chair, which is often regarded as one of the most iconic tourism sites in Sydney.

CASE STUDY: Royal Botanic Gardens: the social construction of zoning

Mrs. Macquarie's Chair is a stone chair designed to immortalize the wife of the former governor of NSW, Governor Macquarie, who was responsible for the gazettal of the Gardens in 1816. Lying just on the northeastern corner of the RBG site on the shore of Sydney Harbour, the area around Mrs. Macquarie's Chair has been open for public use since 1831.

As part of the proposed Master Plan redevelopment, it was suggested that a tidal walk could be constructed around Mrs. Macquarie's Point. It was also proposed to construct new viewing platforms and other amenities at Mrs. Macquarie's Point. As such, it was essentially proposed that an evolution should occur in the nature of tourist usage of a site that is listed on the State Heritage Register (NSW Office of Environment and Heritage, ND-a).

In the period following the release of the Master Plan, there was almost universal agreement that tourists (and locals) should be able to use the headland precinct. Where debate occurred was over the appropriateness of different types of usage. In public submissions to the Master Plan, the City of Sydney (local council) applauded the intention to plant significant numbers of "indigenous plants and restored Eucalypt/Bush typology". In contrast, other stakeholders voiced concern over the potential for any increase in tourism infrastructure to result in tourists swamping the site.

Arguments for or against particular land uses in a zone of the Botanic Gardens are framed on the basis of selective reading of culture. The challenge for policy makers, however, is that culture is an evolving concept. When Keating suggested, "the trust would better leaving municipal park benches strewn throughout the gardens and Domain, to allow people's quiet enjoyment and contemplation, rather than this grotesque alienation to the private events and party hire industry" (Needham, 2014), he was tapping into the importance of a communal space that became a popular idea in Sydney in the late nineteenth century (Hoskins, 2003).

With the opening up of the Domain and nearby Botanic Gardens, however, came a simultaneous policy of exclusion – the removal of those undesirable parts of society. In 1907 the composer, barrister and politician John Fitzgerald wrote a description of civic space in Sydney for the journal *The Lone Hand*. Accompanying his description, the illustrator Lionel Lindsey drew "an open air restaurant in the Domain at which well-dressed adults and children enjoyed alfresco dining and views of the Harbour" (Hoskins, 2003, pp. 8, 10).

Hoskins (2003) goes on to note that there is a substantial disjunction between an almost Parisian-style setting on the one hand and the continued use of the wider Domain site as a location for public oratory, civil disobedience and the like. If, however, we look at the whole modern history of the site, we can observe that throughout the Domain there has been constant challenge of what constitutes respectable usage (see Hoskins, 2003). Is an outdoor dining area necessarily more or less appropriate than tidal walkways? Are viewing platforms necessarily more or less appropriate than Mrs. Macquarie's Chair would have been to those members of the Sydney population that found themselves marginalized from the Domain area on account of their position in society?

Botanic gardens, just like other categories of protected areas that are popular with ecotourists, are social constructions. Determinations of the composition of land-use zones and the wider appropriateness of tourism policy cannot be divorced from the area's greater context.

Conclusion

Any move to understand the sustainability potential of ecotourism must involve careful consideration of the policy context in which the industry is developed. Joppe (2018, p. 201) recently argued that the behaviour of travelling means that we are subject to the effects of a wide variety of policies, many written for other purposes, "such as controlling or facilitating the flow of capital and investments, the transportation of passengers and goods, worker rights, safety and security, or environmental protection". While Joppe goes on to note that this means we are often subject to the effect of decision makers "who have little regard for, or knowledge of, tourism" (2017, p. 1), this does not mean that we can downplay the role of government in determining the sustainability of the ecotourism sector. Goodwin(1995) argued that ecotourism must embrace discussions of policy if it is to ensure that its development is consistent with the needs of both the environment and the local people. In the present chapter, we have sought to unpack aspects of tourism policy formation in a contested environmental setting. In the next chapter, we will move on to consider ecotourism in a wider resource management context.

Further reading

Bramwell's work, Bramwell and Lane's work and Fennell and Dowling's edited text explore the range of challenges that ecotourism managers and policy makers face in delivering sustainable tourism experiences. They outline policies and procedures based on case studies and documentation from around the world and how these affect the business of ecotourism.

Bramwell, B. (2012). Interventions and policy instruments for sustainable tourism. In W. F. Theobald (Ed.), *Global Tourism* (pp. 406–425). New York: Elsevier.

Bramwell, B. & Lane, B. (2011). Critical research on the governance of tourism and sustainability. *Journal of Sustainable Tourism, 19*(4–5), 411–421.

Fennell, D. A. & Dowling, R. K. (Eds.) (2003). *Ecotourism Policy and Planning*. Oxford: CABI International.

Wight uses the provincial government of Alberta, Canada, as a case study and tracks its involvement in ecotourism from the early to the late 1990s. She contrasts the government's initial 'strong sustainability' mode with its later 'weak sustainability' mode and its lack of support for the principles of sustainable development.

Wight, P. A. (2003). Supporting the principles of sustainable development in tourism and ecotourism: Government's potential role. In M. Lück & T. Kirstges (Eds.), Global Ecotourism Policies and Case Studies: Perspectives and Constraints (pp. 50–57). Clevedon: Channel View Publications.

These two articles provide case study indicators of how governance is working in the expanding role ecotourism is playing in both government and communities internationally.

Dinica, V. (2017). Tourism concessions in National Parks: Neo-liberal governance experiments for a conservation economy in New Zealand. *Journal of Sustainable Tourism*, 25(12), 1811–1829.

Noh, A. F. M., Shui, A., Tai, S. Y., & Noh, K. M. (2018). Indicators of governance of marine ecotourism resources: Perception of communities in Pulau Perhentian, Terengganu. *International Journal of Business and Society*, 19(S1), 17–25.

Question

The contentious nature of ecotourism means that governance and policy must encompass a wider range of values. Should government be the sole arbitrator of these?

References

Atkin, M. (2014). *Eco-tourism on agenda in Tasmania as government accepts proposals for development in national parks, World Heritage Areas. ABC News, 1 December*. Retrieved from www.abc.net.au/news/2014-12-01/ec-tourism-on-agenda-in-tasmania/5932342.

Ballantyne, R. & Packer, J. (2013). *International Handbook on Ecotourism*. Cheltenham: Edward Elgar Publishing.

Barlass, T. (2014). Five-star 150–room hotel blooms in radical Botanic Gardens and Domain revamp. *Sydney Morning Herald*. Retrieved from www.smh.com.au/nsw/fivestar-150room-hotel-blooms-in-radical-botanic-gardens-and-domain-revamp-20140405-365qo.html.

Benfield, R. (2013). *Garden Tourism*. Boston: CABI.

Bramwell, B. (2012). Interventions and policy instruments for sustainable tourism. In W. F. Theobald (Ed.), *Global Tourism* (pp. 406–425). New York: Elsevier.

Brockway, L. H. (1979). Science and colonial expansion: The role of the British Royal Botanic Gardens. *American Ethnologist*, 6(3), 449–465.

Buckley, R. (2002). Tourism ecocertification in the international year of ecotourism. *Journal of Ecotourism*, 1(2–3), 197–203.

Buckley, R. & Pannell, J. (1990). Environmental impacts of tourism and recreation in national parks and conservation reserves. *Journal of Tourism Studies*, 1(1), 24–32.

Buckman, G. (2008). *Tasmania's Wilderness Battles: A History*. Crows Nest: Allen & Unwin.

Clark, R. N. & Stankey, G. H. (1979). *The recreation opportunity spectrum: A framework for planning, management, and research*. US Department of Agriculture Forest Service and Pacific Northwest Forest and Range Experiment Station - General Technical Report PNS-98.

Cobbinah, P. B. (2015). Contextualising the meaning of ecotourism. *Tourism Management Perspectives, 16*, 179–189.

Das, M. & Chatterjee, B. (2015). Ecotourism: A panacea or a predicament? *Tourism Management Perspectives, 14*, 3–16.

Day, J. C. (2002). Zoning: Lessons from the Great Barrier Reef marine park. *Ocean & Coastal Management, 45*(2), 139–156.

Diamantis, D. (2011). *Ecotourism*. United Kingdom: South Western Cengage Learning.

Dinica, V. (2017). Tourism concessions in National Parks: Neo-liberal governance experiments for a conservation economy in New Zealand. *Journal of Sustainable Tourism, 25*(12), 1811–1829. doi:10.1080/09669582.2015.1115512.

Dodd, J. & Jones, C. (2010). *Redefining the Role of Botanic Gardens: Towards a New Social Purpose*. Leicester: Research Centre for Museums and Galleries (RCMG).

Dodds, R. (2007). Sustainable tourism and policy implementation: Lessons from the case of Calvià, Spain. *Current Issues in Tourism, 10*(4), 296–322.

Dowling, R. & Fennell, D. (2003). The context of ecotourism policy and planning. In D. Fennell & R. Dowling (Eds.), *Ecotourism Policy and Planning* (pp. 1–20). Wallingford: CABI.

Dredge, D. & Jenkins, J. (2011). New spaces of tourism planning and policy. In D. Dredge & J. Jenkins (Eds.), *Stories of Practice: Tourism Policy and Planning* (pp. 1–12). Farnham: Ashgate.

Duffy, R. (2006). The politics of ecotourism and the developing world. *Journal of Ecotourism, 5*(1–2), 1–6.

Dumas, D. (2016, June 11). Win for Sydneysiders as Royal Botanic Garden Masterplan shelved on its 200th birthday. *Sydney Morning Herald*. Retrieved from www.smh.com.au/nsw/win-for-sydneysiders-as-royal-botanic-garden-masterplan-shelved-on-its-200th-birthday-20160609–gpfe71.html.

Farsari, Y., Butler, R., & Prastacos, P. (2007). Sustainable tourism policy for Mediterranean destinations: Issues and interrelationships. *International Journal of Tourism Policy, 1*(1), 58–78.

Fennell, D. (2008). Ecotourism and the myth of indigenous stewardship. *Journal of Sustainable Tourism, 16*(2), 129–149.

Fennell, D., Butler, R., & Boyd, S. (2004). The polar framework and its operation in an ecotourism setting. In D. Diamantis (Ed.), *Ecotourism: Management and Assessment* (pp. 110–134). Australia: South-Western CENGAGE Learning.

Font, X. (2007). Ecotourism certification: Potential and challenges. *Critical Issues in Ecotourism: Understanding a Complex Tourism Phenomenon*, 386–405.

Font, X. & Harris, C. (2004). Rethinking standards from green to sustainable. *Annals of Tourism Research, 31*(4), 986–1007.

Font, X., Sanabria, R., & Skinner, E. (2003). Sustainable tourism and ecotourism certification: Raising standards and benefits. *Journal of Ecotourism, 2*(3), 213–218. doi:10.1080/14724040308668145.

Ginn, F. (2009). Colonial transformations: Nature, progress and science in the Christchurch Botanic Gardens. *New Zealand Geographer, 65*, 35–47.

Goodwin, H. (1995). Tourism and the environment. *Biologist (London), 42*(3), 129–133.

Goodwin, H. (1996). In pursuit of ecotourism. *Biodiversity & Conservation, 5*(3), 277–291.

Gunn, C. A. (1994). *Tourism Planning: Basics, Concepts, Cases*. Washington, DC: Taylor & Francis.

Haase, D., Lamers, M., & Amelung, B. (2009). Heading into uncharted territory? Exploring the institutional robustness of self-regulation in the Antarctic tourism sector. *Journal of Sustainable Tourism, 17*(4), 411–430.

Hall, C. (1994). *Tourism and Politics: Policy, Power and Place*. Chichester: John Wiley & Sons.

Hall, C. (2003). Institutional arrangements for ecotourism policy. *Ecotourism Policy and Planning*, 21–38.

Hall, C. (2006). Tourism, governance and the (mis-)location of power. In A. Church & T. Coles (Eds.), *Tourism, Power and Space* (pp. 247–260). London: Routledge.

Hall, C. (2011). Ecotourism policy. In D. Diamantis (Ed.), *Ecotourism* (pp. 135–150). Australia: South-Western CENGAGE Learning.

Harvey, D. (2007). Neoliberalism as creative destruction. *The Annals of the American Academy of Political and Social Science, 610*(1), 21–44.

Henty, C. (1988). *For the People's Pleasure: Australia's Botanic Gardens*. Richmond Victoria: Greenhouse Publications.

Holden, A. (2013). Protected areas and tourism. In A. Holden & D. Fennell (Eds.), *The Routledge Handbook of Tourism and the Environment* (pp. 276–284). Abingdon: Routledge.

Honey, M. (2002). *Ecotourism & Certification: Setting Standards in Practice*. Washington: Island Press.

Hoskins, I. (2003). 'The core of the city': Public parks, respectability and civic regulation in Sydney. *National Identities, 5*(1), 7–24.

Inskeep, E. (1991). *Tourism Planning: An Integrated and Sustainable Development Approach*. New York: Van Nostrand Reinhold.

Jamal, T., Borges, M., & Stronza, A. (2006). The institutionalisation of ecotourism: Certification, cultural equity and praxis. *Journal of Ecotourism, 5*(3), 145–175.

Johnston, J. & Clegg, S. (2012). Legitimate sovereignty and contested authority in public management organization and disorganization: Barangaroo and the grand strategic vision for Sydney as a globalizing city. *Journal of Change Management, 12*(3), 279–299.

Joppe, M. (2017). Tourism policy and governance: Quo vadis? *Tourism Management Perspectives, 25*, 201–204.

Karlsson, L. & Dolnicar, S. (2016). Does eco certification sell tourism services? Evidence from a quasi-experimental observation study in Iceland. *Journal of Sustainable Tourism, 24*(5), 694–714.

King, B. & Pearlman, M. (2009). Planning for tourism at local and regional levels: Principles, practices, and possibilities. *The SAGE Handbook of Tourism Studies*, 416–431.

Kirkpatrick, J. (2001). Ecotourism, local and indigenous people, and the conservation of the Tasmanian Wilderness World Heritage Area. *Journal of the Royal Society of New Zealand, 31*(4), 819–829.

Law, G. (2001). *History of the Franklin River Campaign 1976–83*. Hobart: The Wilderness Society.

MacLaren, F. T. (2002). The international year of ecotourism in review. *Journal of Sustainable Tourism, 10*(5), 443–448.

Mason, P. (2013). Zoning, land-use planning and tourism. In A. Holden & D. Fennell (Eds.), *The Routledge Handbook of Tourism and the Environment* (pp. 266–275). Abingdon: Routledge.

McCool, S. F. & Cole, D. N. (1997). Experiencing limits of acceptable change: Some thoughts after a decade of implementation. *United States Department of Agriculture Forest Service General Technical Report Int*, 72–78.

Medina, L. K. (2005). Ecotourism and certification: Confronting the principles and pragmatics of socially responsible tourism. *Journal of Sustainable Tourism, 13*(3), 281–295.

Michael Hall, C. & Boyd, S. (2005). Nature based tourism in peripheral areas: An introduction. In C. Michael Hall & S. Boyd (Eds.), *Nature-based Tourism in Peripheral Areas: Development or Disaster?* (pp. 3–20). Clevedon: Channel View Publications.

Morrison, K. (2014, April 9). Why the Botanic Gardens and Domain need a plan for the future. *Sydney Morning Herald*. Retrieved from www.smh.com.au/comment/why-the-botanic-gardens-and-domain-need-a-plan-for-the-future-20140409-zqsnu.html.

Moyle, B. D., McLennan, C.-l. J., Ruhanen, L., & Weiler, B. (2014). Tracking the concept of sustainability in Australian tourism policy and planning documents. *Journal of Sustainable Tourism*, 22(7), 1037–1051.

Murphy, P. (1985). *Tourism: A Community Approach*. New York: Methuen.

Myanmar Ministry of Environmental Conservation and Forestry & Myanmar Ministry of Hotels and Tourism. (2015). Myanmar: Ecotourism Policy and Management Strategy for Protected Areas 2015–2025.

Needham, K. (2014, May 26). Gardens not for raising cash: Keating. Sydney Morning Herald. Retrieved from www.smh.com.au/national/nsw/gardens-not-for-raising-cash-keating-20130525-2n3r1.html.

Nicholls, S. (2014, April 6). Paul Keating attacks Sydney Botanic Gardens plan. *Sydney Morning Herald*. Retrieved from www.smh.com.au/nsw/paul-keating-attacks-sydney-botanic-gardens-plan-20140406-366o5.html.

Noh, A. F. M., Shui, A., Tai, S. Y., & Noh, K. M. (2018). Indicators of governance of marine ecotourism resources: Perception of communities in Pulau Perhentian, Terengganu. *International Journal of Business and Society*, 19(S1), 17–25.

NSW Office of Environment and Heritage. (ND-a). Domain (Including Mrs Macquaries Chair). Retrieved from www.environment.nsw.gov.au/heritageapp/ViewHeritageItemDetails.aspx?ID=2424819.

NSW Office of Environment and Heritage. (ND-b). Royal Botanic Gardens and Domain. Retrieved from www.environment.nsw.gov.au/heritageapp/ViewHeritageItemDetails.aspx?ID=5045297.

Ostrom, E., Burger, J., Field, C. B., Norgaard, R. B., & Policansky, D. (1999). Revisiting the commons: Local lessons, global challenges. *Science*, 284(5412), 278–282.

Parker, S. (2001). The place of ecotourism in public policy and planning. In D. Weaver (Ed), *The Encyclopaedia of Ecotourism* (pp. 509–520). Wallingford: CABI.

Reinmuth, G. (2014, April 14). Keating's wrong about the plans for Sydney's Botanic Gardens. *The Conversation*. Retrieved from http://theconversation.com/keatings-wrong-about-the-plans-for-sydneys-botanic-gardens-25473.

Rettie, K., Clevenger, A., & Ford, A. (2009). Innovative approaches for managing conservation and use challenges in the National Parks: Insights from Canada. In T. Jamal & M. Robinson (Eds.), *The SAGE Handbook of Tourism Studies* (pp. 396–413). Los Angeles: SAGE.

Royal Botanic Gardens and Domain Trust. (2014a). Royal Botanic Garden and Domain Masterplan: Community Consultation Report. Retrieved from www.rbgsyd.nsw.gov.au/About-Us/Major-Projects/Draft-Master-Plan.

Royal Botanic Gardens and Domain Trust. (2014b). Royal Botanic Gardens and Domain Trust ANNUAL REPORT.

Sakata, H. & Prideaux, B. (2013). An alternative approach to community-based ecotourism: A bottom-up locally initiated non-monetised project in Papua New Guinea. *Journal of Sustainable Tourism*, 21(6), 880–899. doi:10.1080/09669582.2012.756493.

Schweinsberg, S., Darcy, S., & Cheng, M. (2017). The agenda setting power of news media in framing the future role of tourism in protected areas. *Tourism Management*, 62, 241–252.

Shafer, C. L. (1999). US national park buffer zones: Historical, scientific, social, and legal aspects. *Environmental Management, 23*(1), 49–73.

Shani, A., Polak, O., & Shashar, N. (2012). Artificial reefs and mass marine ecotourism. *Tourism Geographies, 14*(3), 361–382.

Sharpley, R. (2006). Ecotourism: A consumption perspective. *Journal of Ecotourism, 5*(1–2), 7–22.

Spenceley, A. & Manning, E. (2013). Ecotourism: Planning for rural development in developing nations. In R. Ballantyne & J. Packer (Eds.), *International Handbook for Ecotourism* (pp. 292–311). Cheltenham: Edward Elgar.

Stankey, G. H., McCool, S. F., & Stokes, G. L. (1984). Limits of acceptable change: A new framework for managing the Bob Marshall Wilderness complex. *Western Wildlands, 10*(3), 33–37.

Stevenson, N., Airey, D., & Miller, G. (2008). Tourism policy making: The policymakers' perspectives. *Annals of Tourism Research, 35*(3), 732–750.

Sutherland, L. (2013). Botanic Gardens as ecotourism sites. In R. Ballantyne & J. Packer (Eds.), *International Handbook of Ecotourism* (pp. 470–484). Cheltenham: Edward Elgar.

Telfer, D. (2012). The Brundtland Report (Our Common Future) and tourism. In A. Holden & D. Fennell (Eds.), *The Routledge Handbook of Tourism and the Environment* (pp. 213–226). London: Routledge.

Timothy, D. & Boyd, S. (2015). *Tourism and Trails: Cultural, Eological and Management Issues.* Bristol: Channel View.

Torres-Delgado, A. & Palomeque, F. L. (2012). The growth and spread of the concept of sustainable tourism: The contribution of institutional initiatives to tourism policy. *Tourism Management Perspectives, 4*, 1–10.

Wai, K. (2017, March 15). Ecotourism plan still faces challenges to implement. Myanmar Times. Retrieved from www.mmtimes.com/national-news/mandalay-upper-myanmar/25332-ecotourism-plan-still-faces-challenges-to-implement.html.

Wearing, S. & Neil, J. (2009). *Ecotourism Impacts Potentials and Possibilities* (2nd ed.). Oxford: Butterworth-Heinemann.

Weaver, D. (2011). *Ecotourism* (2nd ed.). Milton: Wiley.

Wegner, A. & Macbeth, J. (2011). How the use of power impacts on the relationship between protected area managers and tour operators. In D. Dredge & J. Jenkins (Eds.), *Stories of Practice: Tourism Policy and Planning* (pp. 295–309). Farnham: Ashgate Publishing.

World Commission on Environment and Development (1987). *Our Common Future.* Oxford: Oxford University Press.

Wu, W., Zhang, X., Yang, Z., Qin, W., Wang, F., & Wang, C. (2015). Ecotourism Suitability and Zoning from the Tourist Perspective: A Nature Reserve Case Study. *Polish Journal of Environmental Studies, 24*(6), 2683–2697.

Yochim, M. J. (2007). A water wilderness: Battles over values and motorboats on Yellowstone Lake. *Historical Geography, 35*, 185–213.

Notes

1 Tourism Transport Forum – An Australian national member-funded CEO forum, advocating public policy interests in the tourism, aviation and investment sectors (see www.ttf.org.au).
2 For further information, see www.barangaroo.com.

Chapter 4

Ecotourism and natural resource management

Introduction

Historically, ecotourism and nature-oriented tourism often took place in protected and remote regions – areas of exceptional beauty, ecological interest and cultural importance. These areas were established to conserve biodiversity and to halt the large-scale loss of natural ecosystems. In 1962, there were 1,000 protected areas covering 3% of the earth's surface; in 2003, there were 102,100 covering 18.8 million square kilometers, or 11.5% of the earth's land surface (Bushell, 2003) and they now encompass 15.4% of the earth's land surface and 3.4% of oceans (IUCN-WCMC, 2014). The IUCN has pledged that these amounts will rise to at least 17% of land and 10% of marine areas by 2020. This chapter will provide an outline of protected areas and their often-complex relationship to the pressures and opportunities afforded by ecotourism. This pressure is due to the expansion of ecotourism and its commodification on a range of fronts, including:

- the demands of overuse brought about by 'overtourism', which also call for 'multiple use' management that occurred in the past in parks that had to allow for extractive industries
- the demands of neoliberal-based enterprise as lobby groups seek access for a wider range of tourism activities in a wider range of sensitive natural-resource management areas. These activities (e.g., four-wheel driving, horse riding, hunting, fishing, mountain biking, bushwalking and skiing) are now becoming apparent in a wider range of land areas due to new tourism trends such as 'last-chance tourism' (LCT) and the wider expectations of indigenous and local community groups for an active role in the ecotourism planning process.

The globalization and transition of protected areas and ecotourism to a more neoliberal consumption means a need for better management. Additionally, despite the recent rhetoric by the United States government under President Trump and despite Britain voting to leave the E.U., the global neoliberal economic order continues to underpin microeconomic activity in the majority of Western countries and many developing countries impacted by tourism. There are two main reasons for this: the first is the influence that large, multinational corporations engaged in tourism wield over domestic and international government, ensuring the political and economic status quo remain in place as it best serves their interests (Couch, 2011). Secondly, as Anderson (2017) and Mirowski (2014) find, the corporations' influence is exerted in a number of ways, which is significant given the extraordinary levels of wealth that are now concentrated in some multinational companies (Couch, 2011). These companies are now major players in the global business of tourism, indeed dictating what is developed in tourism and where, and so the resistance to the commodification of ecotourism (see Wearing & Wearing, 2016) is no longer relevant, for it has essentially occurred. Now in seeking to de-commodify ecotourism (see Wearing, McDonald, & Ponting, 2005; Wearing & Wearing, 1999), we might find in the tools used in protected area management a better means of managing the 'overtourism' that has resulted from the commodification of ecotourism. This is the focus of this chapter.

Overtourism, which is described as the tourism to destinations where hosts or guests, locals or visitors, feel that there are too many visitors and that the quality of life in the area or the quality of the experience has deteriorated unacceptably (see for example Joppe, 2018). The first concerns in the management of too much tourism occurred most obviously in national parks when they exceeded their carrying capacity (Ovington, Groves, Stevens, & Tanton, 1974; Sinden, 1975). In the second edition Wearing and Neil (2009) suggested that the preservationist position at an ideological level was under attack from the opposite end of the spectrum by those who believe nature has one primary value or function – for human use. 'Use' adherents range from industry representatives seeking access to park resources, such as the logging, grazing and mining industries, to the many diverse special interest groups who are generally hostile to nature-centered management, such as hunters and off-road vehicle enthusiasts, and in some cases, tourism operators.

Historically, protected area policy has moved significantly in the direction of human use with a move to wise use and better management. In the Caracas Action Plan, the major strategy document to come out of the IV World Congress on National Parks and Protected Areas in Venezuela in 1992, the shift away from an overt preservationist position toward a human-needs orientation is unambiguous: "Protected areas must be managed so that local communities, the nations involved and the world community all benefit" (Thorsell & Sawyer, 1992, p. 14). These sentiments were echoed in the Durban Action Plan, which stated that protected areas cannot be managed without regards to the communities and the economic activities within and around them (IUCN, 2004).

We can see here, in both the use and preservationist positions, the centrality of the anthropocentric premise. Nature conservation's most acceptable and prevalent form is a utilitarian one, in that such areas are deemed necessary to preserve or protect for their potential human benefits, such as 'aesthetic', 'gymnasium', 'cathedral' or 'laboratory' potential. Thus, the use and preservationist positions are constrained by two orientations: at one extreme lies the emphasis on human needs being met in parks, while at the other lies overt opposition to the preservation and protection of natural areas, seeing it as valueless 'locking up' of land. This conflict intensified with the pressures of an exponentially increasing global population and the concomitant consumption of resources this entails. The debate then spilled over as ecotourism became a global phenomenon (Dowling, 2000) and the debates moved to natural land areas beyond the boundaries of protected areas and national parks.

The growth and success of ecotourism has allowed it to move to areas of land beyond protected areas, and so to forms of governance that were much more market based (see Medina, 2015; Wearing & Wearing, 2016). The preservation vs. use debate, prevalent in protected areas like national parks, then moved to the wider sphere of neoliberalist society, with debates around the use of nature and how eco-centrically oriented philosophies have raised significant challenges to the neoliberal anthropocentric focus, which places nature's value more directly aligned to its relation to human needs. An extreme ecocentrist approach would actually challenge the fundamental rationale of protected areas themselves as a 'Noah's Ark solution', for they see protected areas as, in effect, isolated islands of biodiversity. An ecocentric perspective would argue that we would not need protected areas if we did not have such an exploitative relationship with nature. This was the heart of the protected area debate, particularly in relation to ecotourism, and now has moved to the debates around ecotourism and its interaction with nature in the wider neoliberal societies that dominate the tourism industry.

Tourism and natural resource management

Nowhere are the conflicting views over intrinsic and utilitarian value more evident than the debate over the function and purpose of protected areas. It is a conflict over two primary orientations, preservation versus use, and tourism in protected areas embodies precisely this dilemma. However, for ecotourism this debate has moved to the wider society as ecotourism has moved to the marketplace in its governance (Medina, 2015). However, some of the essential elements in that debate underlie ecotourism's success and are now played out in the use of natural resources (nature) in a wider spectrum beyond just protected areas, where they are also still essentially played out.

The consumption of nature is not now rendered passive in the market system – a system in which "the hyperreality of consumption codes, simulates and replaces the social in its entirety"[1] (Slater, 2005, p. 141). The superficial nature of this hyperreality is countered by the codification and categorisation of touristic experience by the marketing, mass media and advertising industries. The guidebook, magazine and brochure are symptomatic of texts and technology coded as 'the entryway into eco-tourist reality' and used to convince consumers that nature through an ecotourism experience is 'real'; this explains the obsession with genuineness and authenticity in much of advertising for nature and ecotourism. However, the consumer is now more aware of the 'rights of nature' in their use of it, because they have become educated. This centralization of ecotourism as a means to engage consumers with nature has also raised consumers' awareness and demand for practices that ensure the sustainability of natural resources used in tourism, such as destinations and the communities associated with those destinations.

Society then, in this case via tourism enterprise focused on ecotourism, provides a value for nature that ecotourists have come to align with their travel experience, this being both the nature encompassing the experience and the communities aligned to that experience. In previous decades, protected areas that had been seemingly incompatible with such activities, because their primary function lies in the preservation of natural ecosystems (Żarska, 2006), have had to transition to this use value, where ecotourism becomes a mainstay of ongoing revenue streams and management. Such an interaction brought both opposition and support and was illustrated and reinforced through accepted institutional arrangements in which tourism and conservation goals were pursued by independent organizations. That debate on tourism in parks was the extension of a long controversy, a controversy that had existed since the conception of protected areas and equivalent reserves. The originating conception of national parks placed recreation rather than conservation at the center of park functions (Nash, 1990). Yellowstone National Park in the United States of America, for example, was originally conceptualized as "pleasuring grounds for the benefit and enjoyment of the people. For gaining great profit from tourists and pleasure seekers" and as "a national domain for rest and recreation" (Strom, 1980, p. 3). Similarly, the Royal National Park, established in Australia in 1879, was originally established as an area for leisure. Historically, then, parks were established for utilitarian reasons, but since the early conception of parks there has been a significant reorientation away from a predominant recreational or tourism focus toward conservation objectives. Recreation and tourism were only minor threats to parks because of the distance, difficulty in access and low levels of visitation. However, this has changed significantly in the last forty years as protected areas are becoming much more popular through increases in mobility, leisure and environmental awareness (Eagles & McCool, 2004; Sheppard, 1987).

To accept increased levels of visitation as the price of support significantly compromises the natural qualities upon which parks and our natural resource use are founded. Every day we witness increasing pressure on natural resources and a need for escalated protection of resources, particularly those found in protected areas and equivalent reserves. The major problem is in deciding what directions and actions should be taken to ensure the future of such areas.

Although protected areas are not conceived identically across the world, the International Union of the Conservation of Nature (IUCN) provides a general definition:

> An area of land and/or sea especially dedicated to the protection and maintenance of biological diversity, and of natural and associated cultural resources, and managed through legal or other effective means. (Sustainable Tourism Alliance, 2018)

Within the definition, six different categories have been identified, which provide an underlining approach to management for protected areas (see Table 4.1).

These definitions clearly identify nature conservation values as a major objective for protected area management. This includes the protection of genetic and biological diversities and the provision of settings for baseline measurements of biological conditions for the comparison of effects associated with development. However, the main definition also recognizes the legitimate right of public entry "under special conditions" – recreational purposes, for example.

Table 4.1 Categories of protected areas

Category Ia	Strict Nature Reserve: protected area managed mainly for science
Category Ib	Wilderness Area: protected area managed mainly for wilderness protection
Category II	National Park: protected area managed mainly for ecosystem protection and recreation
Category III	Natural Monument: protected area managed mainly for conservation of specific natural features
Category IV	Habitat/Species Management Area: protected area managed mainly for conservation through management intervention
Category V	Protected Landscape/Seascape: protected area managed mainly for landscape/seascape conservation and recreation
Category VI	Managed Resource Protected Area: protected area managed mainly for the sustainable use of natural ecosystems

Nature, protected areas and capitalist realism

Across the industrialized West the role of government is shrinking, with many formerly government-controlled sectors – insurance, health, education, energy, water, transport and banking – being increasingly removed from public owner-ship and control and shifting toward a corporate or profit model rather than a public interest model (see Case Study: Cockscomb Basin Wildlife Sanctuary). The impacts of this change have seen no sphere of government exempt from the market-based rationale. In this way, protected-area agencies have also found them-selves under intense pressure to be more 'commercial' and 'customer focused', and to produce more of their revenue from the services provided by parks. This has now extended to most geographical areas that involve nature-human interactions via ecotourism.

As we have found in the previous editions, contemporary questions about whether to utilize or conserve are really questions about who controls natural resources (Stretton, 1976; Worboys, Lockwood, & De Lacy, 2005; Worboys, Lockwood, Kothari, Feary, & Pulsford, 2015). They are therefore like any other question of distributive justice and are inherently political (for politics of ecotourism see Duffy, 2006a; Duffy, 2006b) In our current economically rationalist worldview, natural resources used for ecotourism, including protected areas and now a wider variety of land resources, are considered as no different from competing land-use claims, and most argue for their survival on these terms.

The imperative for conservation advocates is still *how* to conserve rather than whether or not to conserve. Even with a wider influence on natural resources, and in fact because of the influence of market-driven outcomes, ecotourism still needs to wake people up to physical and ecological changes. Environmental reformers also need political philosophies (Stretton, 1976), for quite practical purposes (Weaver, 2001), that are effective in neoliberal-driven societies (Wearing & Wearing, 2016). In this way ecotourism is increasingly being turned to as a sustainable development strat-egy and as part of a political philosophy, not only for protected-area managers and conservation agencies, but also for communities, investors and ecotourists. This is a

CASE STUDY: managing governance by the market, Cockscomb Basin Wildlife Sanctuary, Belize

This case study demonstrates how the market domination of ecotourism impacts the way nature is viewed and managed. It demonstrates that just as protected areas management agencies had to become more market-aware in the changing view of their use from intrinsic to utilitarian value, or 'preservation' to 'use', in an attempt to make themselves more profitable, so the market is not driving how nature is used in ecotourism. Medina (2015) finds that neoliberalism is now impacting Belize's market, and by association, its ecotourism market, which has seen the responsibility for governing nature devolve from states to non-state entities. With this, the further commodification of tourism has the impact of reconfiguring the contexts that nature and human interactions are controlled by – in this case, neoliberal forms of 'government' which privilege markets as mechanisms of indirect rule. In Medina's study in Belize, the state assigned responsibility for managing a wildlife sanctuary and nearby Maya communities to a conservation non-governmental organization (NGO). However, through ecotourism, management of both the sanctuary and the surrounding villages devolved to become more fundamentally the purview of 'the market': as villagers became incorporated into global ecotourism markets, they came to apply market rationalities to govern their own conduct in relation to the sanctuary. The logics of devolution and commodification have reoriented

Figure 4.1 Cockscomb Basin Wildlife Sanctuary, Belize: an example of new ecotourism market-orientated cooperation through NGOs, communities and government. © Kcaples | Dreamstime Stock Photos & Stock Free Images

the use and view of nature, and we believe this case study would be replicated globally. In a new regime, better management tools are needed to ensure that overtourism due to market demand does not exceed the carrying capacity of the resource. These tools have been developed through a similar need in earlier decades through protected area examples.

This unique sanctuary in southern Belize covers an area of about 150 square miles of tropical forest and is the world's only jaguar preserve. Declared a forest preserve in 1984 and finally a jaguar preserve in 1986, the park is the culmination of many years of work and perseverance by individuals and national and international organizations.

means of providing practical outcomes in the struggle to provide a basis for continued protection for the area used. These practical outcomes include:

- a source of finance for destination communities, protected areas and conservation, and therefore an economic justification for the protection of destination resources
- an alternative form of economic development to extractive industry-related forms
- the broadening of conservation knowledge within organizations dealing with ecotourism and the general public
- the facilitation of a private conservation ethic in market-driven neoliberalism.

To operationalize conservation goals in the context of a more neoliberal market-driven approach involves decisions on the allocation of scarce resources and dictates that arguments for natural resources, such as those used for ecotourism, including protected areas, will almost inevitably involve economic, rationalist and utilitarian premises. Being realistic (some would say pessimistic), it also seems unlikely that the potential value of protected areas to future generations will be a sufficiently strong argument to convince current generations to set aside scarce resources for their progeny.

However, to allow the continued growth of ecotourism, particularly in protected areas that are resources that can be enjoyed for recreation and tourism, still poses a serious dilemma, particularly the more market-driven ecotourism becomes. This dilemma is ongoing even in a wider market-driven approach, which poses the issues of current protections based on utilitarian objectives and of future conservation based on intrinsic value. Are these approaches compatible or, more importantly, can either contribute toward conservation?

With such a variety of pressures on natural resources, the need for more and more intensive protection of those resources which are currently found in protected areas and equivalent reserves is all too evident. The manpower and financial resources which are needed for the protection of the 2% of the Earth's terrestrial surface that are currently in protected areas are far from adequate. Can we rest with any confidence that the 98% of the globe which is not covered by the UN list of protected areas and Equivalent Reserves is adequately managed? [P]rotected areas are but one mechanism for attaining conservation objectives. They are an important mechanism but in themselves they are inadequate. (Eidsvik, 1980, p. 187)

A number of authors (for example, Nash, 1997) suggest that the use versus preservation question is an 'appropriate use' dilemma. This dilemma of 'appropriate use' is a conflict of values that will always arise in any anthropocentric approach to conservation and management of ecosystems:

> Wilderness, however defined, belongs to all Americans, yet to enjoy the wilderness is to destroy it – particularly if the enjoyment is seen in terms of mass recreation. (Coppock & Rogers, 1975, p. 510)

Although protected areas are considered as primarily conservation based (e.g., Bruggemann, 1997; Runte, 1997; Strom, 1980), there will always be conflicts between use and conservation.

> Protected areas have been, are, and will continue to be used by people, irrespective of what park management agencies say and do. (Sheppard, 1987, p. 23)

Section 72(4)(e) of the New South Wales (Australia) National Parks and Wildlife Act (1974) requires of protected areas:

> The encouragement and regulation of the appropriate use, understanding and enjoyment of each national park, historic site and state recreation area by the public.

Why ecotourism is a key

A neoliberal society expects an optimal use of natural resources as an integral part of the process of continual economic development, and this has been pursued by a dominant neoliberalist valuing. Historically, in these circumstances the economic justification of ecotourism in protected areas has offered a means of providing outcomes that can demonstrate to society the benefits of protected areas. This has seen ecotourism used to provide an economic rationale to preserve natural areas rather than develop them for alternative uses, such as agriculture or forestry (see for example Schweinsberg, Wearing, & Darcy, 2012). In current analyses of natural or protected areas it is this element that has become central, pushing debate onto the question of maintaining an area in its natural state, as opposed to exploiting the resources it contains and centralizing neoliberal business practices into a global ecotourism.

This economic valuation is being used to justify the maintenance of nature in its more natural state and the existence of protected areas through the demonstrable 'value' of both the wildlife and the ecosystem features for ecotourist use. Ecotourism is central to these strategies, given that tourists are willing to pay to experience these natural areas, while those seeking to preserve or conserve them seek to educate the consumer through the experience in the desire to increase society's support for them (Wearing & Wearing, 2016).

In the past a range of studies have been used to show that protected areas make an economic contribution of some significance (e.g., Bushell, 2003; Butler et al., 1994; Buultjens & Luckie, 2004; Herath & Kennedy, 2004; Prideaux & Falco-Mammone, 2007). These studies have variously used econometric modeling, input–output analysis and multiplier analysis to estimate the impact of natural resource-based recreation and tourism on local and regional economies.

CASE STUDY: Amboseli National Park

Mount Kilimanjaro is the majestic backdrop for this park, which features five different wildlife habitats: the seasonal lake bed of Lake Amboseli, sulfur springs surrounded by swamps and marshes, open plains, woodlands and lava rock thornbush country. These habitats support elephants, black rhino, lion and cheetah, as well as Masai giraffe, eland, Coke's hartebeest, waterbuck, impala and gazelle.

Even early valuations of Amboseli National Park estimated it to be worth 18 times the annual income of a fully developed commercial beef industry covering the same area. Estimates indicate that Amboseli National Park brings in US$3.3 million a year from park fees and related tourist activities. The value of a single lion as a tourist attraction is estimated at US$27,000 a year, while an elephant herd may be worth as much as US$610,000 per year – thus they are worth more alive than dead (MacKinnon, MacKinnon, Child, & Thorsell, 1986). The total net return for a park such as Amboseli in utilizing tourism is estimated to be fifty times more per hectare per year than the most optimistic agricultural returns.

In fact, there are many potential economic benefits related to the park. For example, Okello (2005) estimates that extending wildlife tourism and conservation beyond the park boundaries of Amboseli and through an adjoining community conservation area could potentially generate US$147,867 annually for surrounding villages.[2]

Ecotourism in protected areas can lead to increased economic benefits through both the direct expenditures of ecotourists and the associated employment opportunities it generates, both within and adjacent to the natural resource (Gosling, Shackleton, & Gambiza, 2017). This can be capitalized upon in promotional strategies. For example, a poster in Tanzania reads: "Our protected areas bring good money into Tanzania – Protect them" (Nash, 1989, p. 344). The Terai Arc Landscape, a UNESCO World Heritage Site in Nepal, carries a slogan that shares the same sentiments: "People for natural resources and natural resources for the people" (Gajurel, 2004). This economic rationale in support of parks (for example, Machlis & Tichnell, 1985; MacKinnon et al., 1986) is especially important where competing resource uses, such as agriculture and forestry, are involved and in moving towards support to ensure ecotourists will choose to avoid overtourism (Joppe, 2018) in order to ensure sustainable use of natural resource-based destinations.

The economic benefits of ecotourism have the potential to provide additional support for park protection and to give parks a role in supporting rural development. However, there are continuing questions about the distribution of the economic benefits of ecotourism. Large-scale developments involving millions of dollars may appear to contribute to local or regional economies but, in fact, such benefits may only be illusory. Rates of leakage of tourist expenditures can be very high and are generally found to range from 30% to 45% in first-round leakages, thus leaving limited income for local communities (see for example, Lea, 1988; Mowforth & Munt, 2008) and for directly adjacent communities (Badola et al., 2018; Chirenje, 2017; Mazibuko, 2007; Rylance & Spenceley, 2017).

The question of who gets the benefits and who pays the costs is complex. Although visitors expect some tourism money to directly benefit the local population, in some cases little of that money is actually distributed to the local communities. Moreover, much of the economic impact literature focuses only on benefits. Limited attention has been given to the economic costs of developing the infrastructure to attract, accommodate and facilitate ecotourism, or to the costs of maintaining or restoring park resources that are adversely affected by tourists. This raises the concern of whether the perceived economic returns of ecotourism, in or associated with pro-tected areas, will lead to inappropriate developments or use levels that threaten the conservation objectives upon which parks are founded.

Arguments for tourism's ability to generate employment are also problematic, as often employment goes to persons residing outside of the area. Wages also are typically low and tourism is highly seasonal in many areas. Economic benefits are also subject to external changes, such as shifts in exchange rates that can rapidly change the attractiveness of a location, as the cost of holidaying is one of the most important factors in determining the desirability of a region.

This illustrates several key limitations in the economic justification of natural resources used for ecotourism, such as protected areas. Current economic analy-ses are capable of extending only to those more tangible economic measurements, such as willingness to pay, travel costs and expenditure rates. These methods have been effective to an extent in evaluating some human behavior associated with natural destinations, national parks and protected areas (Job, Becken, & Lane, 2017; Libosada Jr, 2009; Walpole, Goodwin, & Ward, 2001), and in the last decade have provided more accurate measurement of the value of nature-based destinations, national parks and protected areas (Akinyemi & Mushunje, 2017; Castley, Hill, & Pickering, 2009; Koontz, Thomas, Ziesler, Olson, & Meldrum, 2017).

Economics is by definition a zero-sum equation and must, therefore, take account of all costs that are associated with a particular project in order for the economic equation to balance fully. In terms of natural areas, a large proportion of the costs in changing the use of an area are social costs, which in many cases are intangible and difficult, if not impossible, to measure.

Economic concepts do not readily adapt to measurement of the intangible values of natural areas. The valuation of natural areas has its basis in the framework for land-use planning in developed countries, which centers on the idea of 'highest and best use'. For an economic cost, the highest and best use of land invariably refers to the most economically viable purpose. Inherent in this judgment are the limita-tions of economic indicators to value all relevant factors with a consistent degree of accuracy. Clearly it is easier to quantify the value of raw materials, land (as private real estate) or development opportunities in accurate monetary terms than it is to identify the more intangible social impacts of utilizing a resource.

When an economic valuation of a natural area is proposed, it is usually done in order to compare alternative uses of the resource. This comparison is almost always for the purpose of decision making, and this decision-making process is inherently political. While the concept of economic cost seeks to produce a figure that provides a platform upon which a political argument is built, almost inevitably this argument moves to analysis of noneconomic matters or the concept of 'social cost' – in eco-nomic terms, externalities.

In basic economic terms, a quality environment is a 'good' producing 'satis-faction' and therefore must be accounted for in some way. Environmental impact assessment has been developed as a mechanism to begin accounting for these less tangible values. However, the consideration of social costs presents significant problems for economic analyses. Economic analysis has, in the last decade, expanded its theoretical parameters to include nonfinancial benefits (Job et al., 2017) and a movement towards evaluation benefits beyond those that are solely measurable in economic returns (Maroudas & Kyriakaki, 2001; Strzelecka, Boley, & Woosnam, 2017; Tisdell & Wilson, 2002).

It is found that although global property rights in biodiversity and ecotourism can provide some positive support for biodiversity conservation, they cannot be relied on to conserve biodiversity to the extent desired globally. This is because they only allow appropriation of economic use values, and then probably do this only partially (Tisdell, 2004). The solution to the problem should not be based on the development of better economic and social indexes alone and is now being recognized (Strzelecka et al., 2017).

The way we value differently (just as in the 'appropriate use' debates discussed earlier) means indexes cannot alter the fact that what one citizen sees as goods another sees as costs or waste. What one wants to consume, another wants to leave in the ground. Indexes of net welfare have to be constructed by controversial judgments of good and bad. They are still worth having, though every person may want their own. Better accounting can serve all sorts of good purposes and reconcile some mistaken conflicts of opinion, but it cannot reconcile real conflicts of interest for use (Stretton, 1976, p. 314). Ecocentrically informed management recognizes that modern science and technology cannot prevent environmental degradation if the current economic growth and resource use trends continue, and that a change in philosophy, politics and economics is needed to ensure that a sustainable human population can exist in balance with its environment. This is a preservationist position that reemphasizes the need for prior macro-environmental constraints, such as government legislation. Such an approach is based on the idea of ecological economics (or full-cost accounting), which comprehensively takes resource depletion and environmental damage into consideration and thereby addresses issues of natural debt (ShuYang, Freedman, & Cote, 2004).

Conservation then involves the management or control of human use of resources (biotic and abiotic) and human activities on the planet in an attempt to restore, enhance, protect and sustain the quality and quantity of a desired mix of species, ecosystem conditions and processes for present and future generations (Dunster & Dunster, 1996).

Resource conservation is thus a form of restrained development in that, at a minimum, development must be sustainable in not endangering the natural systems that support life on earth – the atmosphere, the waters, the soils and all living beings. An ecocentric systems approach to protected areas management allows a shift from the utilitarian and instrumental justification toward the intrinsic values of the natural resources. However, without this change in values, the long-term future of those natural resources used by ecotourism could be placed in jeopardy.

Sustainable management techniques

While more conventional forms of tourism modify the surrounding environment to suit the specific needs of their clients, ecotourists do not necessarily expect or even desire substantial modifications of the natural environment (Chand, Singh, Parappurathu, Roy, & Kumar, 2015; Fredman, Wall-Reinius, & Grundén, 2012). Rather than measuring the quality of the tour by conventional standards, such as predictability and uniformity of experience, "ecotourism's success is based on the unexpected" (Williams, 1990, p. 84). Ecotourism is built on providing the tourist with opportunities to discover, actively participate in and interact with the surrounding environment, encouraging tourists to assume a proactive role in creating their own tourism experience.

Despite increasing interest from larger tour operators, ecotourism remains largely an activity of small operators (O'Neill, 1991). Thus it occurs at a different scale to traditional mass tourism, as small operators are restricted in the number of clients that they are able to handle at any one time (see for example, Choegyal, 1991, p. 94; Williams, 1990, p. 84). Due to the small scale of operations, political support, market stability, business costs and employment are not as reliable as they are in conventional tourism (Orams, 2003). However, limited group size provides a higher quality experience for the tourist (Chao & Chao, 2017). There is concern, however, that ecotourism will act much in the same manner as mass tourism, only destroying resources at a slower rate (Bauer, 2001; Butler, 1992; Cater, 1993). In the short term, ecotourism is viewed as less conducive to causing change in destination areas than mass tourism is, in part because of its dimensions and in part because of the need for fewer and smaller facilities (Butler, 1990). However, it is thought that, over time, the cumulative effects of this activity may penetrate deeper into the environment and the surrounding communities, paving the way for mass tourism development (Duffy, 2002). For example, many forms of alternative tourism, such as ecotourism, are located in highly sensitive and vulnerable environments, some of which cannot withstand even moderate levels of use, and which often have little or no infrastructure to deal with development (Butler, 1999; Serrano, 2008). This is a fundamental issue for ecotourism and protected areas

Ecotourists prefer to experience natural areas in an unspoilt state; therefore, there is a significant crossover of interest for conservation objectives. However, although ecotourism to natural areas may have positive outcomes, it is important for management to be aware of possible adverse effects so that they might be addressed through careful planning and effective management strategies (Buckley, 2003; Hornoiu, Hociung, & Frăncu, 2015; Ljubičić, 2016; Penteriani et al., 2017; Wang, Cater, & Low, 2016). The overriding aim for managers is to carefully plan for and monitor tourist movement in order to achieve a balance between the use and conservation (Żarska, 2006). Protected area agencies may be attracted to the economic benefits of tourism that may significantly compromise conservation objectives. Managers must be clear about the park's objectives along with the significant differences between forms of tourism and their impacts. Common issues associated with tourism in natural areas that need to be considered by managers include visitor crowding, user conflict between different types, visitor littering, user fees and information distribution (Eagles, 2004; Eagles & McCool, 2004; Penteriani et al., 2017).

Thus, an important consideration for management involved in ecotourism activities in natural areas is ecological planning to prevent intensive usage from causing future damage (Cengız, 2007). It is essential here to note that even when ecotourism is deployed in order to supply protected areas with economic benefits, the natural resource itself must be strictly managed, monitored and controlled through protective measures to prevent degradation of the site by tourists. Most protected areas with the highest biodiversity are fragile, and even the smallest human impacts have significant environmental effects. Protected areas are themselves areas that are in much demand for nature-based tourism because of the very features that they are designed to protect – their biodiversity, remoteness and pristine ecosystems. However, many of these areas lack infrastructure, and park managers therefore have few resources to cope with increasing tourist levels.

The defense of protected areas for their intrinsic value alone has proven to be difficult. In what can be termed consumer society based on neoliberal free-market economies, expensive and often expansive claims on scarce land resources must be based on broad grounds and integrated within a robust management framework; ecotourism has presented an opportunity to achieve this.

As we have seen in previous chapters, one critical element of ecotourism is sustainability. In theory ecotourism's goal is sustainability, which attempts to provide a resource base for the future and seeks to ensure the productivity of the resource base, maintain biodiversity and avoid irreversible environmental changes while ensuring equity both within and between generations. Ecotourism seeks to capitalize on the increase in tourism to protected areas renowned for their outstanding beauty and extraordinary ecological interest and return the benefits to the host community. Ecotourism is premised on the idea that it can only be sustainable if the natural and cultural assets it is reliant upon survive and prosper. This involves reducing social and biophysical impacts caused by visitors, reducing the leakage of potential benefits away from developing countries, increasing environmental awareness and action among tourists and increasing opportunities for the people who would otherwise depend on the extraction of local resources.

Management guidelines for natural attractions are frequently expected by nature-oriented tourists. Management control serves to protect and conserve the area, ensuring that the expectations of visitors are met, thus ensuring that patronage continues along with the natural resource bases. Factors that should be under management control, which may affect natural attractions as well as tourist expectations, include tourist infrastructure and development, visitor levels, guides, vandalism, souvenir collection, area access, off-road driving, animal feeding and others.

Ecotourism groups ideally should be small in scale in order to provide a higher quality experience to the customer. This aids in keeping environmental stress and impact levels to a minimum as well as allowing the tourists' intrinsic goals to be realized. Ecotourism is able to foster an appreciation of natural areas and traditional cultures by enabling the tourist to experience an area firsthand. It is this firsthand experience with the natural environment combined with the quest for education and other intrinsic enjoyment that constitutes a true ecotourism experience (Butler, 1992).

Carrying capacity, recreation opportunity spectrum (ROS), limits of acceptable change (LAC), visitor impact management (VIM) and visitor activity management process (VAMP) are sustainability decision-making frameworks used in protected area management. When implemented, they help to protect a country's natural and cultural heritage, enhance public appreciation of resources, and manage the conflict between resource and user (Graham, Nilsen, & Payne, 1987; Jenkins & Pigram, 2006; Pigram & Jenkins, 2005). In more recent years, these frameworks have been used in a wider variety of natural resource settings (Uusitalo & Sarala, 2016) and as examples for better management globally (Manning & Anderson, 2012). To gain an appreciation of these strategies and their relationship to managing ecotourism operations, we will elaborate on the specific issues relating to sustainability practices by using protected areas as an example. We will also examine their historical development within the context of an increasing environmental awareness and the consideration of broad social factors.

Beyond protected areas to sustainable management strategies

Balancing the tension between the resource and the user during the late nineteenth century and into the late 1960s was largely achieved by focusing research, planning and management efforts on the resource base in determining infrastructure and facilities in parks. Social and economic factors were not integral components of park planning and management, and little was known about the dimensions and nature of human use. In this respect, management did not have an understanding of the interdependent relationship between social and biophysical systems. There was no overall approach to the selection and management of visitor opportunities, and the effectiveness of services could not be measured with incorrect decisions often being made about the size and location of facilities. There was little public involvement in the development of park plans, and often confusing information was given to the visitors (Graham, 1990).

As we have seen so far in this chapter, increasing recreational and tourism use of protected areas is generally accompanied by negative environmental and social impacts. These impacts have to be managed to conserve ecological and recreational values. Numerous planning and management frameworks have been developed to assist managers in preventing, combating or minimizing the effects of recreational use on natural environments.

The concepts of carrying capacity, the ROS, LAC, VIM, VAMP and the tourism optimization management model (TOMM) are examples of visitor planning and management frameworks. Each is intended to complement existing management and decision-making processes (Pigram & Jenkins, 2005).

Carrying capacity is fundamental to environmental protection and sustainable development. It refers to the maximum use of any site without negatively affecting the resources, reducing visitor satisfaction or adversely impacting the society, economy and culture of the area. Carrying capacity limits can sometimes be difficult to quantify, but they are essential to environmental planning for tourism and recreation.

Carrying capacity

The carrying capacity concept originated in the 1970s. Its central idea "is that environmental factors set limits on the population that an area can sustain. When these limits are exceeded, the quality of the environment suffers and ultimately, its ability to support that population" (Stankey, 1991, p. 12). It was believed that objective, biological studies could determine the capacity of an area's natural resources, establishing how much use the environment could cope with and regulating access to the resource. According to Stankey (1991) this 'scientific' basis explains the wide appeal of carrying capacity as a recreation and tourism management concept.

There are three main elements of tourism carrying capacity:

- biophysical (ecological), which relates to the natural environment
- sociocultural, which relates primarily to the impact on the host population and its culture
- facility, which relates to the visitor experience.

Carrying capacity varies according to the season and, over time, factors such as tourists' behavioural patterns, facility design and management, the environment's dynamic character, and the host community's changing attitudes will all vary in differing ways, thus affecting the carrying capacity's determination. However, carrying capacity has not been as useful as anticipated. Perhaps it was expected to reveal precisely 'how many is too many?' Instead, depending on assumptions and values, the result has been "widely varying capacity estimates" of types and levels of use (Stankey, 1991, p. 12). There is a wide range of differing values and perceptions of what an 'unacceptable impact' is. There are no absolute measurements of the resource's condition that can be defined as constituting 'crowding' or 'resource damage' (Stankey, 1991).

As social issues, management and natural resources affect the calculation of carrying capacity, it is not possible to come up with a number beyond which unacceptable impacts occur: "To prevent most impact it would be necessary to limit use to very low levels" (Stankey, 1985).

Carrying capacity analysis then has been virtually ignored because of the complexity of the parameters, and although tourism operators can be conscious that too many visitors will degrade the environment and diminish the experience of their clients in both recreation and tourism, there are very few examples of carrying capacity analysis being used by agencies to successfully limit tourism (McCool & Lime, 2001).

Solutions to the problems of overuse and crowding differ depending on the policies of agencies managing wilderness (Stankey, 1991, p. 13). People continue to use an area for recreational activities even when it is obviously having an impact on the resource. This stems from the absence of an adequate framework that links visitor expectations, use and impact and management decisions (Stankey, Cole, Lucas, Peterson, & Frissell, 1985). argue that the conditions needed to establish carrying capacity are rarely achieved in the real world and that it is only applicable to limited situations where numerical capacities may be appropriate, such as parking lots. In its stead, they suggest that planning frameworks such as visitor experience, resource protection and LAC are better suited to address the issues of visitor impacts. Canada, for example, recognized the concept's deficiencies, such as ignoring the social aspects, and went on to develop more broad-based concepts.

The recreation opportunity spectrum (ROS)

ROS is based on assumptions and tenets borrowed from other visitor management strategies (Driver, Brown, Stankey, & Gregorie, 1987). Nevertheless, Viñals et al. (2003) an innovative approach to carrying capacity by steering it away from empirical approaches and toward developing a sequenced approach that could be extrapolated to other sites. This approach offers a particular research methodology as opposed to a generalized formula. The methodology involves a sequence of phases for analyzing a protected area's recreational carrying capacity (e.g., physical carrying capacity, actual carrying capacity and permissible carrying capacity). It also considers all components and factors that should be included in the analysis (wetland environment, profile of users, resources involved, type of recreational activity), and includes systems of indicators and quick assessments.

More recent use of ROS in the broader global ecotourism context has occurred, and its use can be seen in a variety of countries (Ly & Nguyen, 2017), settings, such as surf spots (Reineman & Ardoin, 2018) and contexts, such as indigenous tourism (Wu, Wall, & Tsou, 2017).

ROS is a framework for prescribing carrying capacities and managing recreational impacts. The process is largely a judgmental one, but it establishes explicit standards regarding appropriate conditions for each opportunity class. Determining carrying capacities for recreational areas establishes conditions of use that are considered appropriate for each opportunity type and provides a means of assessing the relative numbers of persons as a result of changing opportunity types (e.g., Stankey, 1991).

The ROS approach shifted attention from the type and amount of use an area receives to the biophysical, social and managerial attributes of the park setting (Prosser, 1986). The ROS was further developed to provide a logical series of inter-related steps for natural area planning. This new framework is known as the LAC system (Prosser, 1986).

The ROS focuses on the setting in which recreation occurs. A recreation opportunity setting is the combination of physical, biological, social and managerial conditions that give value to a place (Clark & Stankey, 1979). ROS has been described as a framework for presenting carrying capacities and managing recreational impacts. The ROS provides a systematic framework for looking at the actual distribution of opportunities and a procedure for assessing possible management actions.[3]

Clark and Stankey (1979) initially proposed a series of four levels of development, or management classes, under the ROS system: semi-modern, modern, semi-primitive and primitive. Factors used to describe management classes were

- access
- other non-recreational resource uses
- on-site management
- social interaction
- acceptability of visitor impacts
- acceptable level of regimentation.

The ROS has been used to establish the classification criteria and framework for a local ecotourism venture in Taiwan. A number of opportunity classifications were identified, including specialized and middle adventure, specialized, middle and popular ecotourism experience and cultural scanning (Huang and Lo, 2005). Limitations of the ROS are related to its basis in recreational carrying capacity, which is seen as the product of technical assessments, as opposed to value judgments that weigh resource and social impacts along with human needs and values (McCool, 1990). It has now been used in wider contexts as the basis for management of eco-tourism (Boyd & Butler, 1996; Lamers, Amelung, & Haase, 2008; Sæthórsdóttir, 2010) with its evolution taking on new labels, such as the ecotourism opportunity spectrum (EOS) (see C. P. Dawson, 2008; Huang & Lo, 2005).

Limits of acceptable change (LAC)

LAC methodology is an extension of the ROS concept and recognizes both the social and environmental dimensions of recreational impacts. It involves both resource managers and stakeholders in:

- identifying acceptable and achievable social and resource standards
- documenting gaps between desirable and existing circumstances
- identifying management actions to close these gaps
- monitoring and evaluating management effectiveness (Payne & Graham, 1993).

The LAC planning system consists of nine steps:

1 Identifying concerns and issues.
2 Defining and describing opportunity classes.
3 Selecting indicators of resource and social conditions.
4 Carrying out an inventory of resource and social conditions.
5 Specifying standards for the resource and social indicators.
6 Identifying alternative opportunity class allocations.
7 Identifying management actions for each alternative.
8 Evaluating and selecting an alternative.
9 Implementing actions and monitoring conditions (Stankey et al., 1985).

Like the ROS, the LAC framework offers more opportunity for public participation, which results in a consensus planning approach to natural area management (for example, Ahn, Lee, & Shafer, 2002). However, few LAC systems generated in Australia, for instance, have been implemented with any great success, and this is thought to be due to a lack of political and economic support from stakeholders (Lindberg, Epler Wood, & Engeldrum, 1998). LAC systems also require considerable resources to establish inventories of resource and social conditions, which makes it particularly difficult to implement in developing countries (Rouphael & Hanafy, 2007).

The LAC system is a technical planning system. It provides a "systematic decision-making framework which helps determine what resource and social conditions are acceptable and prescribes appropriate management actions" (Stankey, 1991, p. 14). The LAC framework mitigates the conflict between recreation, tourism and conservation. It defines the impacts associated with different levels of environmental protection. It also helps to set the basis for allowing environmental change consistent with, and appropriate and acceptable to, different types of recreational opportunities (Stankey, 1991). By establishing specific indicators and standards related to conservation values, coupled with monitoring these indicators, it is possible to define what impact levels can be permitted before management intervention becomes necessary (Stankey, 1991).

Significantly, the LAC system does more than develop and extend the ROS framework. It also represents an important reformulation of key elements of the carrying capacity concept (Prosser, 1986). By directing attention away from the question 'how much recreation use is too much?' and toward desired conditions, the LAC approach skirts around the use/impact conundrum. Because the resource and social conditions of an area are most important, the LAC emphasis is on the management of the impacts of use (Lucas & Stankey, 1988). It is also now used in a wider geographical context (see Bentz, Lopes, Calado, & Dearden, 2016; Iliopoulou-Georgudaki, Kalogeras, Konstantinopoulos, & Theodoropoulos, 2016; Iliopoulou-Georgudaki, Theodoropoulos, Konstantinopoulos, & Georgoudaki, 2017) and in more specific ways for ecotourism (Bentz et al., 2016; Higham, 2007; Roman, Dearden, & Rollins, 2007).

Visitor impact management (VIM)

The VIM process involves a combination of legislation and policy review, scientific problem identification (both social and natural) and analysis and professional judgment (Payne & Graham, 1993). The principles of VIM are as follows:

- identifying unacceptable changes occurring as a result of visitor use and developing management strategies to keep visitor impacts within acceptable levels
- integrating VIM into existing agency planning, design and management processes
- basing VIM on the best scientific understanding and situational information available
- determining management objectives that identify the resource condition to be achieved and the type of recreation experience to be provided
- identifying visitor impact problems by comparing standards for acceptable conditions with key indicators of impact at designated times and locations
- basing management decisions to reduce impacts or maintain acceptable conditions on knowledge of the probable sources of, and interrelationships between, unacceptable impacts
- addressing visitor impacts using a wide range of alternative management techniques
- formulating visitor management objectives, which incorporate a range of acceptable impact levels, to accommodate the diversity of environments and experience opportunities present within any natural setting (Graefe et al., 1990).

Both LAC and VIM frameworks rely on indicators and standards as a means of defining impacts that are deemed unacceptable and placing carrying capacities into a broader managerial context. However, VIM makes reference to planning and policy and includes identifying the probable causes of impacts, whereas LAC places more emphasis on defining the opportunity classes (Payne & Graham, 1993; Graefe et al., 1990). LAC is now used in a wider variety of settings internationally (see Farrell & Marion, 2002; Godoy, Conceição, Godoy, & Araújo, 2017; Roe, Hrymak, & Dimanche, 2014; Zanfelice, Etchebehere, & Saad, 2009).

Visitor activity management process (VAMP)

Whereas ROS and LAC rely on management of the resource, the emphasis with VAMP shifts back to the user of the resource. VAMP was built upon the previously developed VIM. VAMP has received relatively little attention in recreation management journals, whereas VAMP has been written about extensively in the USA and

Canada, where it was originally developed (Graham et al., 1988). VAMP relates to interpretation and visitor services. This framework involves the development of activity profiles that connect activities with

- the social and demographic characteristics of the participants;
- the activity setting requirements;
- trends affecting the activity.

The VAMP framework is designed to operate in parallel with the natural resource management processes. It is a proactive, flexible, decision-building framework that can contribute to a more integrated approach to management of protected areas. It has the potential to develop better information about customary users, stakeholders, visitors and non-visitors (Graham, 1990). Information on both natural and social sciences is used to 'build' decisions about access and use of protected areas. It also incorporates a format for evaluating the effectiveness in meeting public needs (Graham, 1990).

VAMP is not a process to justify random development at a site; rather, it is an aid to understand visitor behaviour and, where necessary, to modify it. The questions that guide the process include questions about needs and expectations, interpretive services and educational opportunities, level of service for current and projected use and visitor satisfaction (Graham, 1990).

VAMP provides a framework to ensure that visitor understanding, appreciation and enjoyment of the resources are just as carefully and systematically considered as protection of natural resources. "Its strength is recognizing the demand and supply side of natural area management" (Newsome, Moore, & Dowling, 2002, p. 176). VAMP does not stand alone, but operates within a strong planning and management context, as it represents how social science data are integrated within a park's management planning process.

The application of the basic VAMP concept to management of visitor programs follows the traditional approach to planning used by most resource management agencies. However, a major emphasis throughout each stage is on understanding park visitors (Taylor, 1990). The task is to determine the current situation when comparing the park's expectations to the visitors', and then to assess the actual activity on offer in terms of services, their use and visitor satisfaction (Taylor, 1990). VAMP's proactive approach to profiling visitor activity groups, suggesting target messages and evaluating before the development of interpretive programs may lead to more effective interpretation and environmental education programs (Graham, 1990). Boyd and Butler (1996) provide a sound outline of how VAMP fits with the various other approaches described in this chapter and also go on to show how it has been used in ecotourism; an example of its use for mountain biking in parks can be found in research by Wolf, Wohlfart, Brown, and Bartolomé Lasa (2015).

Tourism optimization management model (TOMM)

The tourism optimization management model was developed by Manidis (1997). It builds on the LAC system to incorporate a stronger political dimension and seeks to monitor and manage tourism in a way that emphasizes optimum sustainable performance, rather than maximum levels or carrying capacities. TOMM involves the following:

- identifying strategic imperatives (such as policies and emerging issues)
- identifying community values, product characteristics, growth patterns, market trends and opportunities, positioning and branding and alternative scenarios for tourism in a region
- identifying optimum conditions, indicators, acceptable ranges, monitoring techniques, benchmarks, annual performance and predicted performance
- identifying poor performance, exploring cause/effect relationships, identifying results requiring a tourism response or other sector response and developing management options to address poor performance (McArthur, 1997).

In Australia the TOMM model has been used to address the tourism impacts on the community, economy and environment of Kangaroo Island, a popular tourist destination that lies off the coast of South Australia (Miller & Twining-Ward, 2005). For other examples of TOMM's use, see Pröbstl et al. (2008) and proceedings of the 6th International Conference on Sustainable Tourism (6th International Conference on Sustainable Tourism, ST 2014, 2014)

Managing visitor use

The frameworks we have discussed above are effective means to assess and project the sustainable and desired limits of human impact on natural ecosystems. Once identified, these limits must be strictly monitored in order to ensure that the baseline sustainability limits are maintained. Protected-area authorities must then implement strategies to ensure that these limits are maintained.

Use limitation

> However much proponents of development may ignore the fact, implicit in the concept of sustainable development is the idea of limits. (Butler, 1999, p. 7)

One fairly common and direct, regulatory type of visitor management is that of 'use limitation'. For instance, in the Grand Canyon National Park, private and commercial rafting parties have been limited to approximately 2,000 per year (Todd, 1989). Also, Skomer Island, Wales, is a bird sanctuary with access controlled by a daily ferry, limiting the quota of visitors to 100 per day (Valentine, 1991). While the small size of ecotour operators serves to limit tourist numbers somewhat, there may also be a need for managers to implement built-in limits to control the size and number of tour operations acting within natural areas (Bunting, 1991). Westwood and Boyd (2005) argue that one way of limiting impacts in areas of high conservation is to offer scenic flights, which have become popular in the South Island of New Zealand. Private operators may also be restricted by permit or other such regulations to guard against excessive or destructive impacts (Ceballos-Lascuráin, 1990). As well as controlling the negative impacts on the natural environment, this would serve to increase the quality of the visitors' experience, as most ecotourists perceive

CASE STUDY: Tomm, Kangaroo Island, South Australia

The implementation of a tourism planning and monitoring model on Kangaroo Island in South Australia has attracted worldwide attention due to its strong focus on involving all relevant stakeholders, from local and state government to tourism operators, the island's community and natural area managers (Manidis, 1997). Its success was largely due to the tourism optimization management model (TOMM), which builds on the LAC system developed by Stankey and McCool (1985). TOMM was designed to serve a multitude of stakeholders with a multitude of interests and can operate at a regional level over a multitude of public and private land tenures. Specifically, TOMM has been designed to monitor and quantify the key economic, marketing, environmental, sociocultural and experiential benefits and impacts of tourism activity. It is also designed to assist in the assessment of emerging issues and alternative future management options for the sustainable development and management of tourism activity (Manidis, 1997).

TOMM is being used to help change the culture of the tourism industry and its stakeholders by generating tangible evidence that the viability of the industry is dependent upon the quality of the visitor experiences it generates and the condition of the natural, cultural and social resources it relies on. A 2008) (see Figure 4.2).

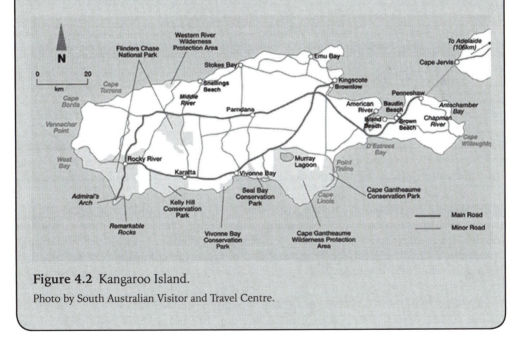

Figure 4.2 Kangaroo Island.

Photo by South Australian Visitor and Travel Centre.

crowding to be a problem. Research indicates that by reducing crowding, particularly in camping areas (for example, Cole, 2001; Farrell & Marion, 2000), the quality of visitor experience tends to increase, although fewer people are able to experience the benefits of this.

Ecotourism and natural resource management

The intensity of use (how many people are engaged in particular activities) is an important consideration for managers of natural areas. Regulations can be used to control the number of visitors entering a particular area in any given time period, their access points and the types of activities they may undertake. As well as implementing these controls, managers may find it necessary to employ some form of deterrent to the breaching of regulations. These deterrents are usually in the form of fines and other penalties, which may be difficult to enforce due to limitations on surveillance.

In order to limit the number of visitors to an area, management must first establish a visitor carrying capacity – an estimate of an area's capacity to absorb visitors so that such use is sustainable (McNeely & Thorsell, 1989; Saveriades, 2000). Environmental, social and managerial resources must be evaluated, as all of these factors represent constraints on the carrying capacity of a given area. One problem associated with the establishment of carrying capacities is that it is a subjective issue, each interest tolerating various levels of environmental degradation. Thus management must determine the level of visitor use that an area can accommodate, "maintaining high levels of visitor satisfaction and few negative impacts on the environment" (McNeely & Thorsell, 1989, p. 33). Butler adds the following:

> While thinking on carrying capacity has been modified greatly since the 1960s, when researchers were seeking the 'magic number' of visitors who could be accommodated at a specific site, the issue of volume still remains. Although it is generally accepted that numbers alone are not an entirely satisfactory measure of the effects of tourism, there is little doubt that, in almost all tourism contexts, there is a maximum number of tourists who can be successfully accommodated (however 'successful' is defined). Once this number is exceeded, a range of negative and sometimes irreversible effects take place. These impacts may take some time to manifest themselves in certain areas (e.g. changes in environmental quality), whereas in others their effects may be felt almost immediately (e.g. resident attitudes). (1999, p. 7)

One method used to achieve a more sustainable level of use is redistribution. Such techniques are most commonly used by managers to reduce the concentration of use in general by shifting some visitors from heavily to lightly used areas (Lucas, 1984), or from peak to off-peak periods (Manning & Powers, 1984). It is believed that tourists tend to confine themselves to small segments of wilderness in accordance with the ease of access and viewing attractions (Todd, 1989). Although this may not be desired by ecotourists, they are often restricted in their experiences by the operators or guides of such tours who, whilst seeking to provide their clients with the best view of wildlife, produce a highly commercial activity. An example of this is the operators in the Serengeti National Park in Tanzania, where tour bus drivers "concentrate on the 'Big 5' – lions, leopards, elephants, buffalos and rhinos" (Todd, 1989, p. 78). Use redistribution has been implemented in East Africa's Amboseli National Park where, in the late 1970s, it was estimated that 80% of visitors used only 10% of the total area of the park. This technique was used to disperse visitor movement throughout the park, allowing carrying capacity to rise from 80,000 to 250,000 visitors annually, for the same level of impact (Todd, 1989). This may not be conducive to the ecotourism experience as impact levels spread, making it more difficult to experience a truly unspoilt wilderness tract.

Managers may wish to shift use in site-specific ways to reduce use in particularly fragile or overused areas and shift some use to specific places that are better able to sustain it. This can be achieved through zoning measures and the restriction of access points to control the movements of ecotourists and other visitors within wilderness areas.

Zoning

Zoning may also be used to control different uses in different parts of the region. It is a multidimensional technique that is driven by ecological data in order to balance the demands between protection and use in determining the most appropriate levels of use for specific areas within the park. Zoning is often used to support wider management frameworks, such as the ROS (for example, Ruschano & Yaotanee, 2007). One of the most important outcomes is to ensure that "activities in one zone do not impinge on the planned functions of another" (Buckley & Pannell, 1990, p. 29). Where tourism is concerned, zoning should include areas that are not open for visitation in order to minimize the impact of infrastructure on wildlife. For example,

> tourism and recreation in the upstream part of a catchment may adversely affect water quality in the downstream region; so if the latter has been zoned purely for conservation, it may suffer water quality deterioration even though there are no recreational activities in the conservation zone itself. (Buckley & Pannell, 1990, p. 29)

Because ecotourism involves low-impact travel and requires few facilities and minimal disturbance to the environment and other wilderness users, it is not so prevalent to zone ecotouristic activity from other users as it is to zone more commercial activities from them. For example, it is necessary for managers to limit or prohibit mechanized recreation, horse riding and other such activities in certain areas in order to minimize the negative impact on the wilderness area, as well as to protect other visitor experiences. Visitor facilities act as a powerful management tool. They allow managing authorities to attract tourists to areas of significance or interest, control activities within these areas and divert visitors from more sensitive areas. Thus, more traditional forms of tourism may be restricted from areas that are important to ecotourism by simply a lack of facilities that adequately satisfy their needs. This indirect management technique of restraint in providing facilities in natural areas seems to be consistent with what is known about wilderness visitor preferences. Wilderness visitors desire a landscape that is natural, wild, uncrowded and free (Cole, 2000). In management terms, this means the absence of built facilities, and in areas where crowding is a problem, a system for limitation (Hendee & Dawson, 2002). In recent years zoning has been used in destination management (Jin, Hu, & Kavan, 2016) and is now extensively used in marine settings (see Bentz et al., 2016; Bentz, Rodrigues, Dearden, Calado, & Lopes, 2015; Roman et al., 2007).

Trail system design

Trail system design has come to prominence in the last decade. It is also an indirect management action that has been effective not only in the redistribution of use, but also in improving the quality of visitor experiences by setting the level of challenge, the scenic quality and opportunities to observe and learn about natural communities and processes (Beeco, Hallo, English, & Giumetti, 2013; Bruno & Perrotta, 2012; Krumpe & Lucas, 1986). In protected areas, trails are the linkage between visitors and the natural ecosystem, so most of the adverse impacts caused by visitors can be concentrated on trails (WenJun, XiaoDong, & ChunYan, 2005).

The design of trail systems may be an important factor in improving the quality of the ecotourists' experience, because they rely on trails to provide an experience in themselves, rather than just a route to attractions. For example, the artificial maintenance of trails, such as the establishment of wooden trails, flagstone trails and bridges can create a point of interest, particularly if signage and construction reflect cultural aesthetics (WenJun et al., 2005). Much of the negative impact that occurs in natural areas can be specifically related to visitor behaviour and actions rather than to sheer number of users. It is the minority "few unskilled, uninformed, careless groups rather than the many typical parties" that cause most of the damage (Lucas, 1984, p. 133). Perceptions of natural areas may be altered through various means of providing visitors with information. This indirect management technique can act to increase the visitors' enjoyment of the area and also to stimulate "modes of behaviour which enhance the environmental quality of the site" (McNeely & Thorsell, 1989, p. 37). It is recognized by Buckley and Pannell (1990) that education may be the most effective of all management techniques, particularly in natural areas where it may well be the only option. Lucas (1984, p. 133) notes that wilderness visitors "tend to be highly educated, most with university educations and often with graduate study, as well as strongly committed to wilderness". Ecotourists possess these same characteristics, and it is thought that these allow education programs to be successful in informing tourists of how to minimize the negative impacts of their visit on the surrounding environment. It is important, however, that the information provided to visitors be interpretive in nature, explaining possible interactions between visitors and the environment as well as methods to reduce any impacts that might occur from these interactions. If possible, it is best that such messages be delivered by trained ecotourism guides (Buckley & Littlefair, 2007; Weiler & Ham, 2001). This information may be provided in such forms as brochures, maps and pamphlets, and visitors prefer it to be distributed prior to entering the resource area. The majority of information aimed at changing visitor behaviour deals with the reduction of environmental impacts through minimal impact camping and hiking information. These education programs commonly address issues such as littering, campfire use and vegetation impacts (Lucas, 1984; Marion & Reid, 2007).

Education

No natural resource can be effectively managed without the support and backing of its users. It follows that no system of natural area reserves can adequately fulfill its roles without the guidance of appropriate management objectives. Failure to fulfill such roles and provide appropriate information is likely to alienate some recreational users and decrease the level of public support for the reserve system as a whole. This would be a very serious situation, for without public support it is unlikely that we would have such a diverse and extensive range of environments protected. The fate of reserve systems is determined largely by social and political pressures (Hall & McArthur, 1996). As Buckley notes,

> Conservation interests hope to use tourism as a tool in conservation, whereas tourism interests want to use conservation as a tool in tourism development. Both promote partnerships, but with different political aims. (2004, p. 75)

Even the best-planned management procedures will fail without public support. A strong base of public support for the aims and objectives of protected areas is one of the first prerequisites for their management. From this comes the political will, the financial support and the staffing necessary to achieve the aims and objectives of management. For this reason it is essential that the natural areas' management provide information that seeks to change behaviour, not just awareness (Forestell, 1990). As we shall see in the following chapter, interpretation and education are the key components of ecotourism and protected areas, and they provide one of the essential ingredients for successful park management. Interpretation provides the opportunities for natural processes to be observed, for the interrelationship of natural ecological systems to be appreciated and for the consequences of human change and ultimate degradation to be understood (Kenchington, 1990). Outdoor recreation has been the major function of all parks and reserve areas, even though conservation may be the more vital and immediately necessary role of these areas (Cameron-Smith, 1977). Recreation in this context is generally limited to those activities that are consistent with preserving the natural state of these areas, although this definition in itself can cause problems. Activities such as bush walking, picnicking, camping and nature photography, for example, are generally considered acceptable within national park and reserve areas; however, even such restricted recreational use can cause problems, including physical damage to ecological and cultural resources. User/user or user/manager conflicts in the perception of what constitutes acceptable recreational behaviour at any given site can and do still arise (for example, Beckmann, 1991; Dear & Myers, 2005).

Priorities in outdoor recreation management should therefore include a balancing of supply and demand – a matching of resource adequacy with human recreational needs and desires (Kenchington, 1990). Management strategies that reconcile recreation with other priorities, such as conservation, have become essential with increasing visitor demand. The visitor, rather than resource management, is now regarded as the most important component of recreation management (Wearing & Gardiner, 1994).

Ecotour operators in wilderness and other protected areas must also assume responsibility for minimizing the impacts of their operations in the destination region. Examples of education techniques that may be applied by tour operators include "slide shows, lectures and discussions to further familiarize guests with the wildlife, history and culture of the remote area in which they find themselves" (Choegyal, 1991, p. 95). It has been identified that a vital component in the successful management of enhanced visitor experiences and appropriate environmental behaviour is the training of the tour guides themselves (Buckley & Littlefair, 2007; McGrath, 2007). It has been argued that in developing countries, such training should form one component of a wider capacity-building program, where the involvement of stakeholders has been found to play an important role in securing positive outcomes for local communities (McGrath, 2007; Strasdas et al., 2008).

A more direct benefit of education and interpretation is as a visitor management tool to manage visitors and reduce visitor impacts. One of the chief criticisms of ecotourism is that it threatens to destroy the environment it is trying to protect. Interpretation is an effective way management can encourage appropriate behaviour, thus alleviating any potentially damaging behaviour of ecotourists. For example, the ecotourist trekking through the Himalayas in Nepal in search of an understanding of subalpine environments may leave trails strewn with toilet paper, empty cans and bottles, which contribute to erosion, and leave ashes from fires used for cooking. However, through education by interpretive means, they may be made aware of on-site problems and learn skills to minimize their own impacts.

While other strategies for reducing environmental impacts from visitor pressure have been developed and implemented in protected areas and national parks, interpretation is a key approach due to its long-term effects (Buckley & Littlefair, 1977). Interpretation can help visitors to understand and appreciate the differences in permitted activities, management practices and conservation values among national parks, state forests, reserves and privately-owned bushland, as such interpretation is an important part of any strategic management plan.

Although interpretation is believed by many to be the most powerful tool for visitor management, it has rarely been incorporated fully into major planning mechanisms (Roggenbuck, 1987). Nonetheless, it is now recognized that the relationship between interpretation and management is fundamental and that such programs should stem directly from management policies (Newsome et al., 2002). For example, interpretation significantly influences the carrying capacity of an area. By limiting the number of unwanted encounters or experiences in a recreational environment, restricting unsuitable behaviour in the area and reducing conflict between users, the current acceptable carrying capacity can be increased

With the growth in ecotourism over the last decade, a significant increase in research and management approaches has occurred using education and interpretation, from dolphin-watching in Fiji (Pratt & Suntikul, 2016) and snorkeling at Marinha Beach in Algarve, Portugal (Rangel et al., 2015) to conservation of biodiversity at Selirong Island Forest Recreation Park in Brunei (Ahmad, 2015), there has been a wide variety of its use in sustainable resource management.

User fees and charges

User fees and charges have been gaining consideration as natural areas have become more popular for recreational use. There is a range of each, and they are the methods of capturing revenue from visitation that is essential to channel back into conservation objectives.

- *User fees*: charges on users of an area or facility, such as park entrance fees and trekking fees.
- *Concession*: a fee for the permission to operate within a location for groups or individuals that provide certain services to visitors, such as food, accommodation and retail stores.

- *Sales and royalties*: fees levied on a percentage of earnings that have been derived from activities or products at a site, such as photographs or postcards.
- *Taxation*: an additional cost imposed upon goods and services that are used by ecotourists, such as airport taxes.
- *Donations*: tourists are often encouraged to contribute to maintaining a facility (Marriott, 1993).

Fees can be an important source of revenue for managers, particularly in developing countries where protected areas are traditionally underfunded (Swanson, 1992). The rationale supporting user fees is that most foreign visitors travel to remote protected areas to experience their very isolation and unspoilt natural features. Research suggests that ecotourists are willing to pay a fee for the conservation of wildlife when observing wildlife that is part of a tour (Tisdell & Wilson, 2005).

> User fees on both the ecotour operators and the ecotourists cover management costs. The visibility of these fees to the operators and the tourists makes an important connection between use and the need for management costs. (Jenkins & Wearing, 2003, p. 215)

Conclusion

This chapter has presented the issues relating to ecotourism and natural resource management, and it has outlined what methods have been used in protected-area management and how these have now coalesced to uses in other ecotourism destinations. It has demonstrated compromise between current views on management of natural resources, and it has demonstrated an evolution toward future sustainable management based on ecocentric management beyond just protected areas where ecotourism has been a catalyst. Given the globalization of ecotourism in neoliberal societies and the dominance of the consumer, the market and economic rationalism, there is a need to ensure the management of these increasingly scarce resources, particularly for protected areas that are going to come under more and more pressure for use.

The managers of natural resources for tourism have much to learn from those of protected areas, who have developed management based around sustaining the environment; this chapter has outlined how this might be achieved. Meanwhile, new trends in tourism must be identified and their impact and management must be explored. One recent development has been last-chance tourism (LCT), which is also termed 'doom' tourism in the popular media, as it is seen as tourism with the aim to witness vanishing landscapes or seascapes and disappearing species. It will have consequences for the management of natural resources; although the nature of these consequences is not clear, last-chance tourism will rely on management techniques developed in protected areas, which have borne the brunt of tourism to these types of landscapes (Lemelin, Dawson, Stewart, Maher, & Lueck, 2013) provide new challenges for natural resources, and ecotourism offers lessons and alternatives to enable a clearer way forward. Park supporters need to join the political debate around a wider sustainability of natural resources, as has occurred in protected areas where ecotourism has been used as a means of achieving economic justification that will ensure the short-term survival of protected areas while developing a political constituency enabling a longer-term perspective. This logic can now be used in debates around natural resource conservation and sustainability. Conservation and preservation of natural resources and cultural heritage are global as well as local concerns. For tourism to be sustainable, the type and extent of tourism activity must be balanced against the capacity of the natural and human-made resources available.

Further reading

Both of these texts provide an introduction to the management of tourism and recreation in natural and protected areas. They describe the potential for environmental impacts and strategies for how managers can plan, develop and deliver appropriate solutions to ensure nature conservation.

Worboys, G., Lockwood, M., & De Lacy, T. (2005). *Protected Area Management: Principles and Practice*, second ed. Oxford: Oxford University Press.
Newsome, D., Moore, S. A., & Dowling, R. K. (2002). *Natural Area Tourism: Ecology, Impacts and Management*. Clevedon: Channel View Publications.

McDonald and Wearing's chapter provides an Australian case study on how the ROS system can be implemented and the way it can take pressure off popular areas experiencing environmental and social impacts.

McDonald, M. & Wearing, S. (2003). Reconciling community's expectations of ecotourism: Initiating a planning and education strategy for the Avoca Beach Rock Platform. In B. Garrod & J. C. Wilson (Eds.), *Marine Ecotourism: Issues and Experiences* (pp. 155–170). Clevedon: Channel View Publications.

The ethics of tourism have received growing attention over the last decade; this chapter explored some of this in relationship to ecotourism.

Wearing, S. L. & Wearing, M. (2016). Ecotourism or eco-utilitarianism: Exploring the new debates in ecotourism. In M. Mostafanezhad, R. Norum, E. J. Shelton, & A. Thompson-Carr (Eds.), *Contemporary Geographies of Leisure, Tourism and Mobility* (pp. 188–206). Abingdon: Routledge.

Exceeding carrying capacity in tourism can be labelled overtourism, which is described as destinations where hosts or guests, locals or visitors, feel that there are too many visitors and that the quality of life in the area or the quality of the experience has deteriorated unacceptably.

Joppe, M. (2018). Tourism policy and governance: Quo vadis? *Tourism Management Perspectives*, 25, 201–204. doi:10.1016/j.tmp.2017.11.011.

Question

Is the current imperative for conservation advocates still *how* to conserve rather than whether or not to conserve?

References

6th International Conference on Sustainable Tourism, ST 2014. (2014). *WIT Transactions on Ecology and the Environment, 187*, 1–350.

Ahmad, A. (2015). Conservation of island biodiversity in Brunei Darussalam: The role of ecotourism in environmental education. *International Journal of Ecology and Development, 30*(1), 51–63.

Ahn, B., Lee, B., & Shafer, C. S. (2002). Operationalizing sustainability in regional tourism planning: An application of the limits of acceptable change framework. *Tourism Management, 23*(1), 1–15.

Akinyemi, B. E. & Mushunje, A. (2017). Willingness to pay for wild coast nature reserves conservation through community-based ecotourism projects. *International Journal of Applied Business and Economic Research, 15*(16), 57–73.

Anderson, P. (2017). Why the system will win. *Le Monde Diplomatique*, pp. 1–2.

Badola, R., Hussain, S. A., Dobriyal, P., Manral, U., Barthwal, S., Rastogi, A., & Gill, A. K. (2018). Institutional arrangements for managing tourism in the Indian Himalayan protected areas. *Tourism Management, 66*, 1–12. doi:10.1016/j.tourman.2017.10.020.

Bauer, T. (2001). *Tourism in the Antarctic: Opportunities, Constraints and Future Prospects*. New York: Haworth Hospitality Press.

Beckmann, E. (1991). Environmental interpretation for education and management in Australian national parks and other protected areas (PhD thesis), University of New England.

Beeco, J. A., Hallo, J. C., English, W. R., & Giumetti, G. W. (2013). The importance of spatial nested data in understanding the relationship between visitor use and landscape impacts. *Applied Geography, 45*, 147–157. doi:10.1016/j.apgeog.2013.09.001.

Bentz, J., Lopes, F., Calado, H., & Dearden, P. (2016). Sustaining marine wildlife tourism through linking limits of acceptable change and zoning in the wildlife tourism model. *Marine Policy, 68*, 100–107. doi:10.1016/j.marpol.2016.02.016.

Bentz, J., Rodrigues, A., Dearden, P., Calado, H., & Lopes, F. (2015). Crowding in marine environments: Divers and whale watchers in the Azores. *Ocean and Coastal Management, 109*, 77–85. doi:10.1016/j.ocecoaman.2015.03.001.

Boyd, S. W. & Butler, R. W. (1996). Managing ecotourism: An opportunity spectrum approach. *Tourism Management, 17*(8), 557–566. doi:10.1016/S0261-5177(96)00076-3.

Bruggemann, J. (1997). National parks and protected area management in Costa Rica and Germany: A comparative analysis. In K. Ghimire & M. P. Pimbert (Eds.), *Social Change and Conservation* (pp. 71–96). London: Earthscan.

Bruno, D. E. & Perrotta, P. (2012). A geotouristic proposal for Amendolara territory (northern ionic sector of Calabria, Italy). *Geoheritage, 4*(3), 139–151. doi:10.1007/s12371-011-0047-8.

Buckley, R. (2003). Australia and New Zealand. In R. Buckley (Ed.), *Case Studies in Ecotourism* (pp. 95–129). Wallingford: CABI.

Buckley, R. (2004). Partnerships in ecotourism: Australian political frameworks. *International Journal of Tourism Research, 6*(2), 75–83.

Buckley, R. & Littlefair, C. (2007). Minimal-impact education can reduce actual impacts of park visitors. *Journal of Sustainable Tourism, 15*(3), 324–325.

Buckley, R. & Pannell, J. (1990). Environmental impacts of tourism and recreation in national parks and conservation reserves. *Journal of Tourism Studies, 1*(1), 24–32.

Bunting, B. (1991). *Nepal's Annapurna Conservation Area*. Paper presented at the Proceedings of the PATA 91 40th Annual Conference, Bali, Indonesia, 12th April.

Bushell, R. (2003). Balancing conservation and visitation in protected areas. In R. Buckley, C. Pickering, & D. B. Weaver (Eds.), *Nature-Based Tourism, Environment and Land Management* (pp. 197–208). Southport: International Centre for Ecotourism Research Griffith University.

Butler, J. R. (1992). *Ecotourism: Its Changing Face And Evolving Philosophy*. Paper presented at the International Union for Conservation of Nature and Natural Resources (IUCN), IV World Congress on National Parks and Protected Areas, Caracas, Venezuela, 10–12 February.

Butler, R. W. (1990). Alternative tourism: Pious hope or Trojan Horse? *Journal of Travel Research, 3*(1), 40–45.

Butler, R. W. (1999). Sustainable tourism: A state-of-the-art review. *Tourism Geographies, 1*(1), 7–25.

Buultjens, J., & Luckie, K. (2004). *Economic Impact of Selected National Parks in North-Eastern New South Wales*. Retrieved from Gold Coast, Australia: http://sustain.pata.org/wp-content/uploads/2015/02/Buultjens31021_NPNSW.pdf.

Cameron-Smith, B. (1977). Educate or regulate? Interpretation in national park management. *Australian Parks and Recreation, Nov*, 34 –37.

Castley, J. G., Hill, W., & Pickering, C. M. (2009). Developing ecological indicators of visitor use of protected areas: A new integrated framework from Australia. *Australasian Journal of Environmental Management, 16*(4), 196–207. doi:10.1080/14486563.2009.972 5235.

Cater, E. (1993). Ecotourism in the third world: Problems for sustainable tourism development. *Tourism Management, 14*(2), 85–90. doi:10.1016/0261–5177(93)90040–R.

Ceballos-Lascuráin, H. (1990). *Tourism, Ecotourism and Protected Areas*. Paper presented at the 34th Working Session of the Commission of National Parks and Protected Areas, Perth, Australia.

Cengız, T. (2007). Tourism, an ecological approach in protected areas: Karagöl-Sahara National Park, Turkey. *International Journal of Sustainable Development and World Ecology, 14*(3), 260–267.

Chand, S., Singh, S., Parappurathu, S., Roy, S. D., & Kumar, A. (2015). Explaining the status and scope of ecotourism development for livelihood security: Andaman and Nicobar Islands, India. *International Journal of Sustainable Development and World Ecology, 22*(4), 335–345. doi:10.1080/13504509.2015.1050478.

Chao, Y. L. & Chao, S. Y. (2017). Resident and visitor perceptions of island tourism: Green sea turtle ecotourism in Penghu Archipelago, Taiwan. *Island Studies Journal, 12*(2), 213–228. doi:10.24043/isj.27.

Chirenje, L. I. (2017). Contribution of ecotourism to poverty alleviation in Nyanga, Zimbabwe. *Chinese Journal of Population Resources and Environment, 15*(2), 87–92. doi:10. 1080/10042857.2017.1319172.

Choegyal, L. (1991). *Ecotourism in National Parks and Wildlife Reserves*. Paper presented at the PATA 40th Annual Conference, Bali, Indonesia, 10–13 April.

Clark, R. & Stankey, G. (1979). *The Recreation Opportunity Spectrum: A Framework for Planning, Management and Research*. Seattle, Washington: General Technical Report, Pacific North-West Forest and Range Experiment Station, United States Department of Agriculture Forest Service.

Cole, D. (2000). Natural, wild, uncrowded, or free? *International Journal of Wilderness, 6*(2), 5–8.

Cole, D. (2001). Visitor use density and wilderness experiences: A historical review of research. In W. A. Ereimund & D. N. Gole (Eds.), *Visitor Use Density and Wilderness Experience: Proceedings (RMRS-P-20)*. Ogden: US Department of Agriculture, Forest Service, Rocky Mountain Research Station.

Coppock, S. T. & Rogers, A. W. (1975). Too many Americans out in the wilderness. *Geographical Magazine, 47*(8), 508–513.

Couch, C. (2011). *The Strange Non-Death of Neoliberalism*. Cambridge: Polity.

Dawson, C. P. (2008). Ecotourism and nature based tourism: One end of the tourism opportunity spectrum? *Tourism, Recreation and Sustainability: Linking Culture and the Environment*, 2nd ed. (pp. 38–49).

Dawson, J., Stewart, E. J., Lemelin, H., & Scott, D. (2010). The carbon cost of polar bear viewing tourism in Churchill, Canada. *Journal of Sustainable Tourism, 18*(3), 319–336. doi:10.1080/09669580903215147.

Dear, C. E. & Myers, O. E. (2005). Conflicting understandings of wilderness and subsistence in Alaskan national parks. *Society & Natural Resources, 18*(9), 821–837.

Dowling, R. K. (2000). Global ecotourism at the start of the new millennium. *World Leisure Journal, 42*(2), 11–19. doi:10.1080/04419057.2000.9674182.

Driver, B., Brown, P. J., Stankey, G. H., & Gregorie, T. G. (1987). The ROS planning system: Evolution, basic concepts and research needed. *Leisure Sciences, 9*(3), 201–212.

Duffy, R. (2002). *A Trip Too Far: Ecotourism, Politics and Exploitation*. London: Earthscan Publications.

Duffy, R. (2006a). Global environmental governance and the politics of ecotourism in Madagascar. *Journal of Ecotourism, 5*(1–2), 128–144.

Duffy, R. (2006b). The politics of ecotourism and the developing world. *Journal of Ecotourism, 5*(1–2), 1–6.

Dunster, J. & Dunster, K. (1996). *Dictionary of Natural Resource Management*. Vancouver: UBC Press.

Eagles, P. (2004). Trends in park tourism: Economics, finance and management. *Journal of Sustainable Tourism, 10*(2), 132–152.

Eagles, P. & McCool, S. (2004). *Tourism in National Parks and Protected Areas*. Wallingford: CABI.

Eidsvik, H. K. (1980). National parks and other protected areas: Some reflections on the past and prescriptions for the future. *Environmental Conservation, 7*(3), 185–190.

Eijgelaar, E., Thaper, C., & Peeters, P. (2010). Antarctic cruise tourism: The paradoxes of ambassadorship, "last chance tourism" and greenhouse gas emissions. *Journal of Sustainable Tourism, 18*(3), 337–354. doi:10.1080/09669581003653534.

Farrell, T. A. & Marion, J. L. (2000). Camping impact management at Isle Royale National Park: An evaluation of visitor activity containment policies from the perspective of social conditions. In D. N. Cole, S. F. McCool, W. T. Borrie, & J. Loughlin (Eds.), *Proceedings – Rocky Mountain Research Station, USDA Forest Service* (pp. 110–114). Fort Collins CO: Rocky Mountain Research Station.

Farrell, T. A. & Marion, J. L. (2002). The protected area visitor impact management (PAVIM) framework: A simplified process for making management decisions. *Journal of Sustainable Tourism, 10*(1), 31–51. doi:10.1080/09669580208667151.

Forestell, P. H. (1990). *Marine Education and Ocean Tourism: Replacing Parasitism with Symbiosis*. Paper presented at the Proceedings of the 1990 Congress on Coastal and Marine Tourism – A symposium and workshop on balancing conservation and economic development, Newport, OR.

Ecotourism and natural resource management

Fredman, P., Wall-Reinius, S., & Grundén, A. (2012). The nature of nature in nature-based tourism. *Scandinavian Journal of Hospitality and Tourism, 12*(4), 289–309. doi:10.1080/15 022250.2012.752893.

Gajurel, D. (2004). Nepal engages local communities to conserve southern plains. Retrieved from www.ens-newswire.com/ens/aug2004/2004-08-18-02.asp.

Godoy, L. P., Conceição, F. T., Godoy, A. M., & Araújo, L. M. B. (2017). Impactos do geoturismo nos atrativos naturais das Águas do polo turÍstico das Águas de SÃo LourenÇo, MT. *Geociencias, 36*(1), 48–64.

Gosling, A., Shackleton, C. M., & Gambiza, J. (2017). Community-based natural resource use and management of Bigodi Wetland Sanctuary, Uganda, for livelihood benefits. *Wetlands Ecology and Management, 25*(6), 717–730. doi:10.1007/s11 273-017-9546-y.

Graefe, A. R., Kuss, F. R., & Vaske, J. J. (1990). *Visitor Impact Management: The Planning Frame-Work* (Vol. 2). Washington, D.C.: National Parks and Conservation Assocation.

Graham, R. (1990). Vistor Management and Canada's National Park. *In Towards Serving our Visitors and Managing our Resources*. Paper presented at the Proceedings of the First Canada/US Workshop on Visitor Management in Parks and Protected Areas, Waterloo, Ontario, Tourism Research and Education Centre, University of Waterloo and Canadian Parks Service.

Graham, R., Nilsen, P., & Payne, R. (Eds.). (1987). *Visitor Activity Planning and Management: Canadian National Parks: Marketing Within a Context of Integration. In Social Science in Natural Resource Management Systems.* Boulder: Westview Press.

Hall, C. M. & McArthur, S. (1996). *Heritage Management in Australia and New Zealand – The Human Dimension* (2nd ed.). Oxford: Oxford University Press.

Hendee, J. & Dawson, C. (2002). *Wilderness Management: Stewardship and Protection of Resources and Values* (3rd ed.). Golden: Fulcrum Publishing.

Herath, A., & Kennedy, J. (2004). Estimating the economic value of Mount Buffalo National Park with the travel cost and contingent valuation methods. *Tourism Economics, 10*(1), pp. 63–78.

Higham, J. (Ed.) (2007). *Critical Issues in Ecotourism: Understanding a Complex Tourism Phenomenon.* Oxford: Butterworth-Heinemann.

Hornoiu, R. I., Hociung, I. G., & Fr ncu, L. G. (2015). The analysis of climate change effects on ecotourism in local communities in protected areas. *Quality – Access to Success, 16*(149), 71–74.

Huang, Y. & Lo, S. (2005). Indicators of ecotourism opportunity spectrum. *Journal of Agriculture and Forestry, 54*(4), 283–296.

Iliopoulou-Georgudaki, J., Kalogeras, A., Konstantinopoulos, P., & Theodoropoulos, C. (2016). Sustainable tourism management and development of a Greek coastal municipality. *International Journal of Sustainable Development and World Ecology, 23*(2), 143–153. doi:10.1080/13504509.2015.1102780.

Iliopoulou-Georgudaki, J., Theodoropoulos, C., Konstantinopoulos, P., & Georgoudaki, E. (2017). Sustainable tourism development including the enhancement of cultural heritage in the city of Nafpaktos–Western Greece. *International Journal of Sustainable Development and World Ecology, 24*(3), 224–235. doi:10.1080/13504509.20 16.1201021.

IUCN-WCMC. (2014). *Protected Planet Report 2014: Tracking Progress Towards Global Targets for Protected Areas.* Retrieved from http://wcmc.io/ProtectedPlanetReport2014.

IUCN. (2004). *The Durban Action Plan.* Retrieved from Gland, Switzerland: https://cmsdata. iucn.org/downloads/durbanactionen.pdf.

Jenkins, J. & Wearing, S. (2003). Ecotourism and protected areas in Australia. In D. A. Fennell & R. K. Dowling (Eds.), *Ecotourism Policy and Planning* (pp. 205–234). Walingford: CABI.

Jenkins, J. M. & Pigram, J. J. (2006). Outdoor recreation. In C. Rojek, S. M. Shaw, & A. J. Veal (Eds.), *A Handbook of Leisure Studies* (pp. 363–385). Basingstoke: Palgrave MacMillan.

Jin, Q., Hu, H., & Kavan, P. (2016). Factors influencing perceived crowding of tourists and sustainable tourism destination management. *Sustainability (Switzerland)*, *8*(10). doi:10.3390/su8100976.

Job, H., Becken, S., & Lane, B. (2017). Protected areas in a neoliberal world and the role of tourism in supporting conservation and sustainable development: An assessment of strategic planning, zoning, impact monitoring, and tourism management at natural World Heritage Sites. *Journal of Sustainable Tourism*, *25*(12), 1697–1718. doi:10.1080/0 9669582.2017.1377432.

Joppe, M. (2018). Tourism policy and governance: Quo vadis? *Tourism Management Perspectives*, *25*, 201–204. doi:10.1016/j.tmp.2017.11.011.

Kenchington, R. A. (1990). *Tourism in Coastal and Marine Settings: The Recreational Perspective*. Paper presented at the Proceedings of the 1990 Congress on Coastal and Marine Tourism – A symposium and workshop on balancing conservation and economic development, Newport, OR.

Koontz, L., Thomas, C. C., Ziesler, P., Olson, J., & Meldrum, B. (2017). Visitor spending effects: Assessing and showcasing America's investment in national parks. *Journal of Sustainable Tourism*, *25*(12), 1865–1876. doi:10.1080/09669582.2017.1374600.

Krumpe, E. & Lucas, R. (1986). Research on recreation trails and trail users. *A Literature Review for the President's Commission on America's Outdoors*. Washington, D.C.: US Government Printing Office.

Lamers, M., Amelung, B., & Haase, D. (2008). Facing the elements: Analysing trends in Antarctic tourism. *Tourism Review*, *63*(1), 15–27. doi:10.1108/16605370810861017.

Lea, J. P. (1988). *Tourism and Development in the Third World*. London: Routledge.

Lemelin, H., Dawson, J., Stewart, E. J., Maher, P., & Lueck, M. (2010). Last-chance tourism: The boom, doom, and gloom of visiting vanishing destinations. *Current Issues in Tourism*, *13*(5), 477–493. doi:10.1080/13683500903406367.

Libosada Jr, C. M. (2009). Business or leisure? Economic development and resource protection – Concepts and practices in sustainable ecotourism. *Ocean and Coastal Management*, *52*(7), 390–394. doi:10.1016/j.ocecoaman.2009.04.004.

Lindberg, K., Epler Wood, M., & Engeldrum, D. (1998). *Ecotourism: A Guide for Planners and Managers* (Vol. 2). North Bennington: The Ecotourism Society.

Ljubičić, D. (2016). Sustainable development analysis of tourist destination case study Dubrovnik. *Nase More*, *63*, 29–35. doi:10.17818/NM/2016/1.11.

Lucas, R. (1984). The role of regulations in recreation management. *Western Wildlands*, *9*(2), 6–10.

Ly, T. P. & Nguyen, T. H. H. (2017). Application of carrying capacity management in Vietnamese national parks. *Asia Pacific Journal of Tourism Research*, *22*(10), 1005–1020. doi:10.1080/10941665.2017.1359194.

Machlis, G. & Tichnell, D. (1985). *The State of the World's Parks*. Boulder: Westview Press.

MacKinnon, J., MacKinnon, K., Child, G., & Thorsell, J. (1986). *Managing Protected Areas in the Tropics*. Gland: IUCN.

Manidis, R. (1997). *Tourism Optimisation Management Model – Final Report*. Retrieved from www.utok.cz/sites/default/files/data/USERS/u28/TOMM%20Tourism%20optimisa-tion%20management%20model.pdf.

Manning, R. E. & Anderson, L. E. (2012). *Managing Outdoor Recreation: Case studies in the National Parks*. Wallingford: CABI.

Manning, R. E. & Powers, L. A. (1984). Peak and off-peak use: Redistributing the outdoor recreation/tourism load. *Journal of Travel Research, 23*(2), 25–31.

Maroudas, L. & Kyriakaki, A. (2001). The perspectives of ecotourism development in small islands of the South Dodecanese. *Anatolia, 12*(1), 59–71. doi:10.1080/13032917.2001 .9687000.

Marion, J. L. & Reid, S. E. (2007). Minimising visitor impacts to protected areas: The efficacy of low impact education programmes. *Journal of Sustainable Tourism, 15*(1), 5–27. doi:10.2167/jost593.0.

Marriott, K. (1993). Pricing policy for user pays. *Australian Parks and Recreation, 29*(3), 42–45.

Mazibuko, S. (2007). Leakages and costs of eco-tourism: The case of AmaZizi in the northern Drakensberg. *Africa Insight, 37*(1), 150–168.

McArthur, S. (1997). Introducing the national ecotourism accreditation program. *Australian Parks and Recreation, 34*(2), 11–13.

McCool, S. F. (1990). Limits of acceptable change: Evolution and future. In R. Graham & G. Lawrence (Eds.), *Towards serving our visitors and managing our resources. Proceedings of the First Canada/US workshop on visitor management in parks and protected areas* (Vol. 185–193). Waterloo, Ontario: Tourism and Recreations Education Center, University of Waterloo, and Canadian Parks Service, Environment Canada.

McCool, S. F. & Lime, D. W. (2001). Tourism carrying capacity: Tempting fantasy or useful reality. *Journal of Sustainable Tourism, 9*(5), 372–388.

McDonald, M. & Wearing, S. (2003). Reconciling communities' expectations of ecotourism: Initiating a planning and education strategy for the Avoca Beach Rock Platform. In B. Garrod & J. C. Wilson (Eds.), *Marine Ecotourism: Issues and Experiences* (pp. 155–170). Clevedon: Channel View Publications.

McGrath, G. (2007). Towards developing tour guides as interpreters of cultural heritage: The case of Cusco, Peru. *Quality Assurance and Certification in Ecotourism* (pp. 364–394).

McNeely, J. A. & Thorsell, J. (1989). *Jungles Mountains and Islands: How Tourism Can Help Conserve Natural Heritage*. Gland: IUCN.

Medina, L. K. (2015). Governing through the market: Neoliberal environmental government in Belize. *American Anthropologist, 117*(2), 272–284. doi:10.1111/aman.12228.

Miller, G. & Twining-Ward, L. (2005). Tourism optimization management model. In G. Miller & L. Twining-Ward (Eds.), *Monitoring for a Sustainable Tourism Transition: The Challenge of Developing and Using Indicators* (pp. 201–231). Wallingford: CABI.

Mirowski, P. (2014). *Never Let a Serious Crisis Go to Waste: How Neoliberalism Survived the Financial Meltdown*. London: Verso.

Mowforth, M. & Munt, I. (2008). *Tourism and Sustainability: Development, Globalization and New Tourism in the Third World* (3rd ed.). London: Routledge.

Munn, C. (1991). *Macaw Biology and Ecotourism, or When a Bird in the Bush is Worth Two in the Hand*. Washington, D.C.: Smithsonian Institution Scholarly Press

Nash, R. (1989). *The Rights of Nature*. Sydney: Primavera Press.

Nash, R. (1990). *The Rights of Nature: A History of Environmental Ethics*. Leichhardt: Primavera/ The Wilderness Society.

Newsome, D., Moore, S. A., & Dowling, R. K. (2002). *Natural Area Tourism: Ecology, Impacts and Management*. Clevedon: Channel View Publications.

O'Neill, M. (1991). Naturally attractive. *Pacific Monthly, September 25*, 1–5

Okello, M. M. (2005). A survey of tourist expectations and economic potential for a proposed wildlife sanctuary in a Maasai Group Ranch near Amboseli, Kenya. *Journal of Sustainable Tourism, 13*(6), 566–589.

Orams, M. B. (2003). Marine ecotourism in New Zealand: An overview of the industry and its management. In B. Garrod & J. C. Wilson (Eds.), *Marine Ecotourism: Issues and Experiences* (pp. 213–248). Clevedon: Channel View Publications.

Ovington, J. D., Groves, K. W., Stevens, P. R., & Tanton, M. T. (1974). Changing scenic values and tourist carrying capacity of national parks: An Australian example. *Landscape Planning, 1*(C), 35–50. doi:10.1016/0304-3924(74)90004-5.

Payne, R. & Graham, R. (1993). Parks and protected areas in Canada: Planning and management. In P. Dearden & R. Rollins (Eds.), *Visitor Planning and Management*. Toronto: Oxford University Press.

Penteriani, V., López-Bao, J. V., Bettega, C., Dalerum, F., Delgado, M. D. M., Jerina, K., … Ordiz, A. (2017). Consequences of brown bear viewing tourism: A review. *Biological Conservation, 206*, 169–180. doi:10.1016/j.biocon.2016.12.035.

Pigram, J. J. & Jenkins, J. (2005). *Outdoor Recreation Management* (2nd ed.). London: Routledge.

Pratt, S. & Suntikul, W. (2016). Can marine wildlife tourism provide an "edutaining" experience? *Journal of Travel and Tourism Marketing, 33*(6), 867–884. doi:10.1080/10548408.2015.1069778.

Prideaux, B. & Falco-Mammone, F. (2007). *Economic Values of Tourism in the Wet Tropics World Heritage Area*. Cairns: Cooperative Research Centre for Tropical Rainforest Ecology and Management.

Pröbstl, U., Prutsch, A., Formayer, H., Landauer, M., Grabler, K., Kulnig, A., … Krajasits, C. (2008). Climate change in winter sport destinations – Transdisciplinary research for implementing sustainable tourism. *WIT Transactions on Ecology and the Environment, 115*, 165–173. doi:10.2495/ST080171.

Prosser, G. (1986). The limits of acceptable change: An introduction to a framework for natural area planning. *Australian Parks and Recreation, 22*(2), 5–10.

Rangel, M. O., Pita, C. B., Gonçalves, J. M. S., Oliveira, F., Costa, C., & Erzini, K. (2015). Eco-touristic snorkelling routes at Marinha beach (Algarve): Environmental education and human impacts. *Marine Policy, 60*, 62–69. doi:10.1016/j.marpol.2015.05.017.

Reineman, D. R. & Ardoin, N. M. (2018). Sustainable tourism and the management of nearshore coastal places: Place attachment and disruption to surf-spots. *Journal of Sustainable Tourism, 26*(2), 325–340. doi:10.1080/09669582.2017.1352590.

Roe, P., Hrymak, V., & Dimanche, F. (2014). Assessing environmental sustainability in tourism and recreation areas: A risk-assessment-based model. *Journal of Sustainable Tourism, 22*(2), 319–338. doi:10.1080/09669582.2013.815762.

Roggenbuck, J. W. (1987). Park interpretation as a visitor management strategy. *In proceedings of the 60th international conference of the Royal Australian Institute of Parks and Recreation – Metropolitan prospectives in parks and recreation*. Canberra: Royal Australian Institute of Parks and Recreation.

Roman, G. S. J., Dearden, P., & Rollins, R. (2007). Application of zoning and "limits of acceptable change" to manage snorkelling tourism. *Environmental Management, 39*(6), 819–830. doi:10.1007/s00267-006-0145-6.

Rouphael, A. B. & Hanafy, M. (2007). An alternative management framework to limit the impact of SCUBA divers on coral assemblages. *Journal of Sustainable Tourism, 15*(1), 91–103.

Runte, A. (1997). *National Parks: The American Experience*. Lincoln: University of Nebraska Press.

Ruschano, R. & Yaotanee, K. (2007). *Application of geographical information system to recreation opportunity spectrum zoning, Chiang Mai Province. Paper presented at the Proceedings of the 44th Kasetsart University Annual Conference, Kasetsart University, Chalermphrakiat Sakon Nakhon Province Campus*, 30 January–2 February.

Rylance, A. & Spenceley, A. (2017). Reducing economic leakages from tourism: A value chain assessment of the tourism industry in Kasane, Botswana. *Development Southern Africa, 34*(3), 295–313. doi:10.1080/0376835X.2017.1308855.

Sæthórsdóttir, A. D. (2010). Planning nature tourism in Iceland based on tourist attitudes. *Tourism Geographies, 12*(1), 25–52. doi:10.1080/14616680903493639.

Saveriades, A. (2000). Establishing the social tourism carrying capacity for the tourist resorts of the east coast of the Republic of Cyprus. *Tourism Management, 21*(2), 147–156.

Schweinsberg, S. C., Wearing, S. L., & Darcy, S. (2012). Understanding communities' views of nature in rural industry renewal: The transition from forestry to nature-based tourism in Eden, Australia. *Journal of Sustainable Tourism, 20*(2), 195–213. doi:10.1080/09669582.2011.596278.

Serrano, I. L. (2008). Challenges and advances at the Brazilian WHSRN sites. *Ornitologia Neotropical, 19*(SUPPL.), 329–337.

Sheppard, D. (1987). *Parks Are for the People – or Are They?* Sydney: NSW National Parks and Wildlife Service.

ShuYang, F., Freedman, B., & Cote, R. (2004). Principles and practice of ecological design. *Environmental Reviews, 12*(2), 97–112.

Sinden, J. A. (1975). Carrying capacity as a planning concept for national parks: Available or desirable capacity? *Landscape Planning, 2*(C), 243–247. doi:10.1016/0304-3924(75)90029-5.

Slater, D. (2005). Consumer culture. In G. Ritzer (Ed.), *Encyclopedia of Social Theory* (Vol. 1, pp. 139–145). Thousand Oaks: SAGE.

Stankey, G., Cole, D. N., Lucas, R. C., Peterson, M. E., & Frissell, S. S. (1985). *The Limits of Acceptable Change (LAC) System for Wilderness Planning*. Retrieved from www.fs.fed.us/cdt/carrying_capacity/lac_system_for_wilderness_planning_1985_GTR_INT_176.pdf.

Stankey, G. H. (1991). Conservation, recreation and tourism: The good, the bad and the ugly. In M. L. Miller & J. Auyan (Eds.), *Proceedings of the 1990 Congress on Coastal and Marine Tourism – A Symposium and Workshop on Balancing Conservation and Economic Development*. Newport: National Coastal Resources Research and Development Institute.

Strasdas, W. (2008). Sustainable transportation guidelines for nature-based tour operators. *Sustainable Tourism Futures: Perspectives on Systems, Restructuring and Innovations*, 258–281.

Stretton, H. (1976). *Capitalism, Socialism and the Environment*. Cambridge: Cambridge University Press.

Strom, A. (1980). Impressions of a Developing Conservation Ethic 1870–1930: *In 100 Years of Parks*. Melbourne: Australian Conservation Foundation.

Strzelecka, M., Boley, B. B., & Woosnam, K. M. (2017). Place attachment and empowerment: Do residents need to be attached to be empowered? *Annals of Tourism Research, 66*, 61–73. doi:10.1016/j.annals.2017.06.002.

Sustainable Tourism Alliance. (2018). Protected areas. Retrieved from www.sustainabletourismalliance.net/resource-center/research-publications/protected-areas/.

Swanson, M. A. (1992). *Ecotourism: Embracing the New Environmental Paradigm*. Paper presented at the International Union for Conservation of Nature and Natural Resources (ICUN) IV World Congress on National Parks and Protected Areas, Caracas, Venezuela, 10–12 February.

Taylor, G. (1990). *Planning and Managing Visitor Opportunities. In Towards Serving Our Visitors and Managing Our Resources*. Paper presented at the Proceedings of the First Canada/US Workshop on Visitor Management in Parks and Protected Areas, Waterloo, Ontario.

Thorsell, J. W. & Sawyer, J. (1992). *World Heritage Twenty Years Later: Based on papers presented at the World Heritage and other workshops held during the IV World Congress on National Parks and Protected Areas, Caracas, Venezuela, February 1992*. Gland: IUCN, the World Conservation Union, in collaboration with UNESCO's World Heritage Committee.

Tisdell, C. (2004). Biodiversity conservation and globalisation: Global economic failures with implications for developing countries. In C. Tisdell & R. K. Sen (Eds.), *Economic Globalisation: Social Conflicts, Labour and Environmental Issues* (pp. 269–279). Cheltenham: Edward Elgar Publishing.

Tisdell, C. & Wilson, C. (2002). Ecotourism for the survival of sea turtles and other wildlife. *Biodiversity and Conservation, 11*(9), 1521–1538. doi:10.1023/A:1016833300425.

Tisdell, C. & Wilson, C. (2005). Perceived impacts of ecotourism on environmental learning and conservation: Turtle watching as a case study. *Environment, Development and Sustainability, 7*(3), 291–302. doi:10.1007/s10668–004–7619–6.

Todd, G. (1989). Tourism and the environment. *Travel and Tourism Analyst (EIU), 5*, 68–86.

Uusitalo, M. T. & Sarala, P. (2016). Indicators for impact management of subarctic mountain resorts: Monitoring built-up areas at high altitudes in northern Finland. *Scandinavian Journal of Hospitality and Tourism, 16*(1), 1–23. doi:10.1080/15022250.2015.1046483.

Valentine, P. S. (1991). Ecotourism and nature conservation: A definition with some recent development in Micronesia. In B. Weiler (Ed.), *Ecotourism: Incorporating the Global Classroom*. Canberra: Bureau of Tourism Research.

Vila, M., Costa, G., Angulo-Preckler, C., Sarda, R., & Avila, C. (2013). Contrasting views on Antarctic tourism: 'Last chance tourism' or 'ambassadorship' in the last of the wild. *Journal of Cleaner Production*. doi:10.1016/j.jclepro.2014.12.061.

Viñals, M. J., Morant, M., El-Ayadi, M., Teruel, L., Herrera, S., Flores, S., & Iroldi, O. (2003). A methodology for determining the recreational carrying capacity of wetlands. In B. Garrod & J. C. Wilson (Eds.), *Marine Ecotourism: Issues and Experiences* (pp. 79–99). Clevedon: Channel View Publications.

Walpole, M. J., Goodwin, H. J., & Ward, K. G. R. (2001). Pricing policy for tourism in protected areas: Lessons from Komodo National Park, Indonesia. *Conservation Biology, 15*(1), 218–227. doi:10.1046/j.1523–1739.2001.99231.x.

Wang, C. C., Cater, C., & Low, T. (2016). Political challenges in community-based ecotourism. *Journal of Sustainable Tourism, 24*(11), 1555–1568. doi:10.1080/09669582.2015.11 25908.

Watson, A. E. (1989). Wilderness visitor management practices: A benchmark and an assessment of progress. In A. E. Watson (Ed.), *Outdoor Recreation Benchmark: Proceedings of the National Outdoor Recreation Forum, 13–14 January*. Tampa: Southeastern Forest Experiment Station.

Wearing, S. & Gardiner, M. (1994). *Outdoor Adventure Programs as a Form of Nature Interpretation. Unpublished report*. Sydney: University of Technology, School of Leisure and Tourism.

Wearing, S., McDonald, M., & Ponting, J. (2005). Building a decommodified research paradigm in tourism: The contribution of NGOs. *Journal of Sustainable Tourism, 13*(5), 424–439.

Wearing, S. & Wearing, M. (1999). Decommodifying ecotourism: Rethinking global–local interactions with host communities. *Loisir et Societe, 22*(1), 39–70.

Wearing, S. L. & Wearing, M. (2016). Ecotourism or eco-utilitarianism: Exploring the new debates in ecotourism. In M. Mostafanezhad, R. Norum, E. J. Shelton, & A. Thompson-Carr (Eds.), *Contemporary Geographies of Leisure, Tourism and Mobility* (pp. 188–206). Abingdon: Routledge.

Weaver, D. (2001). *Ecotourism*. Brisbane: Wiley & Sons.

Weaver, D. (2011). *Ecotourism* (2nd ed.). Milton: Wiley.

Weiler, B. & Ham, S. H. (2001). Tour guides and interpretation. In D. B. Weaver (Ed.), *The Encyclopedia of Ecotourism* (pp. 549–563). Wallingford: CABI.

WenJun, L., XiaoDong, G., & ChunYan, L. (2005). Hiking trails and tourism impact assessment in protected area: Jiuzhaigou Biosphere Reserve, China. *Environmental Monitoring and Assessment, 108*(1–3), 279–293.

Westwood, N. J. & Boyd, S. (2005). Mountain scenic flights: A low risk, low impact ecotourism experience within South Island, New Zealand. In C. M. Hall & S. Boyd (Eds.), *Nature-Based Tourism in Peripheral Areas: Development or Disaster?* (pp. 50–63). Clevedon: Channel View Publications.

Williams, P. (1990). *Ecotourism Management Challenges*. Paper presented at the Fifth Annual Travel Review Conference Proceedings 1990: A Year of Transition, Travel Review, Washington, D.C.

Wolf, I. D., Wohlfart, T., Brown, G., & Bartolomé Lasa, A. (2015). The use of public participation GIS (PPGIS) for park visitor management: A case study of mountain biking. *Tourism Management, 51*, 112–130. doi:10.1016/j.tourman.2015.05.003.

Worboys, G., Lockwood, M., & De Lacy, T. (2005). *Protected Area Management: Principles and Practice* (2nd ed.). Oxford: Oxford University Press.

Worboys, G., Lockwood, M., Kothari, A., Feary, S., & Pulsford, I. (2015). Protected Area Governance and Management. Retrieved from http://press.anu.edu.au/wp-content/uploads/2015/02/WHOLE.pdf.

Wu, T. C., Wall, G., & Tsou, L. Y. (2017). Serious tourists: A proposition for sustainable indigenous tourism. *Current Issues in Tourism, 20*(13), 1355–1374. doi:10.1080/13683500.2014.970143.

Zanfelice, T., Etchebehere, M. L., & Saad, A. R. (2009). Preliminary assessment of the touristic potential of Rifaina municipality (State of São Paulo, Southeastern Brazil) and resulting impacts of the public use of its scenic attractions. *Geociencias, 28*(2), 203–220.

Żarska, B. (2006). Sustainable tourism in natural protected areas: The concept of the set of general planning principles. *Horticulture and Landscape Architecture, 27*, 123–131.

Notes

1 Guy Debord (1967/1994) in his book *Society of the Spectacle* makes a similar claim, arguing the mass mediated image of the commodity has supplanted genuine human interaction in advanced capitalist society.

2 Similar studies abound in the literature: one study in Costa Rica showed that the value of a tropical rain forest reserve in its natural state was at least equal to, up to twice as high as, the economic 'price' of the land itself. A macaw in Peru is estimated as generating between $750 and $4,700 annually in tourist revenues (Munn, 1991, p. 471).

3 For an applied example of the ROS, see McDonald and Wearing's (2003, pp. 163–168) case study of Avoca Beach, Australia.

Chapter 5

Professionalisation and quality assurance

Introduction

Ecotourism, possibly of all the distinct areas of tourism, has achieved a greater industry-wide acceptance and consumer preference from its focus on conservation and nature. This saw its early forms of activity and policy focus on the need for professionalisation and ongoing quality assurance, introducing accreditation, guide-lines and university-based courses as it was being established. This chapter provides an outline of how ecotourism has and can continue to work towards sustainability and how in achieving this, it has developed ways to provide and maintain quality sustainable tourism destinations.

The following will focus on discussion around its professionalisation, which is a mechanism that can be used to move towards sustainability but raises issues that are problematic for it as an activity. This will then lead into, more specifically, an exploration of how a variety of systems of quality assurance based around criteria, mechanisms and indicators have been used to manage ecotourism.

One thing that makes ecotourism unique is the offer of interaction with the natural environment, with experiences that engage with choice, risk and involvement with host communities. In today's urbanised societies, people have less opportunity to participate in these forms of activities, they are likely to have to pay to do so and most desire a guarantee of security and a quality experience from the provider. Thus, the ecotour operator (provider) needs to instil trust in the ecotourist (client) in order to attract and encourage them. But the provider also needs to offer experiences that provide interaction with nature and have meaning for the tourist, while at the same time providing a platform to educate tourists and instil ecotourism's value as an ongoing resource for the future. Professionalisation offers the structures and baseline elements required to achieve this. It introduces elements such as codes of ethics and practice, quality assurance and standardisation of practice, codes of conduct, certification and accreditation; these are examined to demonstrate profes-sionalisation's usefulness as well as some of its weaknesses.

The second objective of this chapter is to explore the tourism industry and its implementation of quality management systems that are seen as being able to obtain the quality improvement of tourism products and services, while achieving the desired economic performance and creating a positive image in the marketplace (Claver-Cortés, Pereira-Moliner, Tarí, & Molina-Azorín, 2008; Claver, Tarí, & Pereira, 2006). This generally would include such things as determining a quality policy, creating and implementing quality planning and assurance, and assuring quality control and quality improvement.

The tension for ecotourism exists between the necessity for customer orientation by tour operators and the need to ensure adherence to the principles of ecotourism of conservation, education and commitment to the host community. This chapter explains how this can be offered through the concepts of professionalism and quality assurance. However, this comes with a cautionary note: professionalism and quality assurance, while providing ecotourists with the security they seek, can in turn reduce the excitement, interaction and learning found in the natural environments visited. As Jacobs and Harms (2014, p. 123) suggest, "The effect of emotion interpretation was larger than were the effects of knowledge interpretation and responsibility interpretation".

Budowski (1976) identified ecotourism as an industry with considerable potential to work symbiotically with conservation forces. Whilst the latter may sometimes view the former with a degree of suspicion on account of often poor standards in tourism planning, when pursued correctly, Budowski (1976, p. 27) notes there is the potential for a partnership that "can contribute greatly to development – the right kind of development involving the right kind of change – leading to a better quality of life for all concerned". This is a fundamental goal of sustainability, and for this reason ecotourism often appeals to advocates of environmental and social responsibility, a core element of Agenda 21 and the Millennium Development Goals (United Nations, 2015; United Nations, 1993). This appeal has become more and more apparent as ecotourism has evolved and studies have shown how "it contributes to tourism studies by engaging a political ecology approach to unpack the concept of 'local people' through a multi-community study of the ripple effects of ecotourism within its immediately surrounding areas" (Gezon, 2014, p. 821). One of the areas that demonstrates this is how ecotourism has become professionalised, which brings both positive and negative outcomes (see for example, Gezon, 2014).

Professionalisation

The notion of a professional is the provision of a service that is best provided by an expert (see for example, Andersson, Lundgren, & Lundén, 2017; Vishlenkova, 2016; Weiler & Black, 2015). The professional approach is developed during training, when individuals acquire a certain self-concept that gives legitimacy to their actions (see Li, 2015). This training consists of absorbing a particular way of thinking about oneself and one's society (see Humburg, 2017). 'Professional' is a term used usually in reference to a group of workers who are prepared by a program of education and training to perform a service and who are sanctioned by the community with a characteristic set of values, skills and knowledge base. Currently ecotourism has no set base of examinable knowledge, nor is it overseen by a professional body. However, a range of international bodies, governments and international non-governmental organizations (NGOs) have engaged in producing tertiary courses and guides to how ecotourism should be practiced (see Butler, 1992; Ceballos-Lascuráin, 1996; World Wide Fund for Nature (WWF), 1992; WWF International, 2001).

The advantages of professionalisation for ecotourism are high standards, reduced risk and better service; this is considered particularly important as many ecotourism activities occur in national parks and protected areas, where there is concern for the impact on these highly valued and vulnerable natural protected area resources. The advantages of the professionalisation of ecotourism in particular for operators and guides include the membership in the professional social status, job satisfaction through control of standards and economic advantages as a result of social status and monopoly positions (see Fennell, 2015; Huang & Weiler, 2010; Weiler & Black, 2015). The disadvantages for ecotourism include the decline in standards once these privileges are granted, so that adherence to the customer's desires becomes more prevalent than the protection of the resource (for example, tourists pressuring guides to get closer to animals in wildlife viewing, leading to the guides ignoring the minimum distances). Most authors writing on the area of leisure in which there exist parallels for ecotourism (see for example, Burton, 1982; Goodale & Witt, 1982; Sky, 1987) offer words of caution, seeing many problems and risks but generally advocating professionalisation to varying degrees (Andersson et al., 2017; Goodale & Witt, 1982; Li, 2015; Simpson, 2005).

The professionalisation of ecotourism can be identified by a number of elements, firstly by an ordered system of knowledge that the profession can be based on. Wearing (1995) goes on to discuss how this then gives ecotourism a professional authority in that area, and so ecotourism professionals are able to advise the ecotourist, are recognised by the community through qualifications and are supported by legal sanctions. The professional body, then, imposes a code of ethics upon its members so as to prevent abuse of the principles of status that the community has conferred upon the profession. This has been outlined for ecotourism guiding (see Weiler & Black, 2015).

However, the idea that one needs a service that is best provided by an expert creates a relationship of mutual dependency and creates a social distance between the ecotourist and the professional (e.g., the ecotour operator who may come from a host or indigenous community). This is essentially a political relationship since it legitimises the professional in the role of policy and decision maker for the customer. Rather than fostering a sense of shared responsibility for ecotourism, the professional behaves in ways that are designed to maintain awe of and respect for it (see Gezon, 2014). This, in the case of ecotourism, could be transferred by the individual professional to the ecotourist in terms of attitude to the natural environment, which in turn becomes distanced.

Professionalisation can lead to encouragement of the status quo and support of bureaucratic rationality, modern technology, centralised authority and scientific control. It can develop a positivist and rationalist way of knowing and organising the world, presupposing the existence of objective knowledge and decision-making processes, which devolve subjectivity in order to maintain control. This approach to ecotourism could legitimise technique at the expense of human interrelationships and nature links, which we see as the key elements of ecotourism. Gezon (2014, p. 281) finds and "argues that a concentration and professionalization of ecotourism services within a region can marginalize neighbouring human communities" and that "as tourist numbers have increased, infrastructure to accommodate them has developed and tour guiding has professionalized". This professionalising of tour guiding is examined by Weiler and Black (2015), who outline the advantages and disadvantages, finding that in some cases "guides actively block or mediate negatively between visitors and the host communities and environments they visit" (2015, p. 34).

Quality assurance measures

Because ecotourism is engaged with protected areas as a primary source for its activities and experiences, it was very quickly regulated. In a neoliberal-dominated global tourism industry, this has generally been done using legislation; for ecotourism, this regulation was used in order to comply with protected-area governance and agencies' directives. Here we outline how this then introduced a range of tools that can be used under the requirements of legislation that creates a regulatory environment, focusing on how this regulation has been labelled and directed towards the idea of quality assurance.

Quality assurance: its tools and instruments

Quality assurance has been used in ecotourism in a variety of ways (see Black & Crabtree, 2007; Chen, 2011; Dietz & Hanemaaijer, 2012; Huang & Weiler, 2010; Merce, Milin, Pet, Sirbu, & Ciolac, 2016; Meyer, 2012; Munanura, Tumwesigye, Sabuhoro, Mariza, & Rugerinyange, 2017; Stockmann, 2012), but generally the first step toward quality assurance is the introduction of legislation that provides the authority to ensure that the industry must meet some form of standard. The alternative is a set of voluntary standards, which are useful, but they have had mixed success in neoliberal societies (see for example, Merger & Pistorius, 2011), as they do not have enforced requirements, so in a competitive tourism industry they can soon be abandoned, while measures that are defined in legislation can be enforced, conveyed and regulated.

In the first instance licensing has been used in ecotourism (see Huang & Weiler, 2010), which is the process of checking compliance with any legislation and regulations, and it conveys a permission to operate (Bassett, 2012; Catlin, Jones, & Jones, 2012; Curtin, 2003; Huang & Weiler, 2010; Rodger, Smith, Newsome, & Moore, 2011; Venables, McGregor, Brain, & Van Keulen, 2016). Explicitly for ecotourism, the purposes of licensing are to protect the public from incompetent practitioners and to ensure sustainable destination management is achieved. For example, the process may require an individual or tourism business to have a licence or a permit to operate, conduct an activity, enter into or practise in a particular location, such as a national park. It is necessary to ensure that mandatory or legislative requirements do not act as barriers to business and that they act mainly to restrict operations to those who meet a minimum acceptable standard. Thus, licensing requirements mainly serve to protect the public from incompetent practice. Minimal standards, whilst necessary and important, do not necessarily demonstrate however a quest or aim for best practice or quality (see Azizi Jalilian, Danehkar, & Shaban Ali Fami, 2012; Font & Harris, 2004).

The use of the measures introduced in the governance of ecotourism have focused on the quality of ecotourism, and, despite the necessary and important role that regulation, policy and other government initiatives play in complementing and supporting ecotourism planning and delivery, these initiatives have been previously outlined and discussed by a range of authors (see Fennell, 2015; Pickering & Weaver, 2003; see Samà, 2011; Weaver & Lawton, 2014; Weaver & Lawton, 2007) and so will not be discussed in any detail here.

The focus in this chapter will be on examining the spectrum of initiatives that may be used to promote and support quality ecotourism. These range from those that are compulsory to those that are voluntary, which means that the initiator is not obliged by law to propose or run the initiative, and the target groups are not obliged to conform or apply; therefore, voluntary initiatives do not restrict trade or operation. The compulsory initiatives have been covered in ecotourism by other authors, with Samà's (2011) overview providing a sound outline. The tools offered by voluntary options can demand best practice and offer a good test for ecotourism rather than accepting a minimum standard, which regulation can impose. Voluntary initiatives must as a minimum meet, but preferably exceed, regulatory compliance. They often indicate practices for which there is no legislation or regulatory control. Voluntary tools include initiatives such as prizes and awards of excellence, codes of conduct or practice, environmental management systems, best-practice guidelines, self-commitments and self-declarations, professional certification programs for individuals such as tour guides, certification and accreditation programs.

Awards for excellence have the potential to become an important catalyst for transforming the tourism industry, enabling it to meet the challenges of the new millennium. The awards not only codify the traditional principles of quality improvements, but also have the ability to provide tourism businesses with a comprehensive framework for assessing their progress towards the new paradigm of quality, which includes environmental considerations. However, there is a danger that winning an award can become the goal rather than the consequence of an organization's quality improvement process. The underlying value of awards lies in the discipline they inspire and not the award itself, a concept that is yet to be understood by many in the tourism industry. The awards' strength lies in their high profile, their weakness lies in their misunderstanding and narrow interpretation of quality. Examples of how awards have been used can be seen in Huang and Weiler (2010, p. 854), who find in talking about tour guiding in China that "'awards-for-excellence schemes could be utilised to advocate sustainable tourism principles and practices, should the government recognise such a need in its policy agenda".' These have also been used successfully in the tourism industry worldwide with varying degrees of success (see Courtenay, 1996; Font, 2002; Fraguell, Martí, Pintó, & Coenders, 2016; Huang & Weiler, 2010; Sasidharan, Sirakaya, & Kerstetter, 2002; Shepherd, 2002; Tubb, 1997; Wheeler, 2003).

Codes of conduct

The use of codes of conduct and guidelines is of interest here as they are part of the attempt to ensure a high level of standard is achieved in ecotourism. However, codes of conduct and guidelines are not the same as regulations; regulations have legal status, while codes and guidelines are voluntary and are a form of self-regulation. The interest here in codes of conduct lies in the idea that if ecotourism is representative of its philosophical basis in sustainability and ethics, then it should in theory respond well to voluntary directives like these. Given that codes of conduct have a wide range of initiators, including governments, NGOs, industry representatives and concerned individuals, and given that they are targeted at tourists, industry, government and host communities, it is of interest to see how they succeed. The message of most codes involves statements, or more usually instructions, about environmental and cultural factors. Codes may be backed up with guidelines and seek sustainable outcomes within the parameters of ecotourism's objectives. However, a number of codes lack supporting guidelines and are largely a set of instructions; as such, they rely on the tour guides, providers and recipient (the ecotourist) to provide interpretation and practice.

If no guidelines are provided, this then raises a range of issues with regard to the use and effectiveness of ecotourism codes. If the codes are not monitored, they become solely reliant on the end users and their understanding and desire to act; additionally, there is a great variability among codes and a general lack of coordination. Codes of conduct have been used in a wider range of settings internationally with varying degrees of success (see Clarke, 2002; Hoover-Miller et al., 2013; Huang & Weiler, 2010; Mason, 1997; Merce et al., 2016; Richards et al., 2015; Smith & Font, 2014; Trave, Brunnschweiler, Sheaves, Diedrich, & Barnett, 2017). It is evident that codes can be ineffective, and 'greenwashing' certainly occurs. For example, an operator might just claim that they have meet the requirements of a code in an attempt to sell more holidays. However, in the research the success seems to be favourable, with some elements of the codes having a low level of success while others much higher (see Quiros, 2007); generally, research suggests they work and should continue to be used (see Bentz, Rodrigues, Dearden, Calado, & Lopes, 2015; Hoover-Miller et al., 2013; Hunt, Harvey, Miller, Johnson, & Phongsuwan, 2013; Quiros, 2007; Smith, Scarr, & Scarpaci, 2010; Smith, Scarpaci, Scarr, & Otway, 2014; Ziegler, Dearden, & Rollins, 2016), and many reviews of specific activities find they have been effective (Trave et al., 2017).

Overall, it appears that the ecotourism industry has taken an ownership of 'codes of practice' that has seen them become effective when used, and research has recommended continued use. It has been claimed that codes that have been designed with the involvement of intended user groups, who thus feel ownership of content and tone, are likely to work better than those created by external bodies (Holmes, Grimwood, & King, 2016). It would appear that relying on the altruistic motives of the ecotourist is not unrealistic, but where operators are provided with codes, some external regulation may be required to strengthen this form of voluntary self-regulation. Historically it seems some have chosen to target the use of codes in ecotourism management, and these codes have been an easy target for those who view such an approach as weak and ineffective. However, research outcomes find codes of conduct in ecotourism to be successful and recommend continued use, as the codes provide education and are concerned more with prevention than cure.

Certification and accreditation

Certification and accreditation have been prominent in ecotourism (Bell & Ruhanen, 2016; Black & Crabtree, 2007; Buckley, 2001; Buckley, 2002; Cretu, 2013; Ecotourism Operators of Australia and the Australian Tourism Operators Network, 2000; Font, 2002; Font, Sanabria, & Skinner, 2003; Fraguell et al., 2016; Griffin & De Lacey, 2002; Huang & Weiler, 2010; Manidis, 1994; Matysek & Kriwoken, 2003; McArthur, 1997; Wearing, Cynn, Ponting, & McDonald, 2002; Wearing, 1995) and were quickly used and became a major part of the ecotourism industry, which used them as a quality assurance mechanism and demonstrated another way of achieving the goal of improving the quality of ecotourism. Weiler and Black (2015) find certification is a voluntary procedure; it is seen as being able to assess and monitor, and it gives written assurance that a business, product, process, service or management system conforms to a specific requirement. Additionally, it can be used as a marketable logo (see for example, Fennell, 2015), as it is given to those that conform or meet the criteria. Black and Crabtree (2007) find that in general for certification and accreditation, the standard is at least meeting, but generally being above, any regulatory requirements. Certification has ongoing relevance because it measures compliance through both initial assessment and subsequent audits (i.e., the certifying body monitors and polices). While certification endorses skilled expertise or best practice rather than regulating for a minimum acceptable standard, accreditation, in contrast, is the procedure by which an authoritative body formally recognizes that a certifier or certification program is competent to carry out specific tasks (i.e., it certifies the certifiers, or demonstrates that they are doing their job correctly). The use of these two elements has to a large degree been successful over the years in ecotourism (Black & Crabtree, 2007; Buckley, 2001; Buckley, 2002; Cretu, 2013; Font, 2002; Font et al., 2003; Fraguell et al., 2016; Huang & Weiler, 2010; Matysek & Kriwoken, 2003), and they have created a successful mix for the ecotourism industry.

Conclusion

Professionalisation and quality assurance have shaped the achievement of sustainable outcomes for ecotourism in a generally positive way. In a neoliberal environment where consumer culture has come to dominate the way we undertake tourism, it is important to understand the forces that drive and shape the changing face of ecotourism and the role certain areas play, and this chapter has outlined one of those areas. This chapter provides the sense that ecotourism is different from more mainstream tourism and has been able to, in small ways, instigate mechanisms that might have struggled in other areas of the industry. Ecotourism has reflected, in its development of professionalisation and quality assurance, the broader sense of its underlying philosophy. The industry has been able to ensure that operators can understand ecotourism's purpose and that conservationists can also appreciate and recognise the wide-ranging tourism industry forces (Black & Crabtree, 2007). The effect of elements such as neoliberalism cannot be ignored and have influenced the instigation of practices in this area; however, it seems ecotourism has to deal with these issues in a realistic manner, with some finding a balanced but positive return:

> The results indicate that 39.4% of respondents knew about the term "ecotourism", and that 22.2% or 12.0 million of the state's visitors in 2008 were ecotourists. By comparison to non-ecotourists, these self-identified ecotourists were found to be more environmentally concerned and responsible, more dedicated to nature, more supportive of tourism accreditation programs, and more likely to patronize businesses with good environmental practices, even at a higher cost. (Deng & Li, 2015, p. 255)

The effectiveness of these measures will continue to be debated in the future, and market-driven decisions will always affect these practices, but generally speaking they have had positive impacts on the ecotourism industry and its engagement with the natural environment. With the increase in ecotourists, the balance of market-driven outcomes will always place pressure on these types of mechanisms and will influence the variety of avenues taken in the future as a wider audience is attracted to the experiences offered.

Further reading

Newson provides a good outline of the frameworks for an ecotourism accreditation program, while Mic and Eagles provide a case study of Costa Rica's certification for sustainable tourism program (CST) and how that is working for the ecolodges brand.

Newson, M. (2001). Encouraging and rewarding best practice: Australia's Nature and Ecotourism Accreditation Programme (NEAP). *Industry and Environment*, 24(3–4), 24–27.
Mic, M. & Eagles, P. F. J. (2018). Cooperative branding for mid-range ecolodges: Costa Rica case study. *Journal of Outdoor Recreation and Tourism*. Doi:10.1016/j.jort.2017.12.001.

Chen outlines how the government seeks to achieve quality assurance of whale- and dolphin-watching tourism by introducing an ecolabelling program.

Chen, C. L. (2011). From catching to watching: Moving towards quality assurance of whale/dolphin watching tourism in Taiwan. *Marine Policy*, 35(1), 10–17.

Question

Has ecotourism achieved a level of professionalisation and quality assurance that positions it as sustainable and enables it to stand out against other forms of tourism?

References

Andersson, B. T., Lundgren, S. M., & Lundén, M. (2017). Trends that have influenced the Swedish radiography profession over the last four decades. *Radiography*, 23(4), 292–297. doi:10.1016/j.radi.2017.07.012.
Azizi Jalilian, M., Danehkar, A., & Shaban Ali Fami, H. (2012). Determination of indicators and standards for tourism impacts in protected Karaj River, Iran. *Tourism Management*, 33(1), 61–63. doi:10.1016/j.tourman.2011.01.024.
Bassett, A. (2012). Reefs, recreation and regulation: Addressing tourism pressures at the Ningaloo Coast World Heritage site. *Environmental and Planning Law Journal*, 29(3), 239–255.
Bell, C. & Ruhanen, L. (2016). The diffusion and adoption of eco-innovations amongst tourism businesses: The role of the social system. *Tourism Recreation Research*, 41(3), 291–301. doi:10.1080/02508281.2016.1207881.

Bentz, J., Rodrigues, A., Dearden, P., Calado, H., & Lopes, F. (2015). Crowding in marine environments: Divers and whale watchers in the Azores. *Ocean and Coastal Management, 109*, 77–85. doi:10.1016/j.ocecoaman.2015.03.001.

Black, R. & Crabtree, A. (2007). *Quality Assurance and Certification in Ecotourism*. Wallingford: CABI.

Buckley, R. (2001). Ecotourism accreditation in Australia. In X. Font & R. Buckley (Eds.), *Tourism Ecolabelling Certification and Promotion of Sustainable Management* (pp. 165–173). Oxford: CABI Publishing.

Buckley, R. (2002). Tourism ecocertification in the international year of ecotourism. *Journal of Ecotourism, 1*(2–3), 197–203.

Budowski, G. (1976). Tourism and environmental conservation: Conflict, coexistence, or symbiosis? *Environmental Conservation, 3*(01), 27–31.

Burton, T. L. (1982). Three views of the leisure professional: Two caricatures and analysis. In T. L. Goodale & P. A. Witt (Eds.), *Recreation and Leisure: Issues in an Era of Change*. State College: Venture Publishing.

Butler, J. R. (1992). *Ecotourism: Its Changing Face and Evolving Philosophy*. Paper presented at the International Union for Conservation of Nature and Natural Resources (IUCN), IV World Congress on National Parks and Protected Areas, Caracas, Venezuela, 10–12 February.

Catlin, J., Jones, T., & Jones, R. (2012). Balancing commercial and environmental needs: Licensing as a means of managing whale shark tourism on Ningaloo reef. *Journal of Sustainable Tourism, 20*(2), 163–178. doi:10.1080/09669582.2011.602686.

Ceballos-Lascuráin, H. (1996). *Tourism, Ecotourism and Protected Areas: The State of Nature-Based Tourism Around the World and Guidelines for Its Development*. Gland: IUCN – The World Conservation Union.

Chen, C. L. (2011). From catching to watching: Moving towards quality assurance of whale/dolphin watching tourism in Taiwan. *Marine Policy, 35*(1), 10–17. doi:10.1016/j.marpol.2010.07.002.

Clarke, J. (2002). A synthesis of activity towards the implementation of sustainable tourism: Ecotourism in a different context. *International Journal of Sustainable Development, 5*(3), 232–249. doi:10.1504/IJSD.2002.003751.

Claver-Cortés, E., Pereira-Moliner, J., Tarí, J. J., & Molina-Azorín, J. F. (2008). TQM, managerial factors and performance in the Spanish hotel industry. *Industrial Management and Data Systems, 108*(2), 228–244. doi:10.1108/02635570810847590.

Claver, E., Tarí, J. J., & Pereira, J. (2006). Does quality impact on hotel performance? *International Journal of Contemporary Hospitality Management, 18*(4), 350–358. doi:10.1108/09596110610665357.

Courtenay, J. (1996). Savannah guides, Australia. Pacific Region, Unpublished paper: *British Airways Tourism for Tomorrow Awards 1996*.

Cretu, R. C. (2013). Sustainable management plan applicable to the certification systems in ecotourism. *Quality – Access to Success, 14*(SUPPL. 1), 177–181.

Curtin, S. (2003). Whale-watching in Kaikoura: Sustainable destination development? *Journal of Ecotourism, 2*(3), 173–195. doi:10.1080/14724040308668143.

Deng, J. & Li, J. (2015). Self-identification of ecotourists. *Journal of Sustainable Tourism, 23*(2), 255–279. doi:10.1080/09669582.2014.934374.

Dietz, J. F. & Hanemaaijer, H. A. (2012). How to select policy-relevant indicators for sustainable development. In A. Von Raggamby & F. Rubik (Eds.), *Sustainable Development, Evaluation and Policy-Making: Theory, Practise and Quality Assurance* (pp. 4–36). Cheltenham: Edward Elgar.

Ecotourism Operators of Australia and the Australian Tourism Operators Network. (2000). The National Ecotourism Accreditation Program. *Issues*, 7–9.

Professionalisation and quality assurance

Fennell, D. A. (2015). *Ecotourism* (4th ed.). Abingdon: Routledge.

Font, X. (2002). Environmental certification in tourism and hospitality: Progress, process and prospects. *Tourism Management, 23*(3), 197–205. doi:10.1016/S0261–5177(01)00084–X.

Font, X. & Harris, C. (2004). Rethinking standards from green to sustainable. *Annals of Tourism Research, 31*(4), 986–1007.

Font, X., Sanabria, R., & Skinner, E. (2003). Sustainable tourism and ecotourism certification: Raising standards and benefits. *Journal of Ecotourism, 2*(3), 213–218. doi:10.1080/14724040308668145.

Fraguell, R. M., Martí, C., Pintó, J., & Coenders, G. (2016). After over 25 years of accrediting beaches, has Blue Flag contributed to sustainable management? *Journal of Sustainable Tourism, 24*(6), 882–903. doi:10.1080/09669582.2015.1091465.

Gezon, L. L. (2014). Who wins and who loses? Unpacking the "local people" concept in ecotourism: A longitudinal study of community equity in Ankarana, Madagascar. *Journal of Sustainable Tourism, 22*(5), 821–838. doi:10.1080/09669582.2013.847942.

Goodale, T. L. & Witt, P. A. (1982). Rethinking Professionalisation: A Word of Caution. In T. L. Goodale & P. A. Witt (Eds.), Recreation and Leisure: Issues in an Era of Change (pp. 377–395). State College: Venture Publishing.

Gössling, S. (2018). Tourism, tourist learning and sustainability: An exploratory discussion of complexities, problems and opportunities. *Journal of Sustainable Tourism, 26*(2), 292–306. doi:10.1080/09669582.2017.1349772.

Griffin, T. & De Lacey, T. (2002). Green Globe: Sustainability accreditation for tourism. In R. Harris, T. Griffin, & P. Williams (Eds.), *Sustainable Tourism: A Global Perspective* (pp. 58–89). Oxford: Butterworth Heinemann.

Holmes, A. P., Grimwood, B. S. R., & King, L. J. (2016). Creating an indigenized visitor code of conduct: The development of Denesoline self-determination for sustainable tourism. *Journal of Sustainable Tourism, 24*(8–9), 1177–1193. doi:10.1080/09669582.2016.1158828.

Hoover-Miller, A., Bishop, A., Prewitt, J., Conlon, S., Jezierski, C., & Armato, P. (2013). Efficacy of voluntary mitigation in reducing harbor seal disturbance. *Journal of Wildlife Management, 77*(4), 689–700. doi:10.1002/jwmg.510.

Huang, S. & Weiler, B. (2010). A review and evaluation of China's quality assurance system for tour guiding. *Journal of Sustainable Tourism, 18*(7), 845–860. doi:10.1080/09669582.2010.484492.

Humburg, L. (2017). The changing teaching personality: From expert on techniques to designer of holistic learning. *Manuelle Medizin, 55*(6), 360–363. doi:10.1007/s00337–017–0322–0.

Hunt, C. V., Harvey, J. J., Miller, A., Johnson, V., & Phongsuwan, N. (2013). The Green Fins approach for monitoring and promoting environmentally sustainable scuba diving operations in South East Asia. *Ocean and Coastal Management, 78*, 35–44. doi:10.1016/j.ocecoaman.2013.03.004.

Jacobs, M. H. & Harms, M. (2014). Influence of interpretation on conservation intentions of whale tourists. *Tourism Management, 42*, 123–131. doi:10.1016/j.tourman.2013.11.009.

Li, G. (2015). Diviners with membership and certificates: An inquiry into the legitimation and professionalisation of Chinese diviners. *Asia Pacific Journal of Anthropology, 16*(3), 244–259. doi:10.1080/14442213.2015.1032999.

Manidis, R. (1994). *An Investigation into a National Ecotourism Accreditation Scheme*. Canberra: Commonwealth Department of Tourism.

Mason, P. (1997). Tourism codes of conduct in the Arctic and Sub-Arctic region. *Journal of Sustainable Tourism, 5*(2), 151–165.

Matysek, K. A. & Kriwoken, L. K. (2003). The natural state. *Journal of Quality Assurance in Hospitality and Tourism, 4*(1–2), 129–146. doi:10.1300/J162v04n01_07.

McArthur, S. (1997). Introducing the national ecotourism accreditation program. *Australian Parks and Recreation, 34*(2), 11–13.

Merce, I., Milin, A., Pet, E., Sirbu, C., & Ciolac, R. (2016). *The Certification of Ecotourism Guesthouses in Romania*. Paper presented at the International Multidisciplinary Scientific GeoConference Surveying Geology and Mining Ecology Management, SGEM.

Merger, E. & Pistorius, T. (2011). Effectiveness and legitimacy of forest carbon standards in the OTC voluntary carbon market. *Carbon Balance and Management, 6.* doi:10.1186/1750–0680–6–4.

Meyer, W. (2012). Should evaluation be revisited for sustainable development? In A. Von Raggamby & F. Rubik (Eds.), *Sustainable Development, Evaluation and Policy-Making: Theory, Practise and Quality Assurance* (pp. 37–54). Cheltenham: Edward Elgar.

Munanura, I. E., Tumwesigye, B., Sabuhoro, E., Mariza, D., & Rugerinyange, L. (2017). The quality and performance nexus of the community-based ecotourism enterprises at Nyungwe National Park, Rwanda: A total quality management perspective. *Journal of Ecotourism,* 1–24. doi:10.1080/14724049.2017.1304945.

Pickering, C. & Weaver, D. B. (2003). Nature based tourism and sustainability: Issues and approaches. In R. Buckley, C. Pickering, & D. B. Weaver (Eds.), *Nature Based Tourism, Environment and Land Management* (pp. 7–11). Wallingford: CABI Publishing.

Quiros, A. L. (2007). Tourist compliance to a code of conduct and the resulting effects on whale shark (Rhincodon typus) behavior in Donsol, Philippines. *Fisheries Research, 84*(1), 102–108. doi:10.1016/j.fishres.2006.11.017.

Richards, K., O'Leary, B. C., Roberts, C. M., Ormond, R., Gore, M., & Hawkins, J. P. (2015). Sharks and people: Insight into the global practices of tourism operators and their attitudes to shark behaviour. *Marine Pollution Bulletin, 91*(1), 200–210. doi:10.1016/j.marpolbul.2014.12.004.

Rodger, K., Smith, A., Newsome, D., & Moore, S. A. (2011). Developing and testing an assessment framework to guide the sustainability of the marine wildlife tourism industry. *Journal of Ecotourism, 10*(2), 149–164. doi:10.1080/14724049.2011.571692.

Samà, D. (2011). The relationship between common management and ecotourism regulation: Tragedy or triumph of the commons? A law and economics answer. *Journal of Advanced Research in Law and Economics, 2*(1), 78–81.

Sasidharan, V., Sirakaya, E., & Kerstetter, D. (2002). Developing countries and tourism ecolabels. *Tourism Management, 23*(2), 161–174. doi:10.1016/S0261–5177(01)00047–4.

Shepherd, N. (2002). How ecotourism can go wrong: The cases of SeaCanoe and Siam Safari, Thailand. *Current Issues in Tourism, 5*(3–4), 309–318.

Simpson, K. (2005). Dropping out or signing up? The professionalisation of youth travel. *Antipode, 37*(3), 447–469.

Sky, P. (1987). *The Leisure Profession: Towards Reality*. KCAE Department of Leisure Studies. Lindfield, Australia.

Smith, K., Scarr, M., & Scarpaci, C. (2010). Grey nurse shark (Carcharias taurus) diving tourism: Tourist compliance and shark behaviour at fish rock, Australia. *Environmental Management, 46*(5), 699–710. doi:10.1007/s00267–010–9561–8.

Smith, K. R., Scarpaci, C., Scarr, M. J., & Otway, N. M. (2014). Scuba diving tourism with critically endangered grey nurse sharks (Carcharias taurus) off eastern Australia: Tourist demographics, shark behaviour and diver compliance. *Tourism Management, 45,* 211–225. doi:10.1016/j.tourman.2014.05.002.

Smith, V. L. & Font, X. (2014). Volunteer tourism, greenwashing and understanding responsible marketing using market signalling theory. *Journal of Sustainable Tourism, 22*(6), 942–963. doi:10.1080/09669582.2013.871021.

Stockmann, R. (2012). Understanding sustainability evaluation and its contributions to policy-making. In A. Von Raggamby & F. Rubik (Eds.), *Sustainable Development, Evaluation and Policy-Making: Theory, Practise and Quality Assurance* (pp. 3–20). Cheltenham: Edward Elgar.

Trave, C., Brunnschweiler, J., Sheaves, M., Diedrich, A., & Barnett, A. (2017). Are we killing them with kindness? Evaluation of sustainable marine wildlife tourism. *Biological Conservation, 209*, 211–222. doi:10.1016/j.biocon.2017.02.020.

Tubb, P. (1997). British Airways Tourism for Tomorrow Awards 1997. [Press release].

United Nations. (1993). Agenda 21: Programme of action for sustainable development: Rio Declaration on environment and development; Statement of Forest Principles: The final text of agreements negotiated by governments at the United Nations Conference on Environment and Development (UNCED), 3–14 June 1992, Rio de Janeiro, Brazil. New York: United Nations Dept. of Public Information.

United Nations. (2015). *The Millennium Development Goals Report*. Retrieved from New York: www.un.org/millenniumgoals/2015_MDG_Report/pdf/MDG%202015%20rev%20 (July%201).pdf.

Venables, S., McGregor, F., Brain, L., & Van Keulen, M. (2016). Manta ray tourism management, precautionary strategies for a growing industry: A case study from the Ningaloo Marine Park, Western Australia. *Pacific Conservation Biology, 22*(4), 295–300. doi:10.1071/PC16003.

Vishlenkova, E. (2016). The state of health: Balancing power, resources, and expertise and the birth of the medical profession in the Russian empire. *Ab Imperio, 2016*(3), 39–75. doi:10.1353/imp.2016.0055.

Wearing, S., Cynn, S., Ponting, J., & McDonald, M. (2002). Converting environmental concern into ecotourism purchases: A qualitative evaluation of international backpackers in Australia. *Journal of Ecotourism, 1*(2–3), 133–148.

Wearing, S. L. (1995). Professionalisation and accreditation of ecotourism. *Leisure and Recreation, 37*(4), 31–36.

Weaver, D. & Lawton, L. (2014). *Tourism Management* (5th ed.). Milton: Wiley.

Weaver, D. B. & Lawton, L. J. (2007). Twenty years on: The state of contemporary ecotourism research. *Tourism Management, 28*(5), 1168–1179.

Weiler, B. & Black, R. (2015). *Tour Guiding Research: Insights, Issues and Implications*. Bristol: Channel View Publications.

Wheeler, P. (2003). Natural high. *Ground Engineering, 36*(7), 16–17.

World Wide Fund for Nature (WWF) (1992). *Beyond the Green Horizon: A Discussion Paper on Principles for Sustainable Tourism*. Retrieved from Surrey (UK): https://trove.nla.gov.au/work/10669337?selectedversion=NBD10355015.

WWF International. (2001). *Guidelines for Community-Based Ecotourism Development*. Retrieved from www.widecast.org/Resources/Docs/WWF_2001_Community_Based_ Ecotourism_Develop.pdf.

Ziegler, J. A., Dearden, P., & Rollins, R. (2016). Participant crowding and physical contact rates of whale shark tours on Isla Holbox, Mexico. *Journal of Sustainable Tourism, 24*(4), 616–636. doi:10.1080/09669582.2015.1071379.

Chapter 6

Interpretation as provocation

Introduction

> It is true that the visitors ... frequently desire straight information, which may be called instruction, and a good interpreter will always be able to teach when called upon. But the purpose of interpretation is to stimulate the reader or hearer toward a desire to widen his [or her] interests and knowledge, and to gain an understanding of greater truths that lie behind any statement of fact ... to search out meanings for his [or her] self. (Tilden, 1957, p. 36)

Earlier chapters in this volume have established that an education agenda remains one of the primary differentiators of ecotourism from other more general forms of nature-based tourism (see also Diamantis, 2011; Orams, 1996). Botha et al. (2016) have observed that interpretation is at its most successful when it fulfills the dual roles of education and entertainment; it is a means of simultaneously managing expectations while aiming to supplement the tourist experience with heightened appreciation and deeper levels of understanding. Numerous works already in the public domain have sought to critique the various on-site and off-site interpretive mechanisms, including tour guides, visitors' centres and interpretive trails, available in a tourism context (see for example, Fallon & Kriwoken, 2003; Ham, 1992; Moscardo, Ballantyne, & Hughes, 2007; Reisinger & Steiner, 2006; Stewart, Hayward, Devlin, & Kirby, 1998; Wearing & Neil, 2009; Weiler & Ham, 2001). Rather than simply re-treading this ground, our aim in the present chapter will be to engage with what Ham (2016) has described as being the quintessential endgame of all interpretive strategies – provocation.

Beyond simply teaching and entertaining, provocation in interpretation aims to challenge. Whilst laudable in essence, the fundamental challenge with provocation is, what justification does any particular stakeholder have to argue for a particular future through interpretation? If the endgame for interpreters is to make a difference (see Ham, 2015), who has the right to say what that difference should be? Wearing, Schweinsberg and Tower (2016) have previously established that the legitimacy of park managers to advance a particular interpretive agenda is often weak. They go on to observe that the success (or not) of interpretive strategies will often be determined through relationship marketing and the establishment of collaborative engagement with message recipients. In the present chapter, we will in essence further this line of inquiry by exploring the evolution of the formation of tourism truths in a national park context.

We explore this evolution on the basis that "although the National Parks Service did not invent interpretation, … [as an] organisation [it] was largely responsible for the broad public recognition of its values in developing understanding and appreciation of nature and history" (Brockman, 1978, p. 24). The involvement of national parks in such an endeavour has been very much a twentieth-century phenomenon. In 1956, forty years after the creation of the US National Park Service, Mission 66 was initiated as a ten-year project to improve the provision of infrastructure in parks to support the mass tourism industry (Strong, 1988). As Strong (1988) observes, groups like the Sierra Club at the time were sceptical of there being too overt a focus on mass recreation. In bemoaning the increased commercialisation of the USA's natural resources, the former Director of the Sierra Club David Bower asked, by what authority does "one generation take another generation's freedom and preclude the right to have wilderness in their civilization" (Strong, 1988, p. 206).

Macnaghten and Urry (1998) once argued, with respect to the integration of notions of history and nature, that the latter is imbued with the contested nature of the former. What this means for the present discussion is that the interpretation that is practiced with an ecotourism destination such as a national park must be seen as a time- and context-specific interpretation of a perceived truth. To illustrate the transient and contested nature of interpretation, we will conclude with a recent example of national park-based interpretation at Mount Rushmore, highlighting the efforts of the first Native American park superintendent, Gerard Barker, as he sought to lean on history and challenge traditional understanding in the community of this iconic tourism location.

Defining the endgame of interpretation

Timothy and Boyd (2003) have observed that the origins of interpretation can be traced back to antiquity and the work of Greek and Roman philosophers, and their work to "interpret the universe, supernatural happenings and various natural phenomena for their students and the general public" (Timothy, 2011, p. 228). While tourists have continued to avail themselves of the benefits of interpretation throughout history, as illustrated through phenomena including the Grand Tour and other pilgrimages, modern understanding of interpretation is very much a twentieth-century phenomenon. The father of modern interpretation, Freeman Tilden (1957), once defined interpretation simply as an "educational activity which aims to reveal meaning and relationships through the use of original objectives, by first-hand experience, and by illustrative media, rather than simply to communicate factual information" (p. 8). Tilden stressed that interpretation was not simply 'jazzed-up information'; it had a larger purpose – that of revelation. Tilden defined interpretation on the basis of six principles (see Tilden, 1957):

1   Any interpretation that does not somehow relate what is being displayed or described to something within the personality or experience of the visitor will be sterile.

2   Information, as such, is not interpretation. Interpretation is revelation based upon information, but they are entirely different things; however, all interpretation includes information.
3   Interpretation is an art that combines many arts, whether the materials presented are scientific, historical or architectural. Any art is in some degree teachable.
4   The chief aim of interpretation is not instruction, but provocation.
5   Interpretation should aim to present a whole rather than a part, and must address itself to the whole person rather than any phase.
6   Interpretation addressed to children (say up to the age of twelve) should not be a dilution of the presentation to adults, but should follow a fundamentally different approach. To be at its best, it will require a separate program.

Timothy (2011) has provided a succinct appraisal of how each of the aforementioned goals of interpretation relate to tourism. In this chapter we have chosen to focus on principle 4 – the chief aim of interpretation is not instruction, but provocation. We have done so because for many years there has been a body of scholarship that has explored the ability of interpretation to act as a mechanism for developing more environmentally responsible tourism products and behaviours (e.g., Moscardo & Pearce, 1997; O'Riordan, Shadrake, & Wood, 1989; Orams, 1996; Orams, 1997; Sharpe, 1982). The present authors are of the belief that the sustainability outcomes to which many modern interpretation proponents aspire can only be successful if those receiving the interpretive message are recognised as being active collaborators in its creation. To be successful in this regard, however, interpretation must be specific with respect to its perceived intent. Hwang et al. (2005) have defined interpretation as both a program of knowledge as well as a set of activities for imparting that knowledge to tourist recipients. An interpretive program articulates the set of objectives for what a visitor should understand; however, to be successful, this knowledge must also be linked to the recipient's life experiences and individual circumstance in which the knowledge is imparted and received (Hwang et al., 2005).

The idea that there is a reciprocal relationship between those imparting and those receiving an interpretive message means that we must consider the role of education in ecotourism, the receptiveness of ecotourists to the interpretive message and its impacts on their behaviour. Education, as we have articulated elsewhere in the present volume, is often seen to be the characteristic that separates ecotourism from other forms of niche tourism. Fennell (2008; 2012) has sought to illustrate the importance of education to ecotourism with respect to the concept of biophilia. Biophilia refers to "the innate tendency to be attracted by other life forms and to affiliate with natural living ecosystems" (Wilson, 1984, p. 214 in Fennell, 2012, p. 329). While ecotourists are often popularly associated with possessing a level of concern for the preservation of the environment, various authors have sought to critique the degree to which interpretation actually translates into long-term changes and sustainability in visitor behaviour (see for example, Walker and Moscardo, 2014).

Moscardo (2014, p. 465) has observed at a definitional level that the words most commonly associated with interpretation are "education, explanation, meaning, understanding, discovery, awareness, enjoyment and inspiration". Taken together, these terms draw attention to the various accepted goals of interpretation in a tourism setting. Binkhorst and Van der Duim (in Markwell, 2004, p. 19) note that "our collective understanding of nature is produced by social and cultural processes and practices involving the interventions of all kinds of producers". From the visitor's perspective, interpretation is a means of adding value to their experience, because most sights become that little bit more interesting when you know a little more about them. As Walker and Moscardo (2014) have identified, most interpretation research continues to focus on interpretation as a form of knowledge creation, which is often couched in the context of theoretical lenses, including the Theory of Planned Behaviour and the Elaboration Likelihood Model. As Walker and Moscardo (2014) acknowledge, "the scientific information processing approach does not [in itself] do value to Tilden's original vision of interpretation as an activity that seeks to create experiences of deeper personal significance".

With this in mind, it is possible to consider what Ham (2016), drawing on earlier scholarship from Tilden, has described as the three different endgames of interpretation: interpretation as teaching, interpretation as entertainment and interpretation as provocation. None of these endgames are mutually exclusive. Much as ecotourism itself is simultaneously seen as a positive force for conservation, a benefit for host communities and a conduit for raising visitor awareness of local environments and culture (Ham, 2003), so too must successful interpretation be seen as an amalgam of entertainment, education and other forces. Ham's (2016) argument, that provocation through interpretation will amount to nothing if we do not also have facts that stand up to scrutiny as well as stories that are interesting to our audience, drives home the idea that ecotourism is first and foremost part of a service industry. While different types of alternative tourism practice (community-based ecotourism, wildlife tourism, adventure tourism, etc.) will highlight participants with different motivations and expectations (see Walter, 2013), the fact remains that ecotourism is a business activity where commercial realities frequently clash with so-called environmental preservation and social development imperatives (see Mckercher, 2010).

Burns (2009) has suggested that it is not, strictly speaking, correct to say that the environment is managed for tourism or that tourism is managed for the environment. Both interpretations are often simultaneously correct, with the final dominant weighting of one management agenda frequently being determined on the basis of wider evolutions in land-use policy. As Wearing et al. (2016) have noted, ecotourism settings like national parks have evolved over the course of their history, at various different times prioritising human usage and environmental preservation agendas. While King, et al. (2012) have identified interpretation to be an essential component of the process of exposing a visitor to the essence of a protected area's brand, how this is to be achieved must be seen in the context of the evolution of that brand. McArthur (1998 in Page & Dowling, 2001, p. 237) notes how, from an ecotourism operator's perspective, interpretation is undertaken in order to "attract high-yield tourists, add value and better position their products, reflect personal or organisational ethics, and/ or to comply with the rules of the property on which they operate". It is with this that we introduce our chapter case study focusing on interpretation in national parks.

Tourism interpretation as provocation: the case of national parks

Interpretation has been a part of the history of national parks since before the formation of the US National Park Service in 1916 or the development of formalised roles of park naturalists, historians or archaeologists. Formalised park interpretation programs are popularly said to have begun in the 1920s in Yellowstone and Yosemite National Parks; however, for more than three decades prior to this, park explorers and advocates of the ilk of John Muir, Nathaniel Langford and Frank Pinkley had advocated for education of visitors to complement the feelings of wonder that were seen as the inevitable consequence of a journey into the wilderness (Brockman, 1978).

Space does not permit us here to provide a full history of interpretation in the national park movement (see Brockman, 1978; Mackintosh, 1986; Tilden, 1957). What is interesting, however, is the way that interpretation strategies evolved to reflect the changing mission of park settings. As Tilden (1957, p. 35) noted, early "educators were concerned primarily with the educational possibilities in the scenic and scientific parks and monuments". Later, Tilden (1957, p. 35) notes, "the [Park] system was to be augmented by the addition of a great number of historic and prehistoric monuments, variously designated, but all presenting chapters in the American story". The early focus on scientific explanation has connections to the positivist doctrines of seeing scientific approaches to management as a safeguard against the perils of subjective bias (English & Lee, 2003). It could also, we would suggest, be an attempt to dehumanize the park, thus removing the deficient human element and allowing the physicality of the natural setting in the United States to compete with established natural tourism settings, like the Swiss Alps. Mackintosh (1986) refers to the development of a more nuanced ethos from the mid- to late 1960s amongst those responsible for the education of visitors; specifically, a departure from the need to catalogue a park's assets and history developed. Through an increased focus on environmental conservation, park interpretation strategies began to align with the growing popularity of environmental ideologies (see Hay, 2002). Today, interpretation within the National Park Service is driven by a philosophy that charges interpreters "to help audiences care *about* park resources so that they might support the care *for* park resources" (National Park Service, 2007, p. 1 [italics in original]).

In the course of discussing the formation of interpretive programs in America's national parks, Tilden (1957, p. 35) argued that if, indeed, "there is a philosophy of interpretation, and basic principles upon which adequate interpretation can be built, the nature of what is being shown and illuminated makes no difference. Interpretation is interpretation anywhere, anytime". Tilden made this observation to draw attention to the fact that even amongst those earliest pioneers of formalized interpretation in national parks, there was a realization that instruction and research do not in themselves constitute interpretation. More pressing priorities included the need to fill what Stephen Mather, then head of the National Park Service, described as a lamentable void and to establish the educational credentials of the park movement (Tilden, 1957). In this sense expediency trumped the need for the articulation of core principles, although Tilden (1957)) leaves his reader with the idea that those responsible for the development of interpretation could have articulated core principles if asked.

While we do not dispute the idea that interpretation is interpretation anywhere, anytime, we must at the same time be careful not to confuse the practice of interpretation with the articulation of its meaning. The practice of interpretation, including its forms, benefits and the like, has been canvassed in detail by a range of sources (e.g., Ham, 1992; Wearing & Neil, 2009). Tim Merriman (past Director of the National Association for Interpretation) recently noted that meaning, and not just successfully employed mechanics, is essential for good interpretation. Merriman (Ham, 2016) notes that information, however it is imparted, is useless without a purpose. By making meaning the foundation of an interpretive message, we are then better able to foster understanding in our recipients. As Tilden (1957, p. 38) once said with respect to the United States National Park Service administrative manual, "through interpretation, understanding; through understanding, appreciation; through appreciation, protection". One of the challenges that meanings present for interpretation, however, is that they are not static. Staiff, Bushell and Kennedy (2002) have suggested that rather than having one meaning, landscapes like national parks are sites of "overlapping [or accretions] of [disputed] meanings sometimes described as a palimpsest" (p. 107). The implications of these competing meanings can be illustrated through the case of Mount Rushmore and interpretive endeavors in the Mount Rushmore National Memorial, which is controlled by the United States National Park Service.

CASE STUDY: Mount Rushmore: an evolving interpretive message

Most readers of the present volume would have a general understanding of the history of Mount Rushmore. Located in South Dakota in the United States, the Mount Rushmore National Memorial was built between 1927 and 1941, with the expressed aim of immortalizing four of the most iconic early United States Presidents: George Washington, Thomas Jefferson, Theodore Roosevelt and Abraham Lincoln. Since their creation, the busts of these four presidents have drawn more than 3 million visitors per annum to the South Dakota region (National Park Service, 2017). While the original creator of Mount Rushmore, Gutzon Borglum, saw his work as a "symbol of America's greatest achievements", to another group of Americans, the "Black Hills represented something quite different" (K. Burns, 2009).

Native Americans have been described by Whittlesey (2002, p. 41) as nothing less than "the first national park interpreters". With an ongoing presence in the regions that would eventually come to be designated iconic parks, like Yellowstone, Yosemite and the like, Native Americans sought to pass down tales of how human beings arrived in the region, as well as, allegedly, tales of their early prophecies of the need to preserve the area in perpetuity – tales which, if true, bear a remarkable resemblance to many of the environmental preservation doctrines later espoused by Europeans (Whittlesey, 2002). While Native Americans have had a long-standing and important role to play in the management of land that would later become many iconic national parks, for many years they were treated as being in some way separate from nature (Denzin, 2005; Denzin, 2007; Denzin, 2008). Runte (1987) notes that it was not until the 1960s that "the policy of protecting natural features in national parks exclusive of natural processes [was] widely criticized" (pp. 238–239).

When the Mount Rushmore sculpture was first created, it was built on land that was sacred to the Sioux Native American tribe. While the former President of the United States Calvin Coolidge observed the ancient history of the site at its dedication, the future of the site was said to be tied to the principles the four depicted presidents represented: "the fundamental principles, which they represented, have been wrought into the very being of our country. They are steadfast as our ancient hills" (Coolidge, 1927). The tourism literature has recognised the link between tourism and nationalism, with tourism sites serving as an opportunity to encourage citizenry to embrace national goals (Pretes, 2003). Interestingly, however, Anderson (2004) has described nationalism as an imagined construct, one that is not always founded on the basis of personal experience of history or in terms of current sociocultural circumstance.

The idea that nationalism is imagined helps explain the evolving approach to visitor interpretation at Mount Rushmore. Interpretation has been a part of the Mount Rushmore National Memorial since its inception. At the time, the sculptor Gutzon Borglum was said to have announced whilst viewing the completed sculpture for the first time that "American history shall march along that skyline" (Glass, 1994, p. 267). Whilst not essentially denying Sioux occupation of the site, there is a contention in history, in that "what we choose to remember about the past, where we begin and end our retrospective accounts, and who we include and exclude from them – these do a lot to determine how we live and what decisions we make in the present" (Lipsitz, 1990, p. 34 in Glass, 1994, p. 267).

As Glass (1994) notes, the integration of European sacred and Native American sacred has been an ongoing challenge for the national parks movement. Recently this integration of two worlds was brought home by the experience of the Mandan-Hidatsa Native American Gerard Baker, who was from 2004 to 2010 Superintendent of the Mount Rushmore National Memorial. While Baker's life history has already been told in a range of sources (Shumaker, 2009), what is particularly interesting here is the way that he reinterpreted the endgame of interpretation at the site. In doing so, he did not seek to deny the emotion and the patriotism elicited by people's experience of the four presidents. In fact, he embraced it, once observing that when people "looked at those four Presidents and they'd get teary-eyed, [that this is a good thing] … This place draws emotion. And it should!" (Baker in Shumaker, 2009, p. 255). Instead, Baker challenged not only the consumers of the interpretive message, but also those creating it, to embrace the whole story, not just part of it. Native Americans were charged with redefining their 'warriorness'; there was a need for them to be at the vanguard, not of a physical retaking of their ancestral lands, but of a healing in the American psyche. In Baker's view, this healing could only be achieved by focusing on the stories and histories of all cultures that make up American history in their interpretive endeavors (Shumaker, (2009).

Conclusion

Education is often seen as being one of the primary distinguishing factors that help to determine the sustainability of the global ecotourism industry. Whether it is education of visitors, education of locals or the education of society at large (see also Chapter 8), knowledge is often argued to be essential for the establishment of more sustainable behaviours and mindsets. Drawing largely on examples from the United States' national parks movement, we have sought to shed light in this chapter not on the tools or mechanics of interpretation, but rather on the goal of interpretation. For over four decades there has been a realisation that the principal aim of interpretation is not education per se, but rather provocation. As Ham (2016) observed, the interpreter "wants to leave people thinking and discovering their own meanings and connections" (p. 61). In the present chapter, we have sought to shed light on the social construction of meanings and to portray the development of goals for interpretation as an evolving and historically informed process.

Further reading

Kohl provides an examination of what might be the most effective way to influence ecotourists.

Kohl, J. (2008). Environmental interpretation versus environmental education as an ecotourism conservation strategy. *Ecotourism and Conservation in the Americas* (pp. 127–140).

Powell and Ham investigate whether a well-conceived ecotourism interpretation product could influence tourists' educational outcomes and support of environmental conservation

Powell, R. B. & Ham, S. H. (2008). Can ecotourism interpretation really lead to pro-conservation knowledge, attitudes and behaviour? Evidence from the Galapagos Islands. *Journal of Sustainable Tourism, 16*(4), 467–489.

Walker and Moscardo examine how using ecotourist experiences, especially those focusing on interpretation, may activate or change sustainability-relevant values, beliefs, attitudes and actions both at places visited and elsewhere.

Walker, K. & Moscardo, G. (2014). Encouraging sustainability beyond the tourist experience: Ecotourism, interpretation and values. *Journal of Sustainable Tourism, 22*(8), 1175–1196.

See also the below for a more practical guide to interpretations use:

Although this text is now over 25 years old, it provides one of the best practical guides for managers wanting to institute an interpretation program. The book covers a range of topics, including how to prepare and present a talk, how to use visual aids, how to develop and undertake a guided tour or walk and how to plan and prepare inexpensive exhibits; it also includes case studies on school and community programs.

Ham, S. H. (1992). *Environmental Interpretation: A Practical Guide for People with Big Ideas and Small Budgets*. Golden: North American Press.

Question

Has the education component of ecotourism become more entertainment than interpretation, and does it matter in trying to teach tourists about conservation?

References

Anderson, B. (2004). *Imagined Communities: Reflections on the Origin and Spread of Nationalism.* London: Verso Books.

Botha, E., Saayman, M., & Kruger, M. (2016). Expectations versus experience: The Kruger National Park's interpretation services from a regional approach. *Journal of Ecotourism, 15*(2), 158–183.

Brockman, C. F. (1978). Park naturalists and the evolution of National Park Service interpretation through World War II. *Journal of Forest History, 22*(1), 24–43.

Burns, G. (2009). Managing wildlife for people or people for wildlife? A case study of dingoes and tourism on Fraser Island, Queensland, Australia. In J. Hill & T. Gale (Eds.), *Ecotourism and Environmental Sustainability: Principles and Practice* (pp. 139–156). Surrey: Ashgate.

Burns, K. (2009). The National Parks: America's Best Idea. Retrieved from www.pbs.org/nationalparks/watch-video/#857.

Coolidge, C. (1927). Address at the Opening of Work on Mount Rushmore in Black Hills, SD. Retrieved from www.presidency.ucsb.edu/ws/index.php?pid=24175.

Denzin, N. K. (2005). Indians in the park. *Qualitative Research, 5*(1), 9–33.

Denzin, N. K. (2007). Indians in the park: Part II. *Studies in Symbolic Interaction, 24*(1), 33–44.

Denzin, N. K. (2008). Drawn to Yellowstone. *Qualitative Research, 8*(4), 451–472.

Diamantis, D. (2011). *Ecotourism.* London: South Western Cengage Learning.

English, A. & Lee, E. (2003). Managing the intangible. In D. Harmon & A. Putney (Eds.), *The Full Value of Parks: From Economics to the Intangible* (pp. 43–55). Lanham: Rowman & Littlefield Publishers.

Fallon, L. & Kriwoken, L. (2003). Community involvement in tourism infrastructure: The case of the Strahan Visitor Centre, Tasmania. *Tourism Management, 24*(3), 289–308.

Fennell, D. (2008). *Ecotourism.* London: Routledge.

Fennell, D. (2012). Ecotourism. In A. Holden & D. Fennell (Eds.), *The Routledge Handbook of Tourism and the Environment* (pp. 323–333). London: Routledge.

Glass, M. (1994). Producing patriotic inspiration at Mount Rushmore. *Journal of the American Academy of Religion, 62*(2), 265–283.

Ham, S. (2003). *Ecotourism: Making a Difference by Making Meaning.* Paper presented at the Keynote Address to the Ecotourism Association of Australia.

Ham, S. (2015). Meaning Making as the Endgame of Interpretation – for the Swedish Centre for Nature Interpretation and the Swedish University of Agricultural Sciences. Retrieved from www.youtube.com/watch?v=t1ESBGw0uvE.

Ham, S. (2016). *Interpretation: Making a Difference on Purpose.* Golden: Fulcrum Publishing.

Ham, S. H. (1992). *Environmental Interpretation: A Practical Guide for People with Big Ideas and Small Budgets.* Golden: North American Press.

Hay, P. (2002). *Main Currents in Western Environmental Thought.* Bloomington: Indiana University Press.

Hwang, S.-N., Lee, C., & Chen, H.-J. (2005). The relationship among tourists' involvement, place attachment and interpretation satisfaction in Taiwan's national parks. *Tourism Management, 26*(2), 143–156.

King, L. M., McCool, S. F., Fredman, P., & Halpenny, E. A. (2012). Protected area branding strategies to increase stewardship among park constituencies. *Parks, 18*(2), 54–63.

Mackintosh, B. (1986). Interpretation in the National Park Service: A Historical Perspective. Retrieved from www.nps.gov/parkhistory/online_books/mackintosh2/.

Macnaghten, P. & Urry, J. (1998). *Contested Natures* (Vol. 54). London: Sage.

Markwell, K. (2004). Constructing, presenting and interpreting nature: A case study of a nature-based tour to Borneo. *Annals of Leisure Research, 7*(1), 19–33.

Mckercher, B. (2010). Academia and the evolution of ecotourism. *Tourism Recreation Research, 35*(1), 15–26.

Moscardo, G. (2014). Interpretation and tourism: Holy grail or emperor's robes? *International Journal of Culture, Tourism and Hospitality Research, 8*(4), 462–476.

Moscardo, G., Ballantyne, R., & Hughes, K. (2007). *Designing Interpretive Signs: Principles in Practice*. Golden: Fulcrum Publishing.

Moscardo, G. & Pearce, P. (1997). *Interpretation and sustainable tourism in the wet tropics World Heritage area: A case study of Skyrail visitors*. Townsville: Department of Tourism James Cook University.

National Park Service. (2007). Foundations of Interpretation Curriculum Content Narrative. Retrieved from www.nps.gov/idp/interp/101/FoundationsCurriculum.pdf.

National Park Service. (2017). Mount Rushmore: History and Culture. Retrieved from www.nps.gov/moru/learn/historyculture/index.htm.

O'Riordan, T., Shadrake, A., & Wood, C. (1989). *Interpretation, Participation and National Park Planning*. London: Belhaven.

Orams, M. (1996). Using interpretation to manage nature-based tourism. *Journal of Sustainable Tourism, 4*(2), 81–94.

Orams, M. (1997). The effectiveness of environmental education: Can we turn tourists into 'greenies'?. *Progress in Tourism and Hospitality Research, 3*(4), 295–306.

Page, S. J. & Dowling, R. K. (2001). *Ecotourism*. Harlow: Pearson Education Limited.

Powell, R. B., & Ham, S. H. (2008). Can ecotourism interpretation really lead to pro-conservation knowledge, attitudes and behaviour? Evidence from the Galapagos Islands. *Journal of Sustainable Tourism, 16*(4), 467–489. doi:10.2167/jost797.0.

Pretes, M. (2003). Tourism and nationalism. *Annals of Tourism Research, 30*(1), 125–142.

Reisinger, Y. & Steiner, C. (2006). Reconceptualising interpretation: The role of tour guides in authentic tourism. *Current Issues in Tourism, 9*(6), 481–498.

Runte, A. (1987). *National Parks: The American Experience* (2nd ed.). Lincoln: University of Nebraska Press.

Sharpe, G. (1982). An overview of interpretation. In G. Sharpe (Ed.), *Interpreting the Environment* (pp. 2–27). Hoboken: John Wiley & Sons.

Shumaker, S. (2009). Untold Stories from America's National Parks: National Park Superintendant Gerard Baker. Retrieved from www.pbs.org/nationalparks/media/pdfs/tnp-abi-untold-stories-pt-13-baker.pdf.

Staiff, R., Bushell, R., & Kennedy, P. (2002). Interpretation in national parks: Some critical questions. *Journal of Sustainable Tourism, 10*(2), 97–113.

Stewart, E., Hayward, B., Devlin, P., & Kirby, V. (1998). The "place" of interpretation: A new approach to the evaluation of interpretation. *Tourism Management, 19*(3), 257–266.

Strong, D. (1988). *Dreamers and Defenders: American Conservationists*. Lincoln: University of Nebraska Press.

Tilden, F. (1957). *Interpreting Our Heritage*. Chapel Hill: University of North Carolina Press.

Timothy, D. (2011). *Cultural and Heritage Tourism: An Introduction*. Bristol: Channel View.

Timothy, D. & Boyd, S. (2003). *Heritage Tourism*. Harlow: Pearson Education.

Walker, K. & Moscardo, G. (2014). Encouraging sustainability beyond the tourist experience: Ecotourism, interpretation and values. *Journal of Sustainable Tourism, 22*(8), 1175–1196. doi:10.1080/09669582.2014.918134.

Walter, P. G. (2013). Theorising visitor learning in ecotourism. *Journal of Ecotourism, 12*(1), 15–32.

Wearing, S. & Neil, J. (2009). *Ecotourism and Protected Areas: Visitor Management for Sustainability Ecotourism* (2nd ed.). Oxford: Butterworth-Heinemann.

Wearing, S., Schweinsberg, S., & Tower, J. (2016). *The Marketing of National Parks for Sustainable Tourism*. Clevedon: Channel View.

Weiler, B. & Ham, S. (2001). Tour guides and interpretation. *Encyclopedia of Ecotourism,* 549–563.

Whittlesey, L. H. (2002). *Native Americans, the earliest interpreters: What is known about their legends and stories of Yellowstone National Park and the complexities of interpreting them.* Paper presented at the The George Wright Forum.

Chapter 7

The community perspective

Introduction

In recent years there has been an increasing emphasis on understanding the geographies of tourism (Coles, 2004; Gibson, 2009; Gibson, 2010; Hall & Page, 2009). In addition to serving as one of the traditional parent disciplines for the study of tourism (see Echtner & Jamal, 1997; Leiper, 1981; Leiper, 2000; Tribe, 1997; Tribe, 2000 for a critical discussion of the disciplinarity of tourism studies), geographical perspectives have also bequeathed tourism scholars with a range of theoretical and practice-oriented tools, including the destination area life cycle (Butler, 2006) along with geographic information systems (GIS), which can assist with understanding the spatial factors that correlate with ecotourism's business performance (Weaver & Lawton, 2007). The sheer diversity of tourism forms that exist throughout the world (heritage tourism, volunteer tourism, death tourism, medical tourism, etc.) means that researchers must increasingly grapple with the spatiality of consumption. As Gibson (2009, p. 522) notes, across each variation in the form of tourism consumption are "variform rationales for travel, internal market structures, divisions of labour and methods of destination construction". As Agarwal (2005) has observed with respect to resort developments, tourism exists at scales ranging from the local to the global. Each of these scales influences the other, much in line with the ideas of the influential human geographer Doreen Massey around the global nature of place.

Massey (2010) observed how the increasingly internationalised nature of capital flows has led to what is popularly described as 'time space compression' and the intermixing of local through to global scales. How, Massey (2010, p. 1) asks,

> can we retain any sense of a local place and its peculiarity? An (idealised) notion of an era when places were (supposedly) inhabited by coherent and homogenous communities is set against the current fragmentation and disruption. The counter position is anyway dubious, of course; place and community have only rarely been coterminous. But the occasional longing for such coherence is none the less [*sic*] a sign of geographic fragmentation, the spatial disruption of our times. And occasionally, too, it has been part of what has given rise to defensive and reactionary

responses – certain forms of nationalism, sentimentalised recovering of sanitised heritages, and outright antagonism to newcomers and outsiders.

Over the last few decades there has been evidence of a more nuanced engagement of local voices in the study and operation of ecotourism. Beeton (2006) notes that the interest tourists and the broader global tourism industry have shown in community stems from the need to personalise experience. We are living in an age where the so-called McDonaldisation of society (Ritzer, 1998; Ritzer, 2009) has reduced much of the global tourism industry to a series of packaged experiences produced by a relatively small number of multinational corporations. By placing the community at the forefront of tourism development, we are able to not only demarcate one experience from another, we are also able to make local impacts a central consideration of any discussion of tourism sustainability (see Singh, Timothy, & Dowling, 2003).

Cobbinah (2015) has shown that it was only in the period post-2000 that deliberations around ecotourism began to look beyond the traditional focus on environmental conservation to also encompass socioeconomic concerns, including stakeholder equity, culture and ethics. Fennell (2008a) has observed that ecotourism is increasingly being seen as a community development tool. Through the development of ecotourism types such as community-based ecotourism (hereafter CBET), which we will discuss in the present chapter, the industry is actively encouraged to engage with the heterogeneous nature of the destination (or local place). The relations that exist within such a place have long been identified as the natural terrain of geographers (Hall & Page, 2012; Mitchell, 1979). At the same time, however, efforts to ensure the active involvement of local populations in ecotourism planning and management will often be hamstrung by the reality that "community development initiatives have a better chance of being accepted by locale [sic] people if developers acknowledge that different groups within the community want different things" (Fennell, 2008b, p. 159). Tourism place has been acknowledged for many years as being intrinsically contested (Cohen, 2004; MacCannell, 1973; Relph, 1976). In the present chapter we will seek to articulate the relationship (both positive and negative) of local communities to sustainable ecotourism management. In doing so, we will pay particular attention to the growing scholarly attention being afforded to CBET.

The challenge for host communities

Perhaps on account of its intrinsic concern with the untouched natural environment, ecotourism is often drawn to some of the most remote regions of the world. Whether it is to the volcanic features of Reunion Island in Madagascar, the forests of Indonesia, the Fiordland wilderness of New Zealand's South Island or the rainforest of the Amazon, ecotourism offers tremendous opportunities for the enacting of visitor experiences, but at the same time presents ethical questions of how best to interact with the environment, society and communities that surround us. By way of example, Fennell (2006) refers to unethical practices, including bio-piracy under the guise of ecotourism; this is piracy where animals are often removed from an area altogether for scientific purposes, or alternatively, where wildlife is restrained so it can be reintroduced to the tourists at the optimal time to facilitate the tourist experience. As Fennell (2006) notes, such practices can cause tensions between the industry and host communities, who have often over time built up an intimate knowledge of the biophysical functioning of the tourism system.

Urry (1995 in Telfer and Sharpley, 2015) identified that such tourism communities can be defined on the basis of four interrelated forces:

> The first is a topographical sense ... the second is a sense of community as a social system implying a degree of local social interconnection of local people and institutions. The third is a sense of communion, a human association implying personal ties and a sense of belonging and warmth ... [and the fourth is] the concept of ideology, which can often hide the power relations that inevitably underlie communities. (p. 178)

In perhaps its most basic sense, therefore, community forms part of the spatial framing of tourism destinations. Developing from the pioneering work of Von Bertalanffy and others in the latter half of the twentieth century (see Von Bertalanffy, 1968/2003; Von Bertalanffy, 1972), systems thinking soon began to gain traction in tourism as scholars and practitioners struggled to conceptualise the workings of the phenomena in question (Mill & Morrison, 2002). In the late twentieth century, Leiper (1990) sought to advance the sophistication of the study of supply-side forces that are a component of most tourism systems models when he suggested that rather than being a "wholly industrialised phenomenon, a huge industry but somehow a fragmented one" (p. 601), that perhaps instead tourism is partially industrialised. Leiper et al. (2008) note with respect to partially industrialised tourism systems that the effects of tourism extend beyond the limits of the direct economic effects of tourists' expenditure. Rejecting the conventional notion of a distinct tourism industry, the idea of partial industrialisation seeks to draw attention to the reality that "not all suppliers directly providing goods and services consumed by tourists have, or need to have, an industrialised relationship to tourism" (p. 208). By extending the boundaries of what can be called an industry beyond its traditional limitations, tourism inevitably comes into contact with an increasing array of stakeholder interests. In a pioneering article on the application of chaos theory to the study of tourism, McKercher (1999, p. 427) notes that destinations are perhaps best described as ecological systems with their own "clearly defined hierarchy of dominant and subservient players and clear inter-relationships between entities".

In this way, community is a fundamental component of any tourism destination and many of the supplier functions it encompasses (Tsaur, Lin, & Lin, 2006). While there is often a symbiotic relationship between the community and the natural and cultural resources of a destination, it should not be assumed, however, that the contemporary concerns of local people will necessarily be in line with the economic opportunities historically afforded by the geographic formation of the area. Land uses evolve and rural communities constantly seek to be empowered to change their region's future as they see fit. Zhang and Lei (2012, p. 916) have identified "empowerment of local people and financial benefits to the local communities" as being, in theory, two of the primary differentiators of ecotourism from conventional mass tourism. Timothy (2007) notes that in tourism contexts, social empowerment is said to occur when a community's equilibrium and cohesiveness is enhanced. Much as Timothy (2007) observed the recent trend towards a more sophisticated engagement with the indigenous voice in tourism development discussions, more broadly, over the last forty years or so the study of tourism's social impact has evolved from largely negative ethnographic critiques to more nuanced appraisals of the positive and negative impacts of tourism development (Smith, 2015). Smith observes that "more sophisticated models of sustainable tourism need to pay special attention to context, the culture of specific communities and even to individuals" (2015, p. 177). This is necessary in that, as Simpson (2008) has noted, active involvement of communities in tourism planning and management will not necessarily lead to tangible economic and other gains in the local area. In fact, communities "may become subjected to external pressures, issues of governance and structure, conflicting stakeholder agendas, jealousies and internal power struggles" (p. 177).

Mbaiwa and Stronza (2009) note that many prominent ecotourism destinations are now asking the question, how much is too much? How does one reconcile the conundrum that the future growth of ecotourism may eventually threaten those very characteristics of place that are so valued by travellers? Since the mid-twentieth century a range of management tools (e.g., carrying capacity, limits of acceptable change, visitor impact management) have been employed with the specific aim of quantifying the impact of tourism on host environments (Boyd & Butler, 1996; Buckley, 1994; Crispin, Berovidez, Marín, García, & Fernández-Truan, 2017; Mbaiwa & Stronza, 2009; Ross & Wall, 1999; Wall, 1997). Whilst actively employed in many ecotourism contexts, these and other management tools often suffer from the reality that they are "simply not adequate to address the complexity found in tourism situations" (Lindberg, Enriquez, & Sproule, 1996, p. 561). As we have already stated, host communities are by their nature heterogeneous constructs, and for this reason, personal values and context underpin the way tourists and hosts alike will perceive the merits (or not) of cultural change through tourism. Wheeller (2005, p. 266) summed up the importance of the values these debates brought to ecotourism when he asked,

> if one of the pillars of the new forms of tourism [such as ecotourism] is to respect the wishes and customs of locals, what happens when their customs fail to meet the existing, prevailing moral and/or political agenda of the outside eco/sustainable tourists?

Duffy (2006) has observed that ecotourism is not, as was previously thought, a politically neutral form of development that can be used to ensure the sustainable utilisation of a region's natural and cultural assets. Rather, as Duffy (2006) illustrates with respect to ecotourism in the wilds of Madagascar, ecotourism represents the modern face of neoliberal development policy; it "relies on the idea of the developing countries trading globally on ... [their] competitive advantage in wildlife, sun, sea and sand ... it does not challenge the existing political and economic order in anyway [sic], rather it supports it" (p. 112). Determining who has control of the industry is an important driver of successful indigenous ecotourism operations (Hinch and Butler 1996 in Telfer & Sharpley, 2015). Karst (2017) has observed that ecotourism developments are often managed by external agents, which can result in the ideological, cultural and social values of locals being overlooked. Wearing and McDonald (2002) have previously argued, in relation to the role of intermediaries in the management of ecotourism operations in the Hunstein Range (Papua New Guinea), that managers need to pursue a participatory approach to development (see also Reggers, Grabowski, Wearing, Chatterton, & Schweinsberg, 2016). Doing so, they suggest, allows for a more nuanced understanding of truth. In contrast, popular understandings of ecotourism have tended to have the effect of compartmentalising humans and nature, "serving as western constructs that promote the interests of the global north" (Karst, 2017, p. 746).

Over the last three decades, McKercher (2010) has observed an evolution in academic understanding of ecotourism. During this time, early "idealism, hope, hyperbole and wishful thinking" (p. 15) has given way to a more realistic understanding of what ecotourism can and can't do. With respect to the vexed question of ecotourism's sustainability credentials, McKercher (2010) observes how early on, ecotourism's future was tied to its ability to contribute to environmental and cultural preservation by transforming local livelihood patterns and linking preservation directly to the imperative of financial returns. While numerous studies continue to debate the economic value of ecotourism (Iasha, Yacob, Kabir, & Radam, 2015; Kolahi, Sakai, Moriya, & Aminpour, 2013) and its community development credentials (Duffy, Kline, Swanson, Best, & McKinnon, 2017; Garraway, 2017; Masud, Aldakhil, Nassani, & Azam, 2017), what is also interesting over the last thirty years is the evolution of our understanding of the host community independent variable. McKercher (2010) has shown how people have come to realise that host communities will not always place equal emphasis on the conservation goals of ecotourism, particularly when conservation is juxtaposed against goals for income generation. McKercher (2010) notes how local populations are often hamstrung in their ability to pursue sustainability goals on account of the limited and variable funding that comes from ecotourism and a lack of clarity over the legality of land ownership. To this, Fennell (2008b) has sought to highlight what they see as a myth of successful ecological stewardship in many traditional societies. In doing so, Fennell (2008b) argues that there needs to be more critical understanding amongst tourism interests of the consumptive histories of host communities.

Are we therefore, in our pious attempt to preserve the natural environment through economic development, pursuing growth in the future at the expense of the past? Butler (2015) once argued with respect to sustainable tourism that it is often presumptuous to assume that we can necessarily understand the needs of the future. In much the same way, we would suggest that authenticity, which is so often the lens through which ecotourism is separated from mass tourism, must be viewed through specific historical lenses. The idea of an authentic experience has long been recognised as a component of the marketing and experience of ecotourism. More broadly, in wider tourism scholarship, authenticity of experience has been a focus of concern since the pioneering work of MacCannell (MacCannell, 1973; MacCannell, 1976; Wang, 1999). So-called staged authenticity is said to occur when local cultures may actively 'construct' what appears (to the tourist's camera) to be an authentic cultural display, but which in reality is a staged event specifically for tourist consumption. While staged authenticity certainly serves a management objective, satisfying the tourists' curiosity while allowing 'real' instances of cultural life to avoid the pressure of the tourist gaze (Urry & Larsen, 2011), the question becomes whether staged experiences can ever have the effect of mediating real conflict and understanding in society. Pessimistically, Baudrillard once observed "we are presently living with a minimum of real sociality and a maximum of simulation … tourism being one such simulacrum" (1990 in Jennings, 2006, p. 11). More recently in the context of the confluence of tourism and technology, Neuhofer et al. (2014) have observed the ability of information technology (IT) to enhance the provision of quality tourism experiences, an observation that has led to the increased use of technology in a range of tourism delivery contexts, including interpretation centres (Owen, Buhalis, & Pletinckx, 2006; Reino, Mitsche, & Frew, 2007).

In chapter seven the authors referred to the development of interpretive programs at the Mount Rushmore National Memorial, noting how the western cultural site was built on land previously inhabited and revered by Sioux Native Americans. Park managers are increasingly seeing interpretation in the indigenous cultural context as a mechanism for promoting a dialogue in society. However, to what end? The following paragraphs form part of an anonymous posting on the Native American Netroots site, articulating some indigenous perspectives of the Mount Rushmore site.

> The Black Hills in South Dakota is an area, which is historically linked to several tribes, including the Sioux, Cheyenne, Arapaho, and Kiowa. As a sacred area, it was used for making contact with the spirit world and obtaining spiritual power...By the 1870s, Americans were spreading rumours that that Black Hills were unoccupied, that they were an area which Indian people did not use...

> The theft of the Black Hills from the Sioux has been widely reported by both historians and the popular media. The theft, however, involved more than just taking the land: it also involved renaming it. All of the geographic features within the Black Hills had Indian names in 1877, but over the next couple of decades these names were replaced by non-Indian names.

> In 1884, New York City attorney Charles E. Rushmore came to the Black Hills to check on legal titles to some properties. On coming back to camp one day, he asked Bill Challis about the name of a mountain. Bill is reported to have replied: *"Never had a name but from now on we'll call it Rushmore."* (italics in original) (Ojibwa, 2012)

Much as the US National Park Service today is eager to draw attention to the sociocultural history and environmental assets of the site in the context of community pressures and their management charter, so too do Native Americans still revere the site as an important part of the maintenance of their community. In South America, the "indigenous culture-spiritual-nature connection has been realised as a philosophy ... known as *buen vivir* ... Roughly translated as living well or collective wellbeing" (Karst, 2017, p. 747); *buen vivir* implies concern for the totality of place and community. With recognition of the heterogeneous nature of place comes the realisation that the community benefits (or costs) of ecotourism must be assessed through the eyes of local people. Park et al. (2018) have recently argued that the process of assessing the merits of community participation projects has historically tended to favour the views of people outside the local community; this is in spite of the fact that "fundamentally CBT (community based tourism) aims to be run autonomously by local communities for their long term benefit" (p. 129).

Where researchers seek to actively engage with host communities, it often becomes apparent that the capacity of community members to benefit from tourism is not uniform. Park et al. (2018), in a study of ecotourism development in Laos, observed that capacity in a community was often connected to levels of education and understanding. In those instances where tourism industry proponents made minimal effort to encourage equal participation in tourism industry planning from the beginning of the project, there was evidence of a corresponding reluctance of community members to participate in the decision-making processes (Park et al., 2018). This reluctance can extend as far as to make communities reluctant to take on ownership of community-based tourism operations. Bittar Rodrigues and Prideaux (2017) recently proposed an eight-step model for the development of sustainable, community-led tourism projects. This model is careful not to gloss over what Schweinsberg et al. (2015, p. 102) have described as "the complexities of resident's [sic] value formations". Instead it proposes a series of steps whereby communities can be equipped with the ability to shape their own lives, defining for themselves the type of society they envisage (see Bittar Rodrigues & Prideaux, 2017).

The model of community-based tourism envisaged by Bittar Rodrigues and Prideaux (2017) recognises the need for communities to be in active collaboration with government, non-governmental organizations (NGOs) and the tourism industry. Much as Reggers et al. (2016) suggested with respect to participatory approaches to tourism development in Indonesia, the aim in the Bittar Rodrigues and Prideaux case becomes to treat communities as active players in the development process. This is in stark contrast to historical notions of tourism commoditisation. The seminal work of Cohen (1988) observed that commoditisation in tourism has the effect of allegedly changing the meaning of cultural products, destroying their historical richness and subjectivity with the expressed aim of developing a simple entity that can be consumed by visitors. Cohen (1988) gave the examples of contrived cultural displays and sex tourism as examples of tourism commoditisation at its worst. While, however, there are numerous examples of the harm industries like sex tourism can place on local communities and individuals (Ryan & Hall, 2001), the fact remains that community-based tourism as a general idea is "linked to the growth or employment opportunities, particularly for women, young people and indigenous peoples" (Telfer & Sharpley, 2015, p. 125). Much as scholarship into sex tourism has begun to explore in more critical depth the complex motivations and justifications of participants (Herold, Garcia, & DeMoya, 2001; Omondi & Ryan, 2017), so too must ecotourism, which is a recognised pathway for pro-poor tourism and poverty alleviation, look beyond simply financial security for host communities when determining benefits.

As Wearing (2001, p. 398) has observed, "in principle ecotourism ensures a supportive host community by investing control within the community itself". In the next section we will consider some of the merits of CBET as a mechanism to ensure active community involvement. Before doing so, however, it is worth recognising the power relations that exist both within and external to the communities in question. Firstly, with respect to power relations external to the community, it must be recognised that industries like tourism are often owned and controlled by developed nations with a high return in the form of economic leakage to these nations; for example, conventional package tours, in many cases, utilize local people through the use of their resources and labour at a minimum (or often zero) cost to the operator. Hall (2007, p. 6) has suggested that the commonly held view that "tourism exchanges benefit primarily the countries of the [developing] south is ridiculous ... the reality is that not only is the consumption of tourism the domain of the wealthy, but in many ways so is its production". While ecotourism may be often controlled by developed north, this is not to suggest that ecotourism is not recognised for the employment opportunities it offers local communities (Rijal, & Sapkota, 2015). Stronza (2007) observed how, in addition to the provision of a more consistent wage than may have been possible through alternative employment opportunities, ecotourism can also provide something of a safety net for communities, as they are able to leverage professional networks established with professional tourism staff.

While the employment available in tourism is often seasonal and low in pay in contrast to the profits accruing to investors and operators, such practices are defended on the pretext that if these operators did not initiate tourism, then there would be no money injected into the community at all. As a case in point, take the island of Cuba, which turned to tourism as a source of development following the collapse of the Soviet bloc. In recent years, Cuban tourism has sought to diversify away from traditional mass tourism and to promote ecotourism and other niche operations (Duffy et al., 2017; Honey, 1999; Winson, 2006). Duffy et al. (2017) highlight how agro-ecotourism operations in Cuba have the potential to support local community development goals. Whilst specific examples can therefore be identified of the positive economic benefits of ecotourism, there is debate in the broader literature as to the accuracy of the tourism economic imperative. For example, ecotourism industries in Northern Ireland and Scottish national parks represent the modern face of the post-productivist countryside. The so-called non-production economic benefits that can be accrued from ecotourism-based industries form an important source of revenue as national parks and other ecotourism destinations seek to take their place in an increasingly interconnected global marketplace. As Bell and Stockdale (2015) note, the presence of an economic argument in favour of national parks does not, however, always ensure community support. Deep ideological cleavages will frequently separate stakeholders, who will respond to the commercialisation of parks for tourism on the basis of environmental preservation, public versus private management and other arguments.

Where economic arguments are pursued to the exclusion of all else, there is therefore the potential for planners to deliberately (or inadvertently) obscure significant social dimensions of tourism impact. This can have the effect of exacerbating power struggles within the community. Communities, as we have shown already in this chapter, are complex entities. Hall (2007) notes that within a designated community (however this is defined), the distribution of benefits and costs from tourism will often depend on the structures and institutions that already exist in the community in question. Where appropriate mechanisms exist, community members may feel empowered. Economic empowerment requires that community members have access to the productive resources of an area (Telfer & Sharpley, 2015). Social empowerment, in contrast, refers to the community's sense of cohesion and integrity (Telfer & Sharpley, 2015). In the next section we will discuss CBET as a mechanism for community empowerment through ecotourism.

A future with community-based ecotourism (CBET)

When Urry and Larsen wrote the third edition of the influential work *The Tourist Gaze*, they did so with a focus on the twin themes of risks and futures (see Urry & Larsen, 2011). These themes were brought together to pose a question – in what ways has the tourist gaze, as a driving force in the spread of tourism throughout the world, made the industry "self destructive, that is using up or destroying the very preconditions of its own activity through generating powerful local or global risks or bads". In this section we will use one of the so-called 'bads' identified by Urry and Larsen – positional competition – as a lens to examine the interplay of local and global forces and the creation of a socially sustainable future through community-based ecotourism.

We have already established in the present chapter that tourism systems are complex entities, made up of an array of complementary or conflicted stakeholder groups that must interact at a range of scales, from the global down to the local. Positional competition, as described by Urry and Larsen (2011), draws on the work of the sociologist Fred Hirsch, *Social Limits to Growth* (see Hirsch, 2005). Hirsch's thesis was that

> individual liberation through the exercise of consumer choice does not make those choices liberating for all because of the positional economy. All aspects of goods, services, work, positions and other social relationships are scarce or subject to congestion or crowding. Competition is therefore zero-sum: as any one person consumes more of the good in question, so someone else consumes less or gains less satisfaction. Supply cannot be increased, unlike material goods where economic growth can generate more. People's consumption of positional goods is relational (Urry & Larsen, 2011).

The idea of positionality relates well to the notion of the tourist gaze in the sense that our gaze is subjective, and is defined as much by what we don't see as what we do. Take, for example, Urry and Larsen's description of a tourist's experience of an Alpine mountain, both as a tangible material good and as a subjective positional good.

> As a material good the mountain can be viewed for its grandeur, beauty and conformity to the idealised Alpine horn. There is almost no limit to this good. However, the same mountain can be viewed as a positional good, as a shrine to nature that people wish to enjoy in solitude or in a small team without other tourists being present. (Urry & Larsen, 2011, p. 225)

Urry and Larsen (2011) observe that notions of positional competition tend to work better in the context of discussions such as the one above, where a romantic view of nature assumes an almost obligatory degree of social exclusion. It works less well, they note, in the context of discussions of the collective gaze, where gaze is framed on the basis of the opportunities afforded for social engagement. Whilst the notion of positional competition as it is applied to the tourist gaze is interesting, the question then becomes what lessons exist for discussions of community involvement in ecotourism planning and CBET. Here we are guided by a comment that was made by Urry and Larsen (2011). They observed that "the more its [Romanticism's] adherents proselytise its virtues to others [and seek to position themselves competitively], the more this in effect undermines the Romantic gaze: the romantic tourist is digging his [sic] own grave as he seeks to evangelise others to his own religion" (Walter, 1982, p. 301 in Urry & Larsen, 2011). Urry and Larsen (2011) go on to note how Romanticism is an important ecotourism marketing tool, allowing localities including the Australian Great Barrier Reef to position themselves as an exclusive and competitive destination. In chapter nine we will explore the issue of marketing as it relates to ecotourism. In the rest of this section we will explore the merits of seeing CBET as a mechanism for evening up the competitive positioning that exists in ecotourism management, managing ecotourism to ensure the collaborative and cooperative engagement of stakeholders across different spatial scales.

Before exploring this topic, it is appropriate to acknowledge both the economic size of the industry and its predilection for exclusivity. On the first point, estimating the economic value of the global ecotourism industry is notoriously difficult on account of the vagaries in asking people to measure the value of natural resources, the partially industrialised nature of the ecotourism industry and the definitional ambiguity over what constitutes ecotourism, as opposed to wildlife tourism, nature-based tourism and the like. At the local level, however, numerous studies have sought to use hypothetical measurement tools, like economic contingent valuations, to measure ecotourism's economic impact (Gallagher & Hammerschlag, 2011; Kim, Wong, & Cho, 2007; Samonte, Eisma-Osorio, Amolo, & White, 2016; Vianna, Meekan, Pannell, Marsh, & Meeuwig, 2012). At the global level, ecotourism has been described repeatedly as the world's fastest-growing tourism sector. Balmford et al. (2015) have estimated ecotourism travel to protected areas alone is worth in the order of "US \$600 billion/y in direct in-country expenditure and US \$250 billion/y in consumer surplus" (p. 1). A range of issues contribute to ecotourism's economic value – the exclusivity of experience and attractions, the opportunity for personal connections with nature and the opportunity to learn, etc. None of these issues exist in isolation from each other. If, however, collectively these and other issues demonstrate what Urry and Larsen describe as "environmental good taste", how then does one link these tourist motivations to a form of tourism characterised by grassroots management and active involvement of host populations in ecotourism planning and management?

The exclusivity of experience is a particularly pertinent issue for any discussion of CBET, in the sense that "the visiting elite [can] gain considerable social capital from visiting such exclusive [ecotourism] locations" (Cater, 2006, p. 23) as the Alaskan wilderness, Antarctica and the Borneo rainforest. Cohen (2002) has observed that tourism is perhaps best characterised as an expanding, centrifugal industry, one where the mature centre has historically provided a level of service and attraction far superior to what one would find at the periphery. As Cohen (2002) notes, however, the process of expansion cannot continue indefinitely. In recent years, last-chance tourism has grown in importance to tourists and industry players alike as people begin to recognise the potential for wider environmental forces to destroy the natural attractions that have long served as the bedrock of the global tourism industry (see Eijgelaar, Thaper, & Peeters, 2010; Lemelin, Dawson, & Stewart, 2013; Piggott-McKellar & McNamara, 2017). As the number and quality of sites decrease, the principles of supply and demand tend to dictate that their value will increase in the eyes of tourists, authorities and private tourism industry interests.

While last-chance tourism is often popularly characterised as the desire to visit localities that are under threat from the environmental impacts of climate change, Lemelin and Baikie (2013) have observed the presence of a cultural dimension as well. The rapid expansion of western civilisation in the eighteenth and nineteenth centuries, they note, led to a predilection amongst some colonisers to parade at-risk indigenous populations as historical curiosities. As a case in point, they refer to the instance in the 1880s "when a small group of Inuit from Northern Labrador in Canada were enticed to travel to Europe and appear in several European cities as living examples of an ancient and vanishing culture" (Lemelin & Baikie, 2013, p. 169).

The community perspective

Tragically and somewhat ironically, all eight members of the indigenous travelling group died after succumbing to the effects of smallpox in the early stages of their trip. Not long after, an interesting variation of what we will refer to as last-chance cultures was observed in what are now some of the world's most iconic ecotourism settings. In the early twentieth century, the See America First campaign was launched with the expressed aim of encouraging more Americans to visit regions such as Glacier National Park and Yellowstone National Park (Runte, 1987). The campaign, which we will discuss in greater detail in the context of tourism marketing in Chapter 9 was of vital importance to the regional and national economy on account of the fact that World War I had made many overseas attractions such as the Alps inaccessible to the majority of American travellers. It was around this time that a variation of last-chance tourism was practiced, with Blackfeet and other Native American tribes sent on promotional rail tours to drum up community interest in the tourism experiences on offer (Burns, 2009). By today's standards, the employment of indigenous peoples as tokenistic symbols of a forgotten culture would be considered to be insulting and demeaning. Today there are many examples within national park settings of active involvement of indigenous interests in the sustainable management of park sites (Ban & Frid, 2018; Premauer & Berkes, 2015; Stevens, 2014).

Reimer and Walter (2013, p. 132) have identified CBET as being a particular variant of ecotourism, one that "appears to hold great promise in resolving the contradiction between conservation imperatives and local and native rights to territory". Emerging along with the cautionary platform and the sustainability movement in the 1990s (Weaver, 2008), ecotourism has been described as a practice of tourism "where the local community has a significant control over, participation in its development and management, and a major percentage of the benefits stay within the community" (World Wildlife Fund, 2001, p. 43 in Stone, 2015, p. 166). When applied specifically to indigenous communities, so-called indigenous community-based ecotourism has been said to have the joint objectives of nature conservation and income generation (Farrelly, 2013).

Over the last decade or so, a substantial body of literature has sought to explore aspects of the establishment and management of CBET (see for example, Jones, 2005; Kontogeorgopoulos, 2005; Masud et al., 2017; Nelson, 2004; Okazaki, 2008; Sakata & Prideaux, 2013; Zong, Cheng, Lee, & Hsu, 2017). Of interest to the present discussion is a recent study by Park (2017), which sought to assess community sentiment on the success of a CBET project through a case study of the Houay Kaeng village in Laos. What this study showed is that the ability of CBET to facilitate an active voice for indigenous community members and thus to minimise the effects of positional competition was not uniform. Those community members who were afforded the opportunity to actively participate in CBET planning and management were generally those with higher levels of education, which facilitated their ability to engage with regional governments and to undertake the training required as part of the CBET approvals process. In contrast, the large, so-called passive participant group existed primarily to service the needs of travellers through the provision of handicrafts, sauna and massage services and cooking (Park, 2017).

The study by Park et al. (2017) does not describe the characteristics of community members in each of the aforementioned groups in detail. It does, however, allude to the fact that when the Houay Kaeng village operation was established, it was done in a way to fit in with existing social structures in the community. On the one hand this is laudable, in the sense that CBET is reliant on its ability to work inclusively with existing leadership structures in the community to be effective (Wang, Cater, & Low, 2016). At the same time, however, leaders must be proactive in imbuing the results of good leadership throughout the rest of the community. As Weaver (2008) finds, CBET leadership initiatives must reconcile management "effectiveness with the factors that engender strong leadership, which in traditional societies may include undemocratic, hereditary or clan entitlements and an authoritarian leadership style" (p. 137). In a study of social capital and CBET, Jones (2005, p. 320) observes that:

> social capital appears to have developed from the seeds sown through the commitment and vision of the village founders. But by elders passing on some of this power to family members who may not share the same vision of village solidarity and collective action, the risk that social capital may be rapidly destroyed is high.

The results of a loss of social capital are potentially significant. Sakata and Prideaux (2013) have observed in the context of CBET in the Fergusson Island/ Milne Bay region of Papua New Guinea how the communities in question struggled to get behind the project in the early stages on account of a perceived lack of information filtering through to the wider community from guesthouse owners and managers.

Conclusions

Urry and Larsen (2011) identified three potential scenarios for future tourism development. The second of these scenarios was described in the following terms – it is "what many environmentalists argue for, namely a worldwide reconfiguration of economy and society around the idea of local sustainability" (p. 234). Host communities of one form or another represent an almost universal constant in tourism destinations throughout the world. As we have demonstrated in this chapter, communities may be conceptualised in objective or subjective terms. This distinction is important in the sense that it recognises the geographical framing of communities around topographical features, land-use regimes and the like. At the same time, however, it recognises the importance of a tourism place as lived. Social sustainability "occurs when the formal and informal processes, systems and structures, and relationship actively support the capacity of current and future generations to create sustainable communities" (McKensie, 2004, p. 21 in Messer & Kecskes, 2009, p. 248). Ecotourism, with its focus on reciprocal stakeholder engagement, is in theory well placed to promote sustainable community outcomes. As Wearing and Neil (2009, p. 115) note, much of "the contribution to ecotourism's following has been its potential to deliver benefits to communities remote from centres of commerce, benefits that do not involve widespread social or environmental destruction". In the final part of this chapter, we made reference to community-based ecotourism with the aim of articulating not only its potential benefits to local communities, but also highlighting some of the challenges in setting up participatory management structures in the context of existing community structures.

Further reading

These authors present how ecotourism can assist in the empowerment of communities through linking the local community with international agencies.

Pookhao, N., Bushell, R., Hawkins, M., & Staiff, R. (2017). Empowerment through community-based ecotourism in a globalised world global-local nexus: Three Thai villages as case studies. In I. Borges de Lima & V. T. King (Eds.), *Tourism and Ethnodevelopment: Inclusion, Empowerment and Self-Determination* (pp. 65–81). London: Routledge.

Van Egmond's chapter provides a critical analysis of international tourism discourse by arguing that concepts such as ecotourism, sustainable tourism, 'dark green' environmentalism, ethnic tourism and the search for authenticity are actually Western Protestant middle-class concepts, thereby raising the question of whether or not developing countries can implement these Western concepts and Western tourist practices.

Van Egmond, T. (2007). Planning for the 'right' tourists. In T. van Egmond (Ed.), *Understanding Western Tourists in Developing Countries* (pp. 144-173). Wallingford: CABI.

Lonn et al. conduct a case study of the Chambok ecotourism program in Cambodia to quantify the contribution of ecotourism to the community's household income and livelihood changes.

Lonn, P., Mizoue, N., Ota, T., Kajisa, T., & Yoshida, S. (2018). Evaluating the contribution of community-based ecotourism (CBET) to household income and livelihood changes: A case study of the Chambok CBET program in Cambodia. *Ecological Economics, 151*, 62–69.

Question

Are the power relations that exist both within and external to communities engaging in ecotourism controlled by those interested in sustainable outcomes or by those desiring economic returns?

References

Agarwal, S. (2005). Global–local interactions in English coastal resorts: Theoretical perspectives. *Tourism Geographies, 7*(4), 351–372.

Balmford, A., Green, J. M., Anderson, M., Beresford, J., Huang, C., Naidoo, R., … Manica, A. (2015). Walk on the wild side: Estimating the global magnitude of visits to protected areas. *PLOS Biology, 13*(2), e1002074.

Ban, N. C. & Frid, A. (2018). Indigenous peoples' rights and marine protected areas. *Marine Policy, 87*, 180–185.

Beeton, S. (2006). *Community Development Through Tourism*. Collingwood: Landlinks Press.

Bell, J. & Stockdale, A. (2015). Evolving national park models: The emergence of an economic imperative and its effect on the contested nature of the 'national' park concept in Northern Ireland. *Land Use Policy, 49*, 213–226.

Bittar Rodrigues, C. & Prideaux, B. (2017). A management model to assist local communities developing community-based tourism ventures: A case study from the Brazilian Amazon. *Journal of Ecotourism, 17*(1), 1–19.

Boyd, S. W. & Butler, R. W. (1996). Managing ecotourism: An opportunity spectrum approach. *Tourism Management, 17*(8), 557–566.

Buckley, R. (1994). A framework for ecotourism. *Annals of Tourism Research, 21*(3), 661–665.

Burns, K. (2009). Episode Three: 1915–1919 The Empire of Grandeur. *The National Parks: America's Best Idea*. Retrieved from www.pbs.org/nationalparks/watch-video/#857.

Butler, R. (2006). *The Tourism Area Life Cycle: Applications and Modifications*. Clevedon: Channel View Publications.

Butler, R. (2015). Sustainable tourism: The undefinable and unachievable, pursued by the unrealistic? In T. Singh (Ed.), *Challenges in Tourism Research*. Bristol: Channel View Publications.

Cater, E. (2006). Ecotourism as a western construct. *Journal of Ecotourism, 5*(1–2), 23–39.

Cobbinah, P. B. (2015). Contextualising the meaning of ecotourism. *Tourism Management Perspectives, 16*, 179–189.

Cohen, E. (1988). Authenticity and commoditization in tourism. *Annals of Tourism Research, 15*(3), 371–386.

Cohen, E. (2002). Authenticity, equity and sustainability in tourism. *Journal of Sustainable Tourism, 10*(4), 267–276.

Cohen, E. (2004). *Contemporary Tourism: Diversity and Change*. Amsterdam: Elsevier.

Coles, T. (2004). Tourism and leisure: Reading geographies, producing knowledges. *Tourism Geographies, 6*(2), 135–142.

Crispin, C., Berovidez, Á., Marín, C., García, U., & Fernández-Truan, J. (2017). Limits of acceptable change of ecotourism in Punta del Este, Isla de la Juventud (Cuba). *Investigaciones Turísticas*, (13), 96–113.

Duffy, L. N., Kline, C., Swanson, J. R., Best, M., & McKinnon, H. (2017). Community development through agroecotourism in Cuba: An application of the community capitals framework. *Journal of Ecotourism, 16*(3), 203–221.

Duffy, R. (2006). The politics of ecotourism. In C. Ryan, S. Page, & M. Aicken (Eds.), *Taking Tourism to the Limits: Issues Concepts and Managerial Perspectives* (pp. 99–112). Amsterdam: Elsevier.

Echtner, C. M. & Jamal, T. B. (1997). The disciplinary dilemma of tourism studies. *Annals of Tourism Research, 24*(4), 868–883.

Eijgelaar, E., Thaper, C., & Peeters, P. (2010). Antarctic cruise tourism: The paradoxes of ambassadorship, "last chance tourism" and greenhouse gas emissions. *Journal of Sustainable Tourism, 18*(3), 337–354.

Farrelly, T. (2013). Community based ecotourism as indigenous social entrepreneurship. In A. Holden & D. Fennell (Eds.), *The Routledge Handbook of Tourism and the Environment* (pp. 447–459). London: Routledge.

Fennell, D. (2008a). *Ecotourism*. London: Routledge.

Fennell, D. (2008b). Ecotourism and the myth of indigenous stewardship. *Journal of Sustainable Tourism, 16*(2), 129–149.

Fennell, D. (2006). *Tourism Ethics* (Vol. 30). Clevedon: Channel View Publications.

Gallagher, A. J. & Hammerschlag, N. (2011). Global shark currency: The distribution, frequency, and economic value of shark ecotourism. *Current Issues in Tourism, 14*(8), 797–812.

Garraway, J. (2017). Ecotourism as a means of community development: The case of the indigenous populations of the Greater Caribbean. *Ara: Revista de Investigación en Turismo, 1*(2), 11–20.

Gibson, C. (2009). Geographies of tourism: Critical research on capitalism and local livelihoods. *Progress in Human Geography, 33*(4), 527–534.

The community perspective

Gibson, C. (2010). Geographies of tourism: (Un)ethical encounters. *Progress in Human Geography, 34*(4), 521–527.

Hall, C. (2007). Tourism, governance and the (mis-)location of power. In A. Church & T. Coles (Eds.), *Tourism, Power and Space* (pp. 247–268). London: Routledge.

Hall, C. & Page, S. (2009). Progress in tourism management: From the geography of tourism to geographies of tourism: A review. *Tourism Management, 30*(1), 3–16.

Hall, C. & Page, S. (2012). Geography and the study of events. In S. Page & J. Connell (Eds.), *Routledge Handbook of Events* (pp. 148–164). London: Routledge.

Herold, E., Garcia, R., & DeMoya, T. (2001). Female tourists and beach boys: Romance or sex tourism? *Annals of Tourism Research, 28*(4), 978–997.

Hirsch, F. (2005). *Social Limits to Growth*. London: Routledge.

Honey, M. (1999). *Ecotourism and Sustainable Development: Who Owns Paradise?*. Washington, D.C.: Island Press.

Iasha, A., Yacob, M. R., Kabir, I., & Radam, A. (2015). Estimating economic value for potential ecotourism resources in Puncak Lawang Park, Agam District, West Sumatera, Indonesia. *Procedia Environmental Sciences, 30*, 326–331.

Jennings, G. (2006). Perspectives on quality tourism experiences: An introduction. In G. Jennings & N. Nickerson (Eds.), *Quality Tourism Experiences* (pp. 1–21). Amsterdam: Elsevier.

Jones, S. (2005). Community-based ecotourism: The significance of social capital. *Annals of Tourism Research, 32*(2), 303–324.

Karst, H. (2017). "This is a holy place of Ama Jomo": Buen vivir, indigenous voices and ecotourism development in a protected area of Bhutan. *Journal of Sustainable Tourism, 25*(6), 746–762.

Kc, A., Rijal, K., & Sapkota, R. P. (2015). Role of ecotourism in environmental conservation and socioeconomic development in Annapurna conservation area, Nepal. *International Journal of Sustainable Development & World Ecology, 22*(3), 251–258.

Kim, S. S., Wong, K. K., & Cho, M. (2007). Assessing the economic value of a world heritage site and willingness-to-pay determinants: A case of Changdeok Palace. *Tourism Management, 28*(1), 317–322.

Kolahi, M., Sakai, T., Moriya, K., & Aminpour, M. (2013). Ecotourism potentials for financing parks and protected areas: A perspective from Iran's parks. *Journal of Modern Accounting and Auditing, 9*(1), 144.

Kontogeorgopoulos, N. (2005). Community-based ecotourism in Phuket and Ao Phangnga, Thailand: Partial victories and bittersweet remedies. *Journal of Sustainable Tourism, 13*(1), 4–23.

Leiper, N. (1981). Towards a cohesive curriculum tourism: The case for a distinct discipline. *Annals of Tourism Research, 8*(1), 69–84.

Leiper, N. (1990). Partial industrialization of tourism systems. *Annals of Tourism Research, 17*(4), 600–605.

Leiper, N. (2000). An emerging discipline. *Annals of Tourism Research, 27*(3), 805–809.

Leiper, N., Stear, L., Hing, N., & Firth, T. (2008). Partial industrialisation in tourism: A new model. *Current Issues in Tourism, 11*(3), 207–235.

Lemelin, H., Dawson, J., & Stewart, E. J. (2013). *Last Chance Tourism: Adapting Tourism Opportunities in a Changing World*. London: Routledge.

Lemelin, R. H. & Baikie, G. (2013). Bringing the gaze to the masses, taking the gaze to the people. In R. Lemelin, J. Dawson, & E. Stewart (Eds.), *Last Chance Tourism: Adapting Tourism Opportunities in a Changing World* (pp. 168–181). London: Routledge.

Lindberg, K., Enriquez, J., & Sproule, K. (1996). Ecotourism questioned: Case studies from Belize. *Annals of Tourism Research, 23*(2), 543–562.

Lonn, P., Mizoue, N., Ota, T., Kajisa, T., & Yoshida, S. (2018). Evaluating the contribution of community-based ecotourism (CBET) to household income and livelihood changes: A case study of the Chambok CBET program in Cambodia. *Ecological Economics, 151*, 62–69.

MacCannell, D. (1973). Staged authenticity: Arrangements of social space in tourist settings. *American Journal of Sociology, 79*(3), 589–603.

MacCannell, D. (1976). *The Tourist: A New Theory of the Leisure Class*. Oakland: University of California Press.

Massey, D. (2010). *A Global Sense of Place*. Retrieved from: www.urbanlab.org/articles/Massey%20global_sense_place.pdf.

Masud, M. M., Aldakhil, A. M., Nassani, A. A., & Azam, M. N. (2017). Community-based ecotourism management for sustainable development of marine protected areas in Malaysia. *Ocean & Coastal Management, 136*, 104–112.

Mbaiwa, J. & Stronza, A. (2009). The challenges and prospects for sustainable tourism and ecotourism in developing countries. In T. Jamal & M. Robinson (Eds.), *The SAGE Handbook of Tourism Studies* (pp. 333–351). London: SAGE Publications.

McKercher, B. (1999). A chaos approach to tourism. *Tourism Management, 20*, 425–434.

McKercher, B. (2010). Academia and the evolution of ecotourism. *Tourism Recreation Research, 35*(1), 15–26.

Messer, E. & Kecskes, K. (2009). Social capital and community: University partnerships. In J. Dillard, V. Dujon, & M. King (Eds.), *Understanding the Social Dimension of Sustainability* (pp. 248–263). New York: Routledge.

Mill, R. C. & Morrison, A. M. (2002). *The Tourism System*. Dubuque: Kendall Hunt.

Mitchell, L. S. (1979). The geography of tourism: An introduction. *Annals of Tourism Research, 6*(3), 235–244.

Nelson, F. (2004). *The Evolution and Impacts of Community-Based Ecotourism in Northern Tanzania*. London: International Institute for Environment and Development.

Neuhofer, B., Buhalis, D., & Ladkin, A. (2014). A typology of technology–enhanced tourism experiences. *International Journal of Tourism Research, 16*(4), 340–350.

Ojibwa. (2012). Mount Rushmore. Retrieved from http://nativeamericannetroots.net/diary/1212.

Okazaki, E. (2008). A community-based tourism model: Its conception and use. *Journal of Sustainable Tourism, 16*(5), 511–529.

Omondi, R. K. & Ryan, C. (2017). Sex tourism: Romantic safaris, prayers and witchcraft at the Kenyan coast. *Tourism Management, 58*, 217–227.

Owen, R., Buhalis, D., & Pletinckx, D. (2006). *Visitors' Evaluations of Technology Used at Cultural Heritage Sites*. In M. Hitz, M. Sigala, & J. Murphy (Eds.), *Information and Communication Technologies in Tourism* (pp. 383–393).Vienna: Springer.

Park, E., Phandanouvong, T., & Kim, S. (2018). Evaluating participation in community-based tourism: A local perspective in Laos. *Current Issues in Tourism, 21*(2), 128–132.

Piggott-McKellar, A. E., & McNamara, K. E. (2017). Last chance tourism and the Great Barrier Reef. *Journal of Sustainable Tourism, 25*(3), 397–415.

Premauer, J. M. & Berkes, F. (2015). A pluralistic approach to protected area governance: Indigenous peoples and Makuira National Park, Colombia. *Ethnobiology and Conservation, 4*(4), 1–16.

Reggers, A., Grabowski, S., Wearing, S. L., Chatterton, P., & Schweinsberg, S. (2016). Exploring outcomes of community-based tourism on the Kokoda Track, Papua New Guinea: A longitudinal study of participatory rural appraisal techniques. *Journal of Sustainable Tourism, 24*(8–9), 1–17.

The community perspective

Reimer, J. K. & Walter, P. (2013). How do you know it when you see it? Community-based ecotourism in the Cardamom Mountains of southwestern Cambodia. *Tourism Management, 34*, 122–132.

Reino, S., Mitsche, N., & Frew, A. J. (2007). *The Contribution of Technology-Based Heritage Interpretation to the Visitor Satisfaction in Museums*. In M. Sigala & M. Murphy (Eds.), *Information and Communication Technologies in Tourism* (pp. 341–352). Vienna: Springer.

Relph, E. (1976). *Place and Placelessness*. London: Pion Ltd.

Ritzer, G. (1998). *The McDonaldization Thesis: Explorations and Extensions*. London: Sage.

Ritzer, G. (2009). *McDonaldization: The Reader*. Thousand Oaks: Pine Forge Press.

Ross, S. & Wall, G. (1999). Ecotourism: Towards congruence between theory and practice. *Tourism Management, 20*(1), 123–132.

Runte, A. (1987). *National Parks: The American Experience* (2nd ed.). Lincoln: University of Nebraska Press.

Ryan, C. & Hall, C. (2001). *Sex Tourism: Marginal People and Liminalities*. London: Routledge.

Sakata, H. & Prideaux, B. (2013). An alternative approach to community-based ecotourism: A bottom-up locally initiated non-monetised project in Papua New Guinea. *Journal of Sustainable Tourism, 21*(6), 880–899. doi:10.1080/09669582.2012.756493.

Samonte, G. P., Eisma-Osorio, R.-L., Amolo, R., & White, A. (2016). Economic value of a large marine ecosystem: Danajon double barrier reef, Philippines. *Ocean Coast Management, 122*, 9–19.

Schweinsberg, S., Wearing, S., & Wearing, M. (2015). Transforming nature's value – cultural change comes from below: Rural communities, the 'Othered' and host capacity building. In Y. Reisinger (Ed.), *Transforming Tourism: Host Perspectives* (pp. 102–113). Wallingford: CABI.

Singh, S., Timothy, D. J., & Dowling, R. K. (2003). *Tourism in Destination Communities*. Wallingford: CABI.

Smith, M. (2015). Tourism and cultral change. In C. M. Hall, S. Gössling, & D. Scott (Eds.), *The Routledge Handbook of Tourism and Sustainability* (pp. 175–184). London: Routledge.

Stevens, S. (2014). *Indigenous Peoples, National Parks, and Protected Areas: A New Paradigm Linking Conservation, Culture, and Rights*. Tucson: University of Arizona Press.

Stone, M. T. (2015). Community-based ecotourism: A collaborative partnerships perspective. *Journal of Ecotourism, 14*(2–3), 166–184.

Stronza, A. (2007). The economic promise of ecotourism for conservation. *Journal of Ecotourism, 6*(3), 210–230.

Telfer, D. J. & Sharpley, R. (2nd Ed.) (2015). *Tourism and Development in the Developing World*. London: Routledge.

Timothy, D. (2007). Empowerment and stakeholder participation in tourism destination communities. In A. Church & T. Coles (Eds.), *Tourism, Power and Space* (pp. 199–216). London: Routledge.

Tribe, J. (1997). The indiscipline of tourism. *Annals of Tourism Research, 24*(3), 638–657.

Tribe, J. (2000). Indisciplined and unsubstantiated. *Annals of Tourism Research, 27*(3), 809–813.

Tsaur, S.-H., Lin, Y.-C., & Lin, J.-H. (2006). Evaluating ecotourism sustainability from the integrated perspective of resource, community and tourism. *Tourism Management, 27*(4), 640–653.

Urry, J. & Larsen, J. (2011). *The Tourist Gaze 3.0*. London: Sage.

Vianna, G., Meekan, M., Pannell, D., Marsh, S., & Meeuwig, J. (2012). Socio-economic value and community benefits from shark-diving tourism in Palau: A sustainable use of reef shark populations. *Biological Conservation, 145*(1), 267–277.

Von Bertalanffy, L. (1968/2003). General system theory. In D. Hammond (Ed.), *The Science of Synthesis: Exploring the Social Implications of General Systems Theory* (pp. 103–142). Boulder: University Press of Colorado.

Von Bertalanffy, L. (1972). The history and status of general systems theory. *Academy of Management Journal, 15*(4), 407–426.

Wall, G. (1997). Is ecotourism sustainable? *Environmental Management, 21*(4), 483–491.

Wang, C., Cater, C., & Low, T. (2016). Political challenges in community-based ecotourism. *Journal of Sustainable Tourism, 24*(11), 1555–1568.

Wang, N. (1999). Rethinking authenticity in tourism experience. *Annals of Tourism Research, 26*(2), 349–370.

Wearing, S. (2001). Exploring socio-cultural impacts on local communities. In D. Weaver (Ed.), *The Encyclopedia of Ecotourism* (pp. 395–410). Oxfordshire: CABI Publishing.

Wearing, S. & McDonald, M. (2002). The development of community-based tourism: Rethinking the relationship between tour operators and development agents as intermediaries in rural and isolated area communities. *Journal of Sustainable Tourism, 10*(3), 191–206.

Wearing, S. & Neil, J. (2009). *Ecotourism Impacts Potentials and Possibilities* (2nd ed.). Oxford: Butterworth-Heinemann.

Weaver, D. (2008). *Ecotourism* (2nd ed.). Milton: Wiley.

Weaver, D. & Lawton, L. (2007). Twenty years on: The state of contemporary ecotourism research. *Tourism Management, 28*(5), 1168–1179.

Wheeller, B. (2005). Ecotourism/egotourism and development. In C. Michael Hall & S. Boyd (Eds.), *Nature Based Tourism in Peripheral Areas: Development or Disaster* (pp. 263–272). Clevedon: Channel View.

Winson, A. (2006). Ecotourism and sustainability in Cuba: Does socialism make a difference? *Journal of Sustainable Tourism, 14*(1), 6–23.

Zhang, H. & Lei, S. L. (2012). A structural model of residents' intention to participate in ecotourism: The case of a wetland community. *Tourism Management, 33*(4), 916–925.

Zong, C., Cheng, K., Lee, C.-H., & Hsu, N.-L. (2017). Capturing tourists' preferences for the management of community-based ecotourism in a forest park. *Sustainability, 9*(9), 1673.

Chapter 8

Marketing ecotourism

Shaping expectations for a sustainable future

Introduction

Ever since the earliest formal definitions of ecotourism, there has been a tendency in popular and industry discourse to frame the sector's *raison d'être* as being to achieve sustainable development. While academics have increasingly sought to constructively critique the sustainability merits of the sector (e.g., Butcher, 2005; Fletcher, 2009; Vanderheiden & Sisson, 2010), influential groups including the United Nations General Assembly have continued to identify ecotourism as a pathway to sustainable development. As a case in point, it is possible to cite the 2016 consensus resolution (71/240) of the United Nations General Assembly: *Promotion of sustainable tourism, including ecotourism, for poverty eradication and environmental protection.* The text of the resolution read in part as follows:

> Recognising that sustainable tourism, including ecotourism, is a cross-cutting activity that can contribute to the three dimensions of sustainable development and the achievement of the Sustainable Development Goals, including by fostering economic growth, alleviating poverty, creating full and productive employment and decent work for all, accelerating the change to more sustainable consumption and production patterns and promoting the sustainable use of oceans, seas and marine resources, promoting local culture, improving the quality of life and the economic empowerment of women and young people and promoting rural development and better living conditions for rural populations. (United Nations General Assembly, 2016)

In the present volume we have tended to be more circumspect with respect to discussions of ecotourism's sustainability potential. We have argued that the intractability of many stakeholder positions on what constitutes sustainability in the global ecotourism industry has led to both the empowerment and disempowerment of ecotourism futures. When Urry and Larsen (2011) wrote speculatively on tourism's future in 2050, they wrote of a reframing of industry boundaries, often a fundamental re-appraisal of social status in new consumer landscapes, and choices that must be made if we are to ever arrive at that sustainability nirvana. While ecotourism does not specifically form a part of Urry and Larsen's (2011) futures discussion, many of the themes we have already mentioned in this volume in connection to eco-tourism do – economic potential, local sense of place, community values and their interrelations.

For ecotourism to play a positive role in the reconciliation of different values and perspectives and thus be a mechanism for pursuing sustainability outcomes, it is vital that it is appropriately planned and managed. Wearing et al. (2012) have written how slow ecotourism and the deliberate application of brakes on capitalism can afford local populations the opportunity to control and self-regulate their indus-tries. Similarly, Conway and Timms (2010) have noted, with respect to slow tourism in the Caribbean, of the need to move beyond the "established mass-tourism infra-structure ... and promote the niche marketing for alternative tourisms that focus on quality upgrading rather than merely increasing the quantity of visitors" (p. 329). This places marketing as a core component of sustainable tourism management dis-cussions. Krippendorf (1987b, p. 138) in his influential work *The Holiday Makers* observed that

> the ultimate pace of tourism depends to a large extent on their business policy and their marketing ... They [tourism] have a special responsibility not only because of the influence they exercise but because – unlike industries producing material goods – they deal in people, cultures, [and] landscapes.

Ecotourism marketing in a tourism marketing tradition

Depending on how its parameters are conceptualised, it would not be unrea-sonable to describe tourism as the world's largest service- or experience-based industry sector. Pine and Gilmore (1998), in their pioneering work on the expe-rience economy, noted that in contrast to those industries that produce mate-rial goods, where attention is understandably focused on the workings of the product, service-based industries like tourism are underpinned by the ability to fulfil experiences (see also Bosangit, Hibbert, & McCabe, 2015; Sharpley & Stone, 2014; Uriely, 2005). Because of the reciprocal interplay of producers and consum-ers in a service environment, the marketing of tourism has become an impor-tant area of academic scholarship over the last four decades (see Hall, 2014; Krippendorf, 1987a; Middleton, 1998; Middleton & Clarke, 2012; Middleton, Fyall, Morgan, & Ranchhod, 2009). Kotler et al. (2017) have observed that the central-ity of marketing to tourism lies in the fact that it is only when we understand the needs and wants of our consumers that we can hope to deliver experiences that are not only satisfactory in the short term (a prerequisite for competitive advantage) but also sustainable in the long term. Page (2015, p. 311) made the following observations on the importance of seeing marketing as a core tourism management function:

> Marketing is widely acknowledged as a vital prerequisite to communicating the product or service offering of business or suppliers to the market ... marketing is a process whereby individuals and groups obtain the type of product they value. These goods are created and exchanged through a process, which requires detailed

understanding of their wants and desires so that the product or service is effectively and efficiently delivered to the client or purchaser.

At its essence marketing, as with interpretation (see Chapter 6), is focused on the provision of knowledge to achieve specific recipient outcomes. While interpretation outcomes are frequently based around the supposedly higher-level values of education and provocation, marketing is traditionally seen as the provision of knowledge aiming to influence purchase intent. How this is achieved has evolved over time. Kotler et al. (2003, p. 6) observed how over the latter half of the twentieth century, marketing evolved from a narrow focus on sales – so-called telling and selling – to a more sophisticated focus on "satisfying consumer needs by interacting and working with the customer". To achieve such outcomes, it is vital that tourism marketers are mindful of a simple reality – one cannot build relationships with consumers without taking into account the business's micro and macro marketing environment.

For a detailed explanation of the components and workings of the microenvironment and macroenvironment, see Kotler et al. (2017). Here we simply wish to make a simple point with respect to the marketing environment – ecotourism is not inherently structurally different from mass tourism on account of the presence of different operating processes or different macroenvironmental forces. All forms of tourism must consider the needs of consumers and suppliers and recognise the presence of evolving natural, demographic and sociocultural forces, etc. Instead, where ecotourism is theoretically different is in the way that power pervades the sector's multi-scalar networks. Stakeholder networks are not static in their form or operation (see Tussyadiah & Sigala, 2018, for a discussion of tourism marketing in the context of the sharing economy). Timothy (2007) has argued that eco-labelling, which we will discuss later in this chapter in the context of ecotourism marketing, seeks to use the process of certification to empower, whether empowerment occurs for tourists, communities or another group entirely. Knowles and Felzensztein (2011) have identified that the ecotourism industry needs to promote greater network synergies between each of its stakeholders – people, institutions and entrepreneurs must band together, stop focusing solely on partisan perspectives on the merits of localised economic development, and instead, package ecotourism under a united brand.

An important requirement for the development of networked synergies is the recognition that consumers are increasingly demanding responsibility from tourism with respect to its relationship to the natural and social world. No longer can the world be seen as a blank canvas for the enactment of personal hedonistic tourist experiences. Tourists themselves are increasingly recognising that they have a responsibility to do good as well as a responsibility to avoid doing harm – a realisation that lies behind the growth of many tourism forms, such as volunteer tourism (Mostafanezhad, 2013; Sin, 2010). Therefore, if we are to understand the manner in which ecotourists' moral predispositions impact their receptiveness to marketing messages, we must understand who the ecotourists are. In Chapter 9, we will consider the motivations and experiences of an iconic and historic ecotourist in more detail. Suffice it to say at this point, however, that Perkins and Grace (2009) have argued that there is a quantifiable difference in the motivations of mainstream tourists and ecotourists. Motivations drawn from a sample of 255 tourists at two iconic Gold Coast (Queensland, Australia) tourism sites (Sea World and the World Heritage Lamington National Park) showed ecotourists to be focused on "immersion in or communion with nature; and in some cases the opportunity to contribute personally to environmental conservation" (Perkins & Grace, 2009, p. 235). In contrast, mainstream tourists were identified as being focused on more "hedonistic-type activities (e.g. fun, relaxation and pampering etc)" (Perkins & Grace, 2009, p. 235). Perkins and Grace use the results of the study to argue that ecotourism is therefore a demand-driven as well as a supply-driven industry.

To understand tourism demand, we must seek to engage with a range of business metrics relating to tourists, including purpose of travel, point of origin, duration of stay, means of transportation, etc. Writing a little over a decade ago, McKercher (2001) bemoaned what he saw as a lack of business acumen amongst many ecotourism operators. While a knowledge of marketing principles can be said to be a key requirement of managers (Cunliffe, 2014), the small operator nature of much of the global tourism industry can make the operation of marketing strategies difficult. Weaver (2008) has identified the financial pressures on businesses to obtain comprehensive market segmentation data and the cost of marketing campaigns as two of the principal impediments. In the course of identifying these and other impediments to marketing amongst small-scale tourism operators, Weaver (2008, p. 161) defines marketing as "an umbrella term that encompasses not just the promotional and advertising functions commonly associated with the word but also market segmentation, new product testing, obtaining customer feedback, assessing competing products, pricing decisions and determining distribution channels and methods". Where there is a lack of understanding of marketing in tourism settings, McKercher observes the tendency for operators to avoid the sensible path of a "targeted marketing approach, allocating scarce resources in such that they optimise the chance to reach their desired markets" (McKercher, 2001, p. 567). Instead, McKercher (2001, p. 567) goes on to note, many adopt a "shotgun marketing-approach … this occurs usually as a function of not knowing who the target market is, not understanding its habits and buying power and not having a clear idea of how to reach that market".

The potential negative effects of a lack of business acumen are often exacerbated in the context of sustainable tourism, where achieving long-term sustainable demand may require a reduction in short-term demand (Edgell, 2016). This reality positions marketing as a component of wider destination management planning. In recent years, demarketing has emerged, with the specific aim of limiting the level of tourism growth that one will allow in light of social and environmental imperatives. Demarketing is often connected to ecotourism in the sense that both ideas are historically premised around how best to create equitable, engaging and maintainable interactions with nature (Wearing, Schweinsberg, & Tower, 2016). Throughout the present volume we have tended to frame ecotourism in quite traditional terms, emphasising the primacy of concern for the natural world, tourist immersion and education (see Atieno & Njoroge, 2018, for a discussion of these and other issues relating to the practice of ecotourism in Kenya). Whilst doing so, however, we must always acknowledge the presence of various niche marketing segments. One example of a niche ecotourism segment is eco-volunteering. The Eco Volunteer Programme (2000 in Chan, 2011, p. 71):

> identifies the specific prominent features used to describe volunteer tourism, which include: meeting the special interests of the volunteer tourist (wildlife, education, authentic experience, participatory in nature, opportunities to meet and work with like-minded people) and his/her purposes or reasons to travel; the participant's

support towards the activities of the host (nature conservation or community development); and making new friends, learning new things and developing new skills.

Marketing to such niche tourist forms will be dependent upon one's ability to generate a profit, whilst tailoring to specific and often unique motivations. In short, it will require an understanding of the processes that help to develop a market orientation – an understanding of the marketing mix, market segmentation, the product life cycle, the value exchange process, etc.

These so-called mechanics of tourism marketing have been the subject of a number of excellent works over the last decade or so (e.g., Dickman, 1999; Godfrey & Clarke, 2000; Kotler, Bowen, & Makens, 2009; Morrison, 2013). Morrison (2013) has argued that success in marketing will ultimately be framed on the basis of the interplay of the components of one's marketing mix. The original conceptualisation of the marketing mix – product, place, promotion and price – was popularised by the work of E. Jerome McCarthy, author of the works Basic Marketing and Essentials of Marketing (see Goeldner, Ritchie, & McIntosch, 2000). To this Morrison (2013) has added other variables, including programming, people and partnerships. Edgell 2016) has in turn proposed the 10Ps of sustainable marketing: product, price, place, promotion, partnerships, packaging, programming, positioning, people, planning. In the 10Ps, we see recognition that marketing goes far beyond the transaction of goods and services to also include the people that make transactions possible.

Drawing on the work of John Tower, Wearing et al. (2016) defined the interplay of many of these and other variables in the context of a tree. Tower's tree model of market delivery (see Figure 8.1) is premised on the notion that the consumer (or

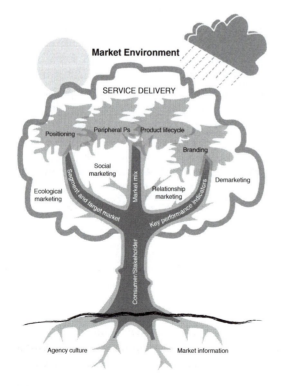

Figure 8.1 Tree model of marketing delivery.

Source: Wearing et al. (2016, p. 17)

recipient stakeholder) is the ultimate recipient of any marketing message; without an understanding of whom a service is for, there is limited capacity to deliver successful services (Zimmermann & Tower, 2017). Understanding this consumer can only be achieved with reference to notions of market segmentation. As Goeldner et al. (2000) note, few vacation destinations are universally acceptable or desired. Therefore, rather than trying to please all travellers, one should aim promotional efforts specifically to the wants and needs of likely prospects.

How such prospects are identified depends upon the segmentation approach one employs. Benckendorff and Moscardo (2000), for instance, refer to the presence of differences in generational responses to environmental and conservation issues that are so intertwined with ecotourism. Generation Xers, they note, are often well-informed and thus often sceptical over perceived inauthenticity in marketing communications. Previous experiences with unscrupulous industry players often makes Generation X "suspicious of products that have an Eco label with the result being that ecotourism has an image problem" (Benckendorff & Moscardo, 2013, p. 147). At this point it is appropriate to note that no group of tourists will be homogenous with resect to their perceptions of the environment and their interactions with the global tourism industry. As a case in point, the decision to climb or not to climb Uluru has been declining in importance for many visitors to Central Australia over the last few decades. James (2007) observed how the actions of tourists at the site (i.e., the decision to climb or not to climb) are influenced by contestation over the importance one should attach to achieving an ephemeral experience on the one hand, and the importance of respecting the views of the Traditional Aboriginal Owners, the Anangu, on the other. In 2017 the Uluru-Kata Tjuta National Park Board made the decision to ban the climbing of Uluru as of 2019. This decision has been identified as being made on the basis of a mutual obligation between tourists and indigenous owners for the responsible use of the site (Norman, 2017). In the Uluru example we see evidence of so-called nonrepresentational geographies of space: geographies that have sought "to reposition the individual, the human, the subject into the making of space and hence into the making of tourism" (Crouch, 2011, p. 45). Tourists are portrayed as active creators of experiences that extend far beyond the prepackaged representations of space, which are presented to them in traditional marketing discourses. In recent years there has been evidence of tourism agencies, like Tourism Australia, moving away from simplistic demographic market segmentation towards psychographic segmentation, where the focus is more on behaviours, attitudes and interests (see also Zografos & Allcroft, 2007). This has allowed them to identify a new class of what are now popularly referred to as high-value travellers, a more discerning class of traveller with clear wants and desires that the industry offerings can then be tailored to.

Market segmentation strategies, therefore, help us to define the trunk of our marketing tree. The trunk will, however, only grow strong if it is supported by a strong root system, which in turn is fed by the external marketing environment. Feeding into the tree are both macro-level market-based information and trends and agency culture. Together these two forces focus our attention on the interplay of capitalist and conservation forces in an ecotourism destination context, examples of which we have already observed throughout this volume. Where the relationship between these forces is pursued innovatively, there is the potential for smart ecotourism marketing outcomes. Boes et al. (2015, p. 391) have defined 'smart', as in smart cities, as a "marketing word for all things that are embedded or enhanced by technology". Recently the Sydney Royal Botanic Gardens, which we discussed extensively in Chapter 3, have sought to partner with telecommunications providers to enhance the ecotourism experience in one of Sydney's oldest institutions through the development of a fully integrated Wi-Fi system. The CEO of Tourism and Transport Forum Australia, Margy Osmond, applauded the move, noting that we live in an interconnected world where smartphones and tablets are becoming the norm.

Once the recipient of a marketing message has been established, Wearing et al. (2016) use the tree model to illustrate how the various modes of marketing delivery that are now common in discussions of ecotourism (e.g., demarketing, ecological marketing, etc.) are underpinned by different interpretations of the interplay of market segmentation, the marketing mix and key performance indicators. For example, when Kotler and Zaltman (1971) first used the term 'social marketing', the phenomenon was defined as the employment of marketing processes to effect social change. Much as demarketing involves the deliberate discouragement of purchase as a response to a decline in supply (see Armstrong & Kern, 2011; Beeton & Benfield, 2002; Kotler & Levy, 1971), social marketing necessitates deliberate decisions on the part of marketing professionals about which segments to target, the manner in which they will be targeted and what success in such an endeavour will look like. As Hall (2014, p. 7) notes:

> Given the size and growth rate of the tourism industry why does tourism need social marketing? Answer: it is exactly because of those growth rates that social marketing is being seen as potentially significant. In some cases social marketing may be used to promote more positive attitudes by a community towards tourists in order to make the tourist experience more welcoming. Such interventions are usually linked with a concern to maximise the economic benefits of tourism at a destination and to create a positive visitor experience and word of mouth.

Buhalis (2000) has observed that the marketing of tourism destinations must always seek to balance the needs of different stakeholder groups. One mechanism by which this can be achieved is the use of new technologies and social media (see Buhalis & Law, 2008). Donohoe and Needham (2008) have witnessed the propensity amongst ecotourism operators to use Internet-based mechanisms as a means of aligning their practices to core ecotourism tenets. At the same time, however, they have also noted the tendency for much Internet marketing to be seen as disingenuous, often falling short of the high standards necessary to convince society at large as to the sector's sustainability benefits. Recent scholarship by Cheng et al. (2017) has identified the importance of blog-based and other online marketing forms for the sustainable growth of new ecotourism areas in China. As they observe,

> Chinese ecotourism has some subtle and important differences to that of the west ... The Ecotourism experience for Chinese visitors is often focused on the unification of one's body with nature and the opportunity to interact with nature by connecting one's present with the past. (Cheng et al. 2017, p. 428).

This is in contrast to many Western ecotourism contexts in which ecotourists, for all their interest in immersive experiences, are still somewhat apart from nature. Through an examination of how ecotourism agencies use social media platforms like

Sina Weibo, Cheng et al. (2017) illustrate how technology can be used to enhance the number of tourists participating, as well as to instil in eco-travellers a more socially conscious and responsible mindset.

Ecotourism marketing for sustainability

The idea that tourism marketing can be discussed in the context of sustainability is, for many, a conceptual oxymoron. After all, how can we continue to grow economically but not have too negative an impact on the society and natural world? In a world where the finite nature of many resources is increasingly being recognised, marketing has come to be seen as one of the many enduring faces of capitalism, one whose primary function remains the promotion of sales and consumption as a pathway towards economic growth (Jamrozy, (Jamrozy, 2007). As Kotler et al. (2017) have noted, however, there is an increasing realisation that marketing can have positive outcomes with respect to sustainability. By looking into the future, not waiting for the inevitable reprimand from legislators for inaction, but rather being proactive with respect to one's social obligations, there is the potential to turn sustainable marketing into a mechanism for gaining a competitive advantage (see Clarke, Hawkins, & Waligo, 2014).

One means by which such outcomes can be achieved is through the alignment of a series of broad sustainability principles to our marketing strategies. Wearing et al. (2016) framed these principles as the 5Rs of Sustainable Marketing: responsible, realistic, regional, relationships and research (see Table 8.1). These principles, which have been previously applied to the development of sustainable tourism marketing strategies in national parks, are premised on an idea that whilst the protection of environmental integrity must be the baseline standard of all marketing strategies, around this baseline there is a series of independent variables that are driven by local conditions. When employed appropriately, the 5R model stipulates adherence to standards in one's own behaviour, as well as recognition of the fact

Table 8.1 5Rs of sustainable tourism marketing

Principle	Description of guiding principle.
Responsible	Sustainable marketing should be designed and undertaken with conservation as a baseline and in a **responsible** ethical manner.
Realistic	To be sustainable, marketing should be done in a manner that disseminates **realistic** images and information to existing and potential visitors.
Regional	Sustainable marketing should be designed and used in a **regional** context.
Relationships	Cooperative **relationships** between relevant land management, industry and community stakeholders can benefit all.
Research	**Research** is a fundamental building block of sustainable marketing. The market environment provides a wealth of data that need to inform market decisions.

Adapted from Wearing et al. (2016, p. 12)

that any marketing strategy we employ (e.g., around eco-certification) must take into account social and environmental conditions.

Eco-certification is often used by tourism operators to distinguish legitimate operators from "counterfeit green washed products" (Medina, 2005, p. 281) and to raise an awareness of a business's sustainability credentials (see Gössling & Buckley, 2016, for a discussion of existing certification schemes). While dozens of certification schemes can be found in different jurisdictions throughout the world, the basic rationale for their use is the ability of certification programs to "standardise the promotion of environmental claims by following compliance to set criteria, generally based on third party, impartial verification" (Font, 2001, p. 3). If implemented properly, certification can assist the establishment of sustainable operating practices (see Font & Harris, 2004) whilst also allowing operators to compete on issues other than price (Font, Epler Wood, Black, & Crabtree, 2007). In increasingly crowded marketplaces, there must be something else that will engender loyalty in consumers. Font et al. (2007) have drawn on work by Epler Wood International to argue that consumers frequently become more loyal as they gain understanding of the significance and impacts of their responsible practices.

Whether it is the values that a business feels it can engender in consumers or the ability of a business to use demarketing practices to strategically control visitor numbers, sustainable marketing is premised on the notion that environmental and sociocultural integrity can occur simultaneously with market growth (Donohoe & Needham, 2018). As Donohoe and Needham (2008, p. 21) note, "Marketing comprises three main elements, consumer behaviour, producer behaviour and the nexus between them". When seen in the context of eco-certification, Honey and Stewart (2002, p. 66) have observed that the marketing of one's credentials necessarily occurs in two directions: "to the wider travel industry to enrol businesses to be certified [on the one hand] and to the travelling public to build patrons who use the certified products [on the other]". No matter how good one's internal business practices are, simply having eco-certification will not necessarily lead to greater patronage. As Honey and Stewart (2002, p. 362) note, consumers must have clarity "as to what an Eco label promises. Certified businesses need to know that if they invest time and money to earn an Eco label, they will gain information on how to improve performance and market advantage".

Micro-level (or firm-oriented) marketing is only one half of sustainable marketing. Kotler (2011, p. 133) makes the following observations on the ways in which the traditional 4Ps of marketing may need to evolve to take into account the so-called sustainability imperative:

Product: Companies will have to consider more questions in the course of developing new products. Designers will have to consider the materials more carefully and their sources and carbon footprints. They will have to develop the packaging more carefully in terms of being biodegradable and disposable. Service firms that do not produce a physical product (e.g., professional firms, hospitals, colleges, airlines) have a chance to compete better by demonstrating their environmental concerns in their use of energy and physical supplies and to contribute to conservation causes.

Price: Companies can create a menu of offerings that differ in their level of environmental friendliness and price them accordingly. Environmentally involved customers may be willing to pay more. Companies will also need to consider how their pricing will be affected by possible new regulations requiring them to cover more of the externality costs they create.

Place: Companies will need to consider where to locate their production and distribution facilities. Environmentalists advocate more locally based production, which would call for more decentralized production. Marketers pursuing sustainability may want to rate the different potential distribution channels for their commitment to sustainable practices. Companies can make greater use of online selling of their products to reduce the amount of consumer driving to outlets.

Promotion: Companies will need to consider how much to shift their promotion from print to online, based on the notion that print uses up paper, ink, and other resources. They will want to communicate their commitment to sustainability (i.e., being a good citizen) in more of their advertisements. Their product labelling might need to be more specific about the ingredients and their carbon footprints. Virtually all companies seek growth, but they need to put more emphasis on sustainable paths to growth. (see Kotler, 2011)

Micro-level strategies such as those above must be seen in the context of the macro-level marketing perspective, where the so-called dominant social paradigm articulates a set of laws, mores and values that broadly define the most common positions in society on a particular issue (Kilbourne, 2004). Clarke et al. (2014) have observed that for many, the dominant social paradigm is one of continuous economic growth. The short-term economic focus that such a mindset often implies has led to a situation where tourism operators will often pursue a narrow, performance-oriented marketing strategy. In such a scenario, marketing efforts will typically be focused on shallow descriptions of product characteristics, as opposed to asking how marketing can be employed to create a dialogue with the information recipient. Where consumers are unable to critically reflect on the relevance of advertised products to their lives, there is the strong potential for scepticism to develop. Writing in relation to the broader tourism accommodation sector, Villarino and Font (2015) observed that sustainability marketing would likely be more successful if it were pursued in a way that engendered an emotional resonance for consumers. How can we use marketing to allow travellers to actively experience the results of sustainability initiatives? How can we link their actions as consumers to wider discussions around accepted behavioural norms? One area where we might start is tourism semiotics.

Semiotics refers to the study of signs and systems of representation (Tresidder, 2014). Signs are "simply anything that stands for something (its object referent), to somebody (interpreter), in some respect its context (i.e. an advert, label, package, service scape or retail environment)" (Mick, 1986, p. 198 in Tresidder, 2014, p. 95). Tourism, in particular tourism marketing, is well placed to seek to capitalise on the power of myths. Whether one is marketing a beach holiday in the Caribbean, a pilgrimage along the Kokoda Track (Papua New Guinea) or an eco-cruise to the Antarctic, each experience is characterised by a series of established words, images and metaphors. As Urry (2002, p. 3) noted, "when tourists see two people kissing in Paris what they capture in the gaze is the timeless romantic Paris. When a small village in England is seen, what they gaze upon is the real old England". If we accept the proposition that all tourists are amateur semioticians, the question becomes how marketing can be used strategically to light a fire amongst visitors, to encourage them to look beyond the shallow framework of their immediate experience and to instead embrace their reciprocal relationship with the business in the development of sustainable outcomes.

One as-yet unexplored mechanism for achieving sustainable outcomes is inter-pretation. Tresidder (2014) observes that often we do not question the meanings of signs we are presented with. Just as Tresidder (2014) notes that a traffic light may be a signifier of traffic control or an ideological or political construct for ensuring a type of behaviour in citizenry, so too can marketing signs be viewed in different ways. For example, an image of a traditionally dressed Polynesian islander can be viewed as the human element in a traditional, picture-perfect postcard representation of an island paradise, or alternatively as an inaccurate, colonial-inspired marketing image, one that seeks to impose idealised representations on complex and evolving local cultures. While neither of these representations is necessarily totally accurate or not, the challenge for ecotourism marketers becomes how best to go beyond a telling and selling approach to marketing. It is the role of interpreters to "awaken people's curiosity", to light a spark that will hopefully lead visitors to open their minds and to be curious as to the complexities of the world (Tilden, 1977, p. xiii). Already, in the field of cultural tourism, it has been demonstrated that interpreta-tion plays a major role in the marketing of heritage sites (see Nuryanti, 1996). As with ecotourism, there are inherent tensions in heritage tourism between the object of study and the means by which heritage is studied. We would suggest that the desire of many ecotourists for an immersive, education-focused experience of nature opens up opportunities for interpreters to challenge existing perspectives of ecology and nature, thus marketing an experience that is thought provoking and reflective (see Packer & Ballantyne, 2013) as well as nature based, as usual.

We will explore the nature of the ecotourist experience in greater detail in the next chapter, when we examine the presidential ecotourist experience of Theodore Roosevelt.

Further reading

Wearing provide a framework for marketing ecotourism and give examples of how the private and public sectors can work together to find solutions in marketing of ecotourism.

Wearing, S., Schweinsberg, S., & Tower, J. (2016). *The Marketing of National Parks for Sustainable Tourism*. Clevedon: Channel View.

Question

Can ecotourism marketing be used strategically to encourage ecotourists to look past the immediate activity to instead embrace their reciprocal relation-ship with the natural environment?

References

Armstrong, E. & Kern, C. (2011). Demarketing manages visitor demand in the Blue Mountains National Park. *Journal of Ecotourism, 10*(1), 21–37.

Atieno, L. & Njoroge, J. M. (2018). The ecotourism metaphor and environmental sustain-ability in Kenya. *Tourism and Hospitality Research, 18*(1), 49–60.

Beeton, S. & Benfield, R. (2002). Demand control: The case for demarketing as a visitor and environmental management tool. *Journal of Sustainable Tourism, 10*(6), 497–513.

Benckendorff, P. & Moscardo, G. (2013). Generational cohorts and ecotourism. In R. Ballantyne & J. Packer (Eds.), *International Handbook on Ecotourism* (pp. 135–154). Cheltenham: Edward Elgar.

Boes, K., Buhalis, D., & Inversini, A. (2015). Conceptualising smart tourism destination dimensions. In I. Tussyadiah & A. Inversini (Eds.), *Information and Communication Technologies in Tourism 2015* (pp. 391–403). New York: Springer.

Bosangit, C., Hibbert, S., & McCabe, S. (2015). "If I was going to die I should at least be having fun": Travel blogs, meaning and tourist experience. *Annals of Tourism Research, 55*, 1–14.

Buhalis, D. (2000). Marketing the competitive destination of the future. *Tourism Management, 21*(1), 97–116.

Buhalis, D. & Law, R. (2008). Progress in information technology and tourism management: 20 years on and 10 years after the Internet: The state of eTourism research. *Tourism Management, 29*(4), 609–623.

Butcher, J. (2005). The moral authority of ecotourism: A critique. *Current Issues in Tourism, 8*(2–3), 114–124.

Chan, J. (2011). Developing and promoting sustainable volunteer tourism sites in Sabah, Malaysia. In A. Benson (Ed.), *Volunteer Tourism: Theoretical Frameworks to Practical Applications* (pp. 71–89). London: Routledge.

Cheng, M., Wong, I. A., Wearing, S., & McDonald, M. (2017). Ecotourism social media initiatives in China. *Journal of Sustainable Tourism, 25*(3), 416–432.

Clarke, J., Hawkins, R., & Waligo, V. (2014). Sustainability and marketing for responsible tourism. In S. McCabe (Ed.), *The Routledge Handbook of Tourism Marketing* (pp. 41–53). London: Routledge.

Conway, D. & Timms, B. F. (2010). Re-branding alternative tourism in the Caribbean: The case for 'slow tourism'. *Tourism and Hospitality Research, 10*(4), 329–344.

Crouch, D. (2011). The power of the tourist encounter. In A. Church & T. Coles (Eds.), *Tourism, Power and Space* (pp. 45–62). London: Routledge.

Cunliffe, A. L. (2014). *A Very Short, Fairly Interesting and Reasonably Cheap Book about Management.* Los Angeles: SAGE.

Dickman, S. (1999). *Tourism and Hospitality Marketing.* Melbourne: Oxford University Press.

Donohoe, H. M. & Needham, R. D. (2008). Internet-based ecotourism marketing: Evaluating Canadian sensitivity to ecotourism tenets. *Journal of Ecotourism, 7*(1), 15–43.

Edgell, D. (Ed.) (2016). *Managing Sustainable Tourism: A Legacy for the Future.* New York: Haworth Hospitality Press.

Fletcher, R. (2009). Ecotourism discourse: Challenging the stakeholders theory. *Journal of Ecotourism, 8*(3), 269–285.

Font, X. (2001). Regulating the green message: The players in ecolabelling. In X. Font & R. Buckley (Eds.), *Tourism Ecolabelling: Certification and Promotion of Sustainable Management* (pp. 1–17). Wallingford: CABI.

Font, X., Epler Wood, M., Black, R., & Crabtree, A. (2007). Sustainable tourism certification marketing and its contribution to SME market access. *Quality Assurance and Certification in Ecotourism, 5*, 147.

Font, X. & Harris, C. (2004). Rethinking standards from green to sustainable. *Annals of Tourism Research, 31*(4), 986–1007.

Godfrey, K. & Clarke, J. (2000). *The Tourism Development Handbook: A Practical Approach to Planning and Marketing.* London: Burns & Oates.

Goeldner, C., Ritchie, J., & McIntosch, R. (2000). *Tourism: Principles, Practices, Philosophies*. New York: John Wiley and Sons, Inc.

Gössling, S. & Buckley, R. (2016). Carbon labels in tourism: Persuasive communication? *Journal of Cleaner Production, 111*, 358–369.

Hall, C. (2014). *Tourism and Social Marketing*. London: Routledge.

Honey, M. & Stewart, E. (2002). The evolution of green standards for tourism. In M. Honey (Ed.), *Ecotourism and Certification: Setting Standards in Practice* (pp. 33–71). Washington, D.C.: Island Press.

James, S. (2007). Constructing the climb: Visitor decision–making at Uluru. *Geographical Research, 45*(4), 398–407.

Jamrozy, U. (2007). Marketing of tourism: A paradigm shift toward sustainability. *International Journal of Culture, Tourism and Hospitality Research, 1*(2), 117–130.

Kilbourne, W. E. (2004). Sustainable communication and the dominant social paradigm: Can they be integrated? *Marketing Theory, 4*(3), 187–208.

Knowles, T. & Felzensztein, C. (2011). Marketing ecotourism: A focus on Chile. In D. Diamantis (Ed.), *Ecotourism: Management and Assessment* (pp. 226–236). London: Thomson.

Kotler, P. (2011). Reinventing marketing to manage the environmental imperative. *Journal of Marketing, 75*(4), 132–135.

Kotler, P., Adam, S., Brown, L., & Armstrong, G. (2003). *Principles of Marketing* (2nd ed.). Frenchs Forest: Prentice Hall.

Kotler, P., Bowen, J., & Makens, J. (2009). *Marketing for Hospitality and Tourism*. Upper Saddle River: Prentice Hall.

Kotler, P., Bowen, J., Makens, J., & Baloglu, S. (2017). *Marketing for Hospitality and Tourism*. Boston: Pearson.

Kotler, P. & Levy, S. (1971). Demarketing, yes, demarketing. *Harvard Business Review, 49*(6), 74–80.

Kotler, P. & Zaltman, G. (1971). Social marketing: An approach to planned social change. *The Journal of Marketing, 35*, 3–12.

Krippendorf, J. (1987a). Ecological approach to tourism marketing. *Tourism Management, 8*(2), 174–176.

Krippendorf, J. (1987b). *Holiday Makers: Understanding the Impact of Travel and Leisure*. London: Heinemann.

McKercher, B. (2001). *The Business of Ecotourism*. Oxfordshire: CABI.

Medina, L. K. (2005). Ecotourism and certification: Confronting the principles and pragmatics of socially responsible tourism. *Journal of Sustainable Tourism, 13*(3), 281–295.

Middleton, V. (1998). *Sustainable Tourism: A Marketing Perspective*. London: Routledge.

Middleton, V. & Clarke, J. (2012). *Marketing in Travel and Tourism* (3rd ed.). London: Routledge.

Middleton, V., Fyall, A., Morgan, M., & Ranchhod, A. (2009). *Marketing in Travel and Tourism*. London: Routledge.

Morrison, A. (2013). *Marketing and Managing Tourism Destinations*. London: Routledge.

Mostafanezhad, M. (2013). The geography of compassion in volunteer tourism. *Tourism Geographies, 15*(2), 318–337.

Norman, J. (2017). Why we are banning tourists from climbing Uluru. Retrieved from https://theconversation.com/why-we-are-banning-tourists-from-climbing-uluru-86755.

Nuryanti, W. (1996). Heritage and postmodern tourism. *Annals of Tourism Research, 23*(2), 249–260.

Packer, J. & Ballantyne, R. (2013). Encouraging reflective visitor experiences in ecotourism. In R. Ballantyne & J. Packer (Eds.), *International Handbook on Ecotourism* (pp. 169–177). Cheltenham: Edward Elgar.

Page, S. (2015). *Tourism Management*. London: Routledge.

Perkins, H. & Grace, D. A. (2009). Ecotourism: Supply of nature or tourist demand? *Journal of Ecotourism, 8*(3), 223–236.

Pine, B. & Gilmore, J. (1998). Welcome to the experience economy. *Harvard Business Review, 76*(4), 97–105.

Sharpley, R. & Stone, P. (2014). *Contemporary Tourist Experience: Concepts and Consequences* (Vol. 27). London: Routledge.

Sin, H. L. (2010). Who are we responsible to? Locals' tales of volunteer tourism. *Geoforum, 41*(6), 983–992.

Tilden, F. (1977). *Interpreting Our Heritage* (3rd ed.). Chapel Hill: North Carolina Press.

Timothy, D. (2007). Empowerment and stakeholder participation in tourism destination communities. In A. Church & T. Coles (Eds.), *Tourism Power and Space* (pp. 199–216). London: Routledge.

Tresidder, R. (2014). The semiotics of tourism marketing. In S. McCabe (Ed.), *The Routledge Handbook of Tourism Marketing* (pp. 94–106). London: Routledge.

Tussyadiah, I. P. & Sigala, M. (2018). Shareable tourism: Tourism marketing in the sharing economy. *Journal of Travel and Tourism Marketing, 35*(1), 1–4.

United Nations General Assembly. (2016). Resolution adopted by the General Assembly on 21 December 2016 – 71/240. Promotion of sustainable tourism, including ecotourism, for poverty eradication and environment protection. Retrieved from www.un.org/en/ga/search/view_doc.asp?symbol=A/RES/71/240.

Uriely, N. (2005). The tourist experience: Conceptual developments. *Annals of Tourism Research, 32*(1), 199–216.

Urry, J. (2002). *The Tourist Gaze*. London: SAGE.

Urry, J. & Larsen, J. (2011). *The Tourist Gaze 3.0*. London: SAGE.

Vanderheiden, S. & Sisson, M. W. (2010). Ethically responsible leisure? Promoting social and environmental justice through ecotourism. *Environmental Philosophy, 7*(2), 33–48.

Villarino, J. & Font, X. (2015). Sustainability marketing myopia: The lack of persuasiveness in sustainability communication. *Journal of Vacation Marketing, 21*(4), 326–335.

Wearing, S., Schweinsberg, S., & Tower, J. (2016). *The Marketing of National Parks for Sustainable Tourism*. Clevedon: Channel View.

Wearing, S., Wearing, M., & McDonald, M. (2012). Slow'n down the town to let nature grow: Ecotourism, social justice and sustainability. In S. Fullager, K. Markwell & E. Wilson (Eds.), *Slow Tourism: Experiences and Mobilities* (pp. 36–50). Bristol: Channel View.

Weaver, D. (2008). *Ecotourism* (2nd ed.). Milton: Wiley.

Zimmermann, J. A. M. & Tower, J. R. (2017). Leisure management: All about the "what" and the "who". *World Leisure Journal, 59*(1), 2–5.

Zografos, C. & Allcroft, D. (2007). The environmental values of potential ecotourists: A segmentation study. *Journal of Sustainable Tourism, 15*(1), 44–66.

Chapter 9

Could the presidential ecotourist please stand up?

Introduction

Over the last decade or so, a number of influential works have considered aspects of ecotourism and the ecotourist (e.g., Ballantyne & Packer, 2013; Diamantis, 2011; Fennell, 2008; Wearing & Neil, 2009; Weaver, 2008). With every new monograph on ecotourism, there exists an almost obligatory chapter highlighting aspects of the ecotourist as a conceptual entity. The reasons for this are easy enough to understand. Ecotourists are the principal consumer of ecotourism products and services. By understanding their motivations, demographic profiles, gaze and experiences, we are better equipped to understand the "differences between ecotourists and other types of travellers" (Fennell, 2008, p. 17). Through such understanding we are in turn able to understand more of the nature of the impacts of ecotourism, the juxtaposition of ecotourist interests to those of host communities and other aspects of the sustainable management of the ecotourism industry.

Over the last half century, research into the nature of the ecotourist has proliferated. Dominant research trajectories relate, amongst other things, to the behavioural differences between hard and soft ecotourists (De Witt, Van der Merwe, & Saayman, 2014; Sheena, Mariapan, & Aziz, 2015; Weaver, 2005) and the evolution of new ecotourism markets in Southeast Asia (Chiu, Lee, & Chen, 2014; Hu & Lu, 2014; Qunming, Rong, Ting, Nijing, & Jia, 2017). This and other academic scholarship has played a major role in the development of public sector plans for the sustainable management of an ecotourism sector that is being forced to respond to rapid market diversification and changing global travel trends (e.g., Queensland Government, 2013). However, in spite of the proliferation of research looking at the categorisation of ecotourists, McCabe (2013) has asked whether the categorisation of tourism has proliferated "without getting any closer to understanding what travel means to people or to understanding how travel tastes and behaviour help explain structural change in societies, the overarching aim of sociological theorizing". Citing the seminal work of Urry, McCabe (2013) goes on to note that the study of the tourist "presupposes a system of social activities and signs which

136

locate the particular tourist practices, not in terms of some intrinsic characteristics, but through the contrasts implied with non-tourists" (p. 19).

Fletcher (2014) has argued that the practice of ecotourism is a social construct in the sense that the embodied habitus of the traveller will be juxtaposed with the realities as perceived by host populations and other stakeholders in the tourism system. Theodore Roosevelt is widely regarded as one of the pioneering influencers on the development of a national approach to wilderness preservation in the United States (Nash, 1967). Over the course of his two terms as president, Roosevelt was responsible for helping to ensure the preservation of 230 million hectares of public lands. While the legacy of 'Green Roosevelt' has been well documented (see Jack, 2010), to date there has been little attention paid to Roosevelt's role as an ecotourism pioneer. Drawing primarily on accounts of Roosevelt's iconic camping trip to what is now Yosemite National Park with the environmentalist John Muir (Roosevelt, 1913; Johnston, 1994; Leidig, 1903/2003), we will seek to explore the way that culture informed the development of a unique tourist gaze for the president, a gaze that in many respects led to the creation of an environmental ethic that underpins the priorities of so many of today's ecotourists.

Roosevelt: an ecotourist of his times

Earlier in the present volume we alluded to one of the most popular definitions of ecotourism – "travelling to relatively undisturbed or uncontaminated natural areas with the specific objective of studying, admiring, and enjoying the scenery with its plants and animals, as well as any existing cultural manifestations (both past and present) found in those areas" (Ceballos-Lascuráin, 1988, p. 13). Widely regarded as one of the first formal definitions in existence, many existing monographs present the definition in the context of a discussion of the etymology of ecotourism. Fennell (2008) observes that while there is debate about ecotourism's precise origins, generally it is accepted that the industry goes back, as a formal entity, as far as the 1970s and 1980s. Blamey argues that the history is a little bit longer, citing the work of Hetzer from 1965, who "identified four pillars or principles of responsible tourism: minimising environmental impacts, respecting host cultures, maximising the benefits to local people, and maximising tourist satisfaction" (Blamey, 2001, p. 5).

In the present chapter we wish to extend this history and look back over a century to May 15, 1903, when President Theodore Roosevelt arrived by train in Raymond, California, for what was to be a four-day camping trip with John Muir in what would later become Yosemite National Park. This trip, which was to have a profound influence on the later establishment of the Antiquities Act and wider nationwide conservation initiatives, was not the first such tourism trip in the Yosemite region. Honey (1999) noted that treks to the area, which were led by luminaries such as James Mason Hutchings and Robert Lamon, date back at least to the mid-nineteenth century. In 1901, the Sierra Club then began organised treks to the high country of the Sierra Nevada mountains.

When President Roosevelt first visited Yosemite, he carried with him private aspirations that would be familiar to ecotourists today. Koy (2003) observes how Roosevelt made confidential arrangements with Muir to deviate from his proposed itinerary, noting the desire to "outskirt and keep away from civilisation ... I want to drop politics absolutely for four days and be out in the open with you" (p. 3). Walker and Moscardo (2014, p. 1188) have observed that effective tourist experiences are characterised by a

> perceived authenticity, variety and diversity in the events ... active participation in these events and activities, novelty and surprise, multisensory components, total immersion in the setting and experience, choice and control over elements of the experience, personal interaction and relevance, reinforcement of self identity, possibilities for exploration and learning, and the inclusion of affective dimensions.

To understand whether any of these aspects of experience were in evidence during President Roosevelt's camping trip, let us deal with select characteristics in turn. Firstly, we have the characteristic of authenticity. At the time of Roosevelt's Yosemite escape in 1903, America was going through a period of change with respect to its engagement with nature. While national parks had existed as a formalised entity since the early 1870s, the National Park Service would not be created for another ten years or so after Roosevelt's trip (Runte, 1997). Simultaneous with the beginning of the national parks movement was the closure of the frontier. As Koy (2003, p. 3) notes, it was an era when the "great herds of bison had been reduced from 60 million to 39. In the Northeast, huge stands of white pine had been decimated. On the Great Plains the open range had been destroyed through overgrazing. Railroads criss-crossed the continent". At around the time of his journey to Yosemite, Roosevelt himself showed a nuanced and historically informed perspective on what was at stake. He recognised that sustainable utilisation of America's resources was a necessity, whilst at the same time acknowledged that long-term (what today would be called intergenerational) perspectives on sustainability were necessary to preserve the "beauties and wonders unspoiled by greedy and short sighted vandalism" (Jack, 2010, p. 25).

It is in this context that the organisation of Roosevelt's trip to Yosemite must be viewed. Charlie Leidig, who was one of the civilian rangers who accompanied the president's party, observed what the early parts of the trip were like, as you would expect for a president of the United States:

> Muir came from San Francisco on the train with the presidential party of eight, including Governor George C. Pardee of California, Benjamin Ide Wheeler, president of the University of California, and Roosevelt's personal secretary Mr Loeb. The group was placed in an eleven passenger coach ... Under Lieutenant Mays, thirty cavalrymen escorted this stage from Raymond directly to the Grizzly Giant in the Mariposa Grove. (Leidig, 1903/2003, p. 4)

Following the dismissal of the cavalrymen, Leidig paints the picture of an intimate journey for the president, one where he made the decision to forgo the trappings of office: "the only cover provided for the president was a 'shelter half' under which about forty blankets were piled to serve as a bed" (Leidig, 1903/2003, pp. 4–5). Throughout the journey the president instructed his guides to actively avoid any route that would bring him into contact with the rest of his official party. Avoiding civilisation was, however, often easier said than done. Leidig (1903/2003) reported how:

The Chris Jorgensen studio home had been set aside for the President's official use. A cook had been arranged from one of the best hotels in San Francisco to serve a banquet. The commissioners had arranged a considerable display of fire-works, which John Degnan claimed amounted to some $1,800 ... [Then later in the journey] there were a number of people awaiting the President at the top of Nevada Falls and in Little Yosemite Valley. Roosevelt requested that everybody be kept at a distance in order that he could carry out his desire for a 'roughing trip'; accordingly the crowd was kept away from the presidential party. (Leidig, 1903/2003, p. 6)

Why would the president do this? The answer can be found in the identity of his principal travelling companion, John Muir. Hall (2010) has described Muir as a bot-anist, geologist, natural historian, conservationist, philosopher and self-confessed tramp. To many, Muir represents one of the founding fathers, not just of the national parks movement, but also of the perceived global imperative of resource conserva-tion (Muir, 1909; Sierra Club, 2015). Curry and Gordon (2017) observe that for Muir, the camping trip with the president was something more than recreation. It was instead an opportunity "to introduce people first hand to the wilderness expe-rience" (Curry & Gordon, 2017, p. 248). In this he was successful, as the following letter penned by President Roosevelt attests:

My dear Mr John Muir ... I trust I need not tell you, my dear sir, how happy were those days in the Yosemite I owed to you and how greatly I appreciated them. I shall never forget our three camps; the first in the solemn temple of the giant se-quoias; the next in the snowstorm among the silver firs near the brink of the cliff; and the third on the floor of the Yosemite, in the open valley, fronting the stupen-dous rocky mass of El Capitan, with the falls thundering in the distance on either hand. Good luck go with you always. (Jack, 2010, p. 286)

For Muir, tourism represented a less evil form of economic development than many of the alternatives, like grazing and commercial clear-cutting of forest (Hall, 2010). Many of his travel writings, such as the aptly named *How Best to Spend One's Yosemite Time* from the work *The Yosemite* (Muir, 1912/2017), aimed to educate visi-tors as to how to experience nature (Hall, 2010). In doing so, Muir was positioning himself at the confluence of a shift in society's perception of nature. Gone were the days of a

gothic perception of wild nature to [be replaced by] one that was not only Romantic and transcendental, but was also experiential ... Muir sought to encourage the reader to get beyond the 'improved' and accessible parts of the Yosemite Valley... In doing so, the tourist may be able to have the same benefits of contact with the sublime as Muir. (Hall, 2010, p. 234)

But is what President Roosevelt experienced ecotourism, and was Roosevelt perhaps an ecotourist? This is not an unnecessary question. National Geographic have listed Theodore Roosevelt National Park as one of the top ten ecotourism spots in the Great Plains (Gerrity, 2012). The National Park Service have gone as far as to draw a direct link between Roosevelt the hunter, and his early work as a rancher in the Badlands of the Dakota Territory, and the enactment of conservation policies that

The presidential ecotourist

America as a nation still benefits from today (National Park Service, ND). Fennell (2012, p. 325) has articulated the typologies of ecotourists as falling broadly into two camps. On the one hand the soft ecotourists:

> the group that is representative of most ecotourists by number, would spend much more time engaged with interests and attractions that fall outside of the natural history attraction realm, that is many of the interests and attractions ... would be spent on other attractions of the destination, including perhaps adventure, culture, shopping, theme parks and so on.

At the other end of the spectrum, so called hard ecotourists are characterised by "a greater emphasis on specialisation, expectations and time spent, less reliance on modified spaces, and fewer numbers of tourists" (2012, p. 325). Which of these characterise Roosevelt must be seen in the context of the times.

As a naturalist, the actions of President Roosevelt would probably sit uneasily today with eco-travellers who ascribe to environmental philosophies like deep ecology (see Chapter 2). Henry Osborn (Director of the American Museum of Natural History) described Roosevelt's trip through Brazil and Paraguay in 1913 and 1914, shortly after the conclusion of his presidency, in terms of its dramatic impact on local wildlife (note: more than 450 mammal and 1,375 bird specimens were added to the museum's collection) (Jack, 2010). Roosevelt had been a hunter for a substantial portion of his life, and in this sense he was aligned to what MacKay and Campbell (2004) have termed traditional tourism markets. Regarding the American West of the late nineteenth century, King (2012) draws a direct connection to the spread of the Transcontinental Railroad (see Dilsaver, 2016, for a discussion of the role of the railroads in the development of the national parks movement) and the increase in the number of hunting safaris:

> Nearly every railroad train, which leaves or arrives at Fort Hays on the Kansas Pacific Railroad, has its race with these herds of buffalo; and a most interesting and exciting scene is the result. The train is 'slowed' to a rate of speed about equal to that of the herd; the passengers get out fire-arms which are provided for the defence of the train against the Indians, and open from the windows and platforms of the cars a fire that resembles a brisk skirmish. Frequently a young bull will turn at bay for a moment. His exhibition of courage is generally his death warrant, for the whole fire of the train is turned upon him, either killing him or some member of the herd in his immediate vicinity. (Harpers Weekly in King, 2012)

Roosevelt's history as a hunter sat uneasily with Muir. Nash (1967, p. 138) reflects on the:

> disarming frankness [with which Muir critiqued the] President's affection for hunting: 'Mr Roosevelt', he asked at one point, 'when are you going to get beyond the boyishness of killing things ... are you not getting far enough along to leave that off'? Taken aback, the President replied, 'Muir, I guess you are right'.

What is interesting about this exchange is not the effect (or lack thereof) that Muir was able to have on Roosevelt's hunting habits; the exchange, after all, preceded by about a decade Roosevelt's eleven-month hunting safari in Africa. Instead, what is interesting is the idea that for Roosevelt, hunting and conservation are indelibly linked. As Jack (2010, p. 5) has suggested, it was:

> hunting that [served] as the impetus by which the young Roosevelt and his generation came into original, revelatory contact with the land. Pursuit of game, then, served as a means to a grander end – close, considered, compassionate, even circumspect contact with nature.

MacKay and Campbell (2004) have shown how community perspectives on the merits of hunting as a tourism form evolve to reflect societal norms. Roosevelt, as with environmental pioneers like Audubon and Leopold, were enthusiastic hunters:

> By tracking an animal, by spending hours in careful consideration of its coloration, concealment and character, the hunter naturalist of the late nineteenth and early twentieth century paved the way and in many instances joined forces with, later day bird watchers, mountaineers, and conservation minded sportsmen. (Jack, 2010, p. 5)

Throughout Roosevelt's camping trip with Muir, it is reported that the president repeatedly demonstrated his great love of birds and ornithological knowledge (Leidig, 1903/2003). He also expressed a desire for the active experience of nature, as the following description from the San Francisco Chronicle describes:

> Avoiding the main road, and long before most of his associates were out of bed ... the President, filled with his usual enthusiasm for adventure, passed rapidly down the narrow defile known as the Lightning Track and struck off for Yosemite Valley. (Johnston, 1994, p. 2)

Both these characterisations of Roosevelt have parallels to wider ecotourism discourse. Kerr (1991) has argued that ecotourists represent a new breed of tourist, those who "require environmentally compatible recreational opportunities ... where nature rather than humanity predominates". What this means in practice, however, varies over time. Hill and Gale (2009) note that notionally, the core charter of ecotourism is to preserve fragile environments whilst also protecting the rights of local people for both current and future generations. In making this observation, Hill and Gale (2009) acknowledge, however, that the attitudes and expectations of ecotourists are an independent variable that may impede ecotourism's achieving its sustainability goals. Wheeler (2006, p. 339) once suggested that "even at the edge, as tourist/travellers in the most authentic Eco lodge we don't experience the 'true' experience of the wild. We are protected cocooned". Roosevelt was cocooned by Muir and his travelling companions, who ensured that he was able to have the time of his life (Johnston, 1994) navigating snow drifts and seeing iconic locations like El Capitan, Glacier Point and the thunderous drop of the Merced River at Ribbon Fall. At a more philosophical level he was also cocooned by the opportunity to converse with and learn from Muir. Renowned for his theories as to the glacial formation of the Yosemite Valley, Muir was able to provide Roosevelt with exposure to his romantic ecological vision of nature (see Hall, 2010) – an ecotourist education that instilled in Roosevelt an appreciation that we must not allow nature to be "vandalized while we slept" (Koy, 2003, p. 4).

Conclusion

Wight (2001, p. 38) once observed that ecotourists are not a homogenous entity. Much as there is a "spectrum of products/experiences which may be termed ecotourism, there is also variation in the activities, motivations and characteristics of markets: a spectrum of demand". In the present chapter, we have made the conscious decision not to provide a comprehensive examination of literature pertaining to ecotourist behaviour, views of nature and experiences (see Ballantyne & Packer, 2013). Instead we have chosen to present a historical case study of a single tourist experience, one that is historically important for the development of the global ecotourism industry and was a product of the societal circumstances in which it occurred.

Barker (2009) has written on the manner in which early tourism in national parks, like Yellowstone, was subject to many of the neoliberal forces that we discussed in Chapter 1. From tourism infrastructure to the natural features of the region, like bears, everything was designed to give the illusion of a landscape that was natural, whilst also appealing to visitor nostalgia for the Old West (Barker, 2009). The 'ecotourism experience', which is at the heart of the present chapter, represents something different. As Roosevelt noted afterwards, his trip afforded him the opportunity to experience and be educated about "those great natural phenomena – wonderful canyons, giant trees, slopes of flower-spangled hillsides – which make California a veritable Garden of the Lord" (Roosevelt, 1915, p. 27).

We have spent much of the present chapter discussing Roosevelt as a person specifically because as Fletcher (2015, p. 338) has suggested, the "practice of ecotourism is informed by a particular ecotourist gaze". It is by this gaze that "the education that providers characteristically offer is implicitly framed" (Fletcher, 2015, p. 338). In the next chapter we will proceed to consider ecotourism's sustainable educational futures.

Further reading

This study investigates and uncovers key antecedents of the intention to engage in ecotourism and to pay premium prices for the experience. It incorporates environmental beliefs, attitudes toward ecotourism, behavioural indications, and willingness to pay in combination with materialism and general tourism motivation.

Hultman, M., Kazeminia, A., & Ghasemi, V. (2015). Intention to visit and willingness to pay premium for ecotourism: The impact of attitude, materialism, and motivation. *Journal of Business Research*, 68(9), 1854–1861.

Wight's chapter provides a comprehensive overview of the market for ecotourism. Particular areas of focus include the identity of ecotourists, their trip characteristics, their origins and destinations, their motivations and their levels of satisfaction.

Wight, P. A. (2000). Ecotourists: Not a homogeneous market segment. In D. B. Weaver (Ed.), *The Encyclopedia of Ecotourism* (pp. 37–62). Wallingford: CABI

Holden and Sparrowhawk investigate the intrinsic motivations of ecotourists visiting the Annapurna area of the Nepalese Himalayas, providing a number of recommendations on how ecotourism destinations can be managed and how the success of such ventures should be measured.

Holden, A. & Sparrowhawk, J. (2002) Understanding the motivations of ecotourists: The case of trekkers in Annapurna, Nepal. *International Journal of Tourism Research, 4*(6), 435–446.

Question

In the typologies of ecotourists, is conservation of nature or attractions and experiences increasing as a motivation for them to visit a destination?

References

Ballantyne, R. & Packer, J. (2013). *International Handbook on Ecotourism*. Cheltenham: Edward Elgar Publishing.

Barker, J. (2009). *Yellowstone: Consuming "Natural" Landscapes*. Retrieved from: https://digital.lib.washington.edu/researchworks/bitstream/handle/1773/15918/jaime%20barker.pdf?sequence=1&origin=publication_detail.

Blamey, R. (2001). Principles of ecotourism. *The Encyclopaedia of Ecotourism*. Retrieved from www.cabi-publishing.org/pdf/Books/0851993680/0851993680ch1.pdf.

Ceballos-Lascuráin, H. (1988). The future of ecotourism. *Mexico Journal, January 27*, 13–14.

Chiu, Y.-T.H., Lee, W.-I., & Chen, T.-H. (2014). Environmentally responsible behavior in ecotourism: Antecedents and implications. *Tourism Management, 40*, 321–329.

Curry, T. J. & Gordon, K. O. (2017). Muir, Roosevelt, and Yosemite National Park as an emergent sacred symbol: An interaction ritual analysis of a camping trip. *Symbolic Interaction, 40*(2), 247–262.

De Witt, L., Van der Merwe, P., & Saayman, M. (2014). Critical ecotourism factors applicable to national parks: A visitor perspective. *Tourism Review International, 17*(3), 179–194.

Diamantis, D. (2011). *Ecotourism*. London: South Western Cengage Learning.

Dilsaver, L. M. (2016). *America's National Park System: The Critical Documents*. Retrieved from www.nps.gov/parkhistory/online_books/anps/anps_toc.htm.

Fennell, D. (2008). *Ecotourism*. London: Routledge.

Fennell, D. (2012). Ecotourism. In A. Holden & D. Fennell (Eds.), *The Routledge Handbook of Tourism and the Environment* (pp. 323–333). London: Routledge.

Fletcher, R. (2014). *Romancing the Wild: Cultural Dimensions of Ecotourism*. Durham: Duke University Press.

Fletcher, R. (2015). Nature is a nice place to save but I wouldn't want to live there: Environmental education and the ecotourist gaze. *Environmental Education Research, 21*(3), 338–350.

Gerrity, S. (2012). Top 10 Ecotourism Spots in the Great Plains. Retrieved from https://voices.nationalgeographic.org/2012/10/19/top-10-ecotourism-spots-in-the-great-plains/.

Hall, C. (2010). John Muir: Pioneer of nature preservation. In R. Butler & R. Russell (Eds.), *Giants of Tourism* (pp. 229–242). Oxfordshire: CABI.

Hill, J. L. & Gale, T. (Eds.) (2009). *Ecotourism and Environmental Sustainability: Principles and Practice*. Surrey: Ashgate Publishing, Ltd.

Honey, M. (1999). *Ecotourism and Sustainable Development: Who Owns Paradise?* Washington, D.C.: Island Press.

Hu, L. & Lu, J. (2014). Exploring characteristics, travel motivation and experiences of tourists in private ecotourism sites: A case study in Zhejiang, China. *TEAM Journal of Hospitality and Tourism, 11*(1), 1–16.

Hultman, M., Kazeminia, A., & Ghasemi, V. (2015). Intention to visit and willingness to pay premium for ecotourism: The impact of attitude, materialism, and motivation. *Journal of Business Research, 68*(9), 1854–1861. doi:10.1016/j.jbusres.2015.01. 013.

Jack, Z. (Ed.) (2010). *The Green Roosevelt: Theodore Roosevelt in Appreciation of Wilderness, Wildlife and Wild Places.* Amherst: Cambria Press.

Johnston, H. (1994). A camping trip with Roosevelt and Muir. *Yosemite, 56*(3), 2–4.

Kerr, J. (1991). *Making Dollars and Sense out of Ecotourism/Nature Tourism.* Paper presented at the First International Conference in Ecotourism, Brisbane, Australia.

King, G. (2012). *Where the Buffalo No Longer Roamed.* Retrieved from https://www.smith sonianmag.com/history/where-the-buffalo-no-longer-roamed-3067904/.

Koy, G. (2003). Theodore Roosevelt and John Muir: 100 years ago and today. *Yosemite, 65*(2), 3–4.

Leidig, C. (1903/2003). Charlie Leidig's report of President Roosevelt's visit to Yosemite in May, 1903. *Yosemite, 65*(2), 4–7.

MacKay, K. J. & Campbell, J. M. (2004). An examination of residents' support for hunting as a tourism product. *Tourism Management, 25*(4), 443–452.

McCabe, S. (2013). Are we all post-tourists now? Tourist categories, identities and post-modernity. In T. Singh (Ed.), *Challenges in Tourism Research (Aspects of Tourism: 70)* (pp. 18–33). Bristol: Channel View Publications.

Muir, J. (1909). *Journeys in the Wilderness: A John Muir Reader (Introduced by Graham White).* Edinburgh: Birlinn.

Muir, J. (1912/ 2017). Chapter 12 How Best to Spend One's Yosemite Time. Retrieved from http://vault.sierraclub.org/john_muir_exhibit/writings/the_yosemite/chapter_12.aspx.

Nash, R. (1967). *Wilderness and the American Mind* (3rd ed.). New Haven: Yale University Press.

National Park Service. (ND). In Honor of a President. Retrieved from www.nps.gov/thro/index.htm.

Queensland Government. (2013). Queensland Ecotourism Plan 2013–2020. Retrieved from www.ecotourism.org.au/assets/Resources-Hub-Ecotourism-Plans/Queensland-Ecotourism-Plan-2013-2020.PDF.

Qunming, Z., Rong, T., Ting, M., Nijing, D., & Jia, L. (2017). Flow experience study of eco-tourists: A case study of Hunan Daweishan Mountain ski area. *Journal of Resources and Ecology, 8*(5), 494–501.

Roosevelt, T. (1913). *In Yosemite with John Muir.* Retrieved from https://vault.sierraclub.org/john_muir_exhibit/life/in_yosemite_by_roosevelt.aspx.

Roosevelt, T. (1915). John Muir: An Appreciation. Retrieved from https://vault.sierraclub.org/john_muir_exhibit/life/appreciation_by_roosevelt.aspx.

Runte, A. (1997). *National Parks: The American Experience.* Lincoln: University of Nebraska Press.

Sheena, B., Mariapan, M., & Aziz, A. (2015). Characteristics of Malaysian ecotourist segments in Kinabalu Park, Sabah. *Tourism Geographies, 17*(1), 1–18.

Sierra Club. (2015). Who was John Muir? Retrieved from http://vault.sierraclub.org/john_muir_exhibit/about/default.aspx.

Walker, K. & Moscardo, G. (2014). Encouraging sustainability beyond the tourist experience: Ecotourism, interpretation and values. *Journal of Sustainable Tourism*, 22(8), 1175–1196.

Wearing, S. & Neil, J. (2009). *Ecotourism Impacts Potentials and Possibilities* (2nd ed.). Oxford: Butterworth-Heinemann.

Wearing, S., Schweinsberg, S., & Tower, J. (2016). *The Marketing of National Parks for Sustainable Tourism*. Clevedon: Channel View.

Weaver, D. (2005). Comprehensive and minimalist dimensions of ecotourism. *Annals of Tourism Research*, 32(2), 439–455.

Weaver, D. (2008). *Ecotourism* (2nd ed.). Milton: Wiley.

Wheeler, B. (2006). Elvis, authenticity, sustainability and TALC. In R. Butler (Ed.), *The Tourism Area Life Cycle* (Vol. 1) (pp. 339–348). Clevedon: Channel View Publications.

Wight, P. (2001). Ecotourists: Not a homogenous market segment. In D. Weaver (Ed.), *The Encyclopaedia of Ecotourism* (pp. 37–52) Oxfordshire: CABI.

Chapter 10

Ecotourism's educational futures

Introduction

To educate a person in mind and not in morals is to educate a menace to society.

(Theodore Roosevelt)

In Chapter 9 we presented a case study of the ecotourist experience of President Theodore Roosevelt in the early twentieth century in Yosemite Valley with the environmentalist John Muir. We justified this focus on the basis that Roosevelt was a key player in the early history of what was to become the United States National Park Service. National parks like Kakadu (Australia) and Yosemite are the sites of some of the world's most iconic ecotourism attractions (see also Lawton, 2001). Through the Antiquities Act of 1906, President Roosevelt "broke with the utilitarian leanings of his administration and won himself the lasting respect of the preservationists" (Runte, 1997, p. 72). The intention of the Antiquities Act was to "by public proclamation [preserve] historic landmarks, historic and prehistoric structures, and or other structures of historic or scientific interest ... to be national monuments" (National Park Service, 1906).

Previous ecotourism scholarship has long emphasised the interplay of scientific and social variables in the cause of offering travellers the opportunity of:

> travelling to relatively undisturbed or uncontaminated natural areas with the specific objective of studying, admiring, and enjoying the scenery and its wild plants and animals, as well as any existing cultural manifestations (both past and present) found in these areas. (Ceballos-Lascuráin, 1987, p. 14)

Kiper (2013) has argued that ecotourism's sustainable development credentials stem from its ability to create a symbiotic connection between the environment and tourists. From an ecocentrically informed perspective, we would argue that ecotourism is not just an activity or industry undertaken in the natural environment; it is intended to be an experience that an individual or group has that affects their attitudes, values and actions.

Fennell (2013) has identified that one of the primary distinguishing features of ecotourism from other forms of nature-based tourism activity is its educational focus. Blamey (2001) has noted that ecotourism education should avoid operating solely at a superficial level to maximise consumer demand; rather, it should aim to achieve a fundamental change in consumer attitude, enhancing consumers' sense of environmental responsibility. It is not, however, just the education of tourists and industry that should be of concern. Ecotourism forms an important component of tertiary tourism programs where the industry leaders of tomorrow are trained. Educators often see ecotourism as the antithesis of unsustainable mass tourism (see McKercher & Prideaux, 2014, for a discussion of why such a viewpoint may amount to nothing more than an academic myth). It is an industry that purports to offer educators unique opportunities to explore the position of tourism in its wider ecological world, whilst also exploring the often-complex interplays of the ecotourism industry (however it is defined) with local communities and cultures. Such learning, we will argue, is important for the development of graduates with the ability to think critically about their place in complex environmental systems.

By forcing students to think critically, we are in a sense asking them to grapple with the most fundamental of questions: what is the purpose of their education? West (2009, p. 22 in Caton, 2015, p. 43), with reference to the concept of *paideia*, has argued that education needs to go beyond the superficial and concern itself with "the cultivation of self, the ways you engage with your own history, your own memories, your own morality, your own sense of what it means to be alive as a critical, loving aware human being". Caton (2015) goes on to suggest that the overtly vocational leaning of tourism education has often, in her view, seen it fall short of such principles. During the preparation of this final chapter, the authors were fortunate to have the opportunity to read Wood's (2017) recent work, *Sustainable Tourism on a Finite Planet: Environmental, Business and Policy Solutions*. In the opening chapter, Wood describes her own efforts to bring environmental management into the tourism classroom at Harvard University. This she achieves in part through the development of a final research project where students are asked to scrutinize, through the use of primary empirical data, the environmental performance of one sector of the industry. Engaging students in the management of a real-world industry has the effect, Wood observes, of "allowing them to learn about the industry and its environmental management before entering into the profession of tourism or hospitality" (2017, p. 8).

Caton (2015) has observed how tourism students "have a hunger for greater meaning in the classroom, even if it is sometimes only latent within them" (p. 52). This makes students one of the principal mechanisms for innovation in sustainable tourism as we move towards the 22nd century. Moscardo (2008) has argued that true innovation comes from the employment of creative thinking methodologies and the challenging of basic assumptions – she asks, is there really ever such a thing as sustainable tourism? As educators, we have a responsibility to challenge the assumptions of our students and develop in them an innovator's mentality. In a personal reflection on the supervisory style of Professor Chris Cooper, the following observation was recently made: he "allowed me to focus the study on what I felt was important rather then [sic] having him impose any strong personal feelings or thoughts that he might have had concerning the topic. This ... made the study much more of a personal issue for me" (Barron, personal communication 2014 in Scott, 2015, p. 125). Whether it is a PhD student or undergraduate student, we must always be mindful of the student's individuality of perspective. As with the tourist gaze (see Urry & Larsen, 2011), the gaze of the student is individual, socially constructed and importantly seen from the perspective of the 'other' (Wilkes, 2008). We will argue with respect to curriculum that we must always strive to understand the evolving student perspective of the 'other'. Ecotourism is a topic of inquiry that, on the basis of its interdisciplinary nature, is innately suited to being used as a mechanism for exposing students not only to vocational considerations of tourism management, like marketing and human resources, but also to ethical and scientific considerations of humankind's relationship to the natural and social world. Fennell 2008a, p. 226) once observed that ecotourism must be grounded in something of a "philosophical rationale, which allows us to consider the bigger picture beyond concerns with our immediate self interest". Over the course of a student's education, the boundaries of that bigger picture will change and the job a student is hiring a degree to complete will evolve. As educators we must actively engage with the evolution of our students if we are to equip them to be ecotourism leaders into the 22nd century and beyond.

Tourism curriculum and the student job to be done

Tribe (2015, p. 20) has defined curriculum as a "whole programme of educational experiences that is packaged as a degree programme. Its constituent parts are a number of modules and courses, which in turn may be specified as a series of syllabi or course contents". In recent years there has been a proliferation in scholarship exploring the nature of the tourism curriculum space (e.g., Inui, Wheeler, & Lankford, 2006; Morgan, 2004; Prebežac, Schott, & Sheldon, 2016; Sigala & Baum, 2003). One of the main threads in this scholarship has been over the interplay and merits of liberal or vocational tourism education (Fidgeon, 2010). These debates are in turn encompassed in wider philosophical discussions over the formulation of tourism knowledge and the presence (or not) of a discipline or indiscipline of tourism (Coles, Hall, & Duval, 2006; Coles, Hall, & Duval, 2016; Leiper, 1981; Leiper, 2000; Tribe, 1997; Tribe, 2000). From Tribe's original conceptualisation of the philosophic practitioner in tourism education (1999), a range of other authors have since sought to position the philosophic practitioner concept in relation to actual curriculum structures (e.g., Dredge et al., 2012; Morgan, 2004; Tribe, 2015).

Taking Tribe's (2015) construction of curriculum space and framing as our starting point, we wish to explore in this concluding chapter the role of the student voice in tourism education. Tribe (2015) designed his views on curriculum around the idea of a forcefield of influences on the way curriculums are packaged. These forcefield influences included a mixture of academic and commercial interests, which, depending on the particulars of the curriculum in question, may steer the tourism degree more towards what Tribe (1999) described as vocational or liberal ends. While the composition of tourism curriculums is perhaps inevitably determined on the basis of a series of power relationships (see Tribe, 2015 and the 12Ps), Dredge et al. (2012) have also recognised the individual journeys of students as they move through the curriculum. Individuality is said to be determined on the basis of how the institution has framed the degree, the effect of lecturers who deliver the course and the subject choices of students. In this chapter, we wish to suggest that this final issue is perhaps underpinned by a more fundamental question: what is the job a student is hiring the degree to do?

To answer this question we will now turn our attention to the theory of jobs to be done (Christensen, Dillon, Hall, & Duncan, 2016; Christensen, Hall, Dillon, & Duncan, 2016; Christensen, Anthony, Berstell, & Nitterhouse, 2007). The essential premise of the jobs idea is that people (in our case students) don't purchase a product (in our case an education). Instead it is suggested that people hire a product that will allow them to complete a job in their day-to-day lives. Christensen, Dillon et al. (2016, p. 27) have defined a job as "the progress a person is trying to make in a particular circumstance". These jobs, or tasks if you will, have a mixture of functional and emotive elements. Christensen, Hall et al. (2016) have observed the applicability of the jobs idea to tertiary education in a case study of Southern New Hampshire University. Southern New Hampshire University was identified as fighting for attention in an increasingly crowded educational marketplace (Christensen, Hall, et al., 2016). While their bread-and-butter market had always been an undergraduate student straight out of school, it was recognised that their online distance learning operation, which offered students an opportunity to return to university later in life, also had an important part to play in their offerings. In the course of reviewing the program, the university discovered that returning students taking part in the online program had very different characteristics from young undergraduates:

> On average, online students are 30 years old, juggling work and family, and trying to squeeze in education. Often they still carry a debt from an earlier college experience. They are not looking for social activities or a campus scene. They need higher education to provide just four things: convenience, customer service, credentials and speedy completion times. (Christensen, Hall, et al., 2016, p. 15)

Characteristics of a consumer do not, Christensen, Hall et al. (2016) have suggested, necessarily correlate to purchase intent. After all, there would be many 30-year-old people in New Hampshire who have work and family obligations and absolutely no interest at all in online learning. Rather, the decision to return to university is made on the basis of a need – a job that needs to be done, which in this case was a qualification that would quickly enable the students to improve their professional standing, whilst also having a personal or emotional objective. "'I got it for me,' one woman says hugging her diploma. 'I did this for my mom,' beams a 30-something man. 'I did it for you, bud,' one father says, holding back tears as his young son chirps, 'Congratulations, Daddy!'" (Christensen, Hall, et al. 2016, p. 17). Once the particular circumstances of a student's job to be done are understood, a service provider is then better able to understand the nature of competition, as well as to more effectively align all of their internal business processes to fulfilling the needs of the consumer.

Crompton (2007, p. 225) once reflected that one of the principal challenges for him as an educator in the fields of leisure and tourism has been the realisation that his early assumptions about student learning, particularly at the undergraduate level, might be wrong: "most young people are not naturally curious and/or they didn't delight in learning – perhaps because the educational system had defused this natural curiosity and it had been replaced by a cynicism that had become habitual and engrained". For Crompton (2007) the joy of learning and the total involvement in a task are recognised as being greater than the "extrinsic rewards associated with it" (p. 227). What, in comparison, are the learning habits of tourism undergraduate students? Hsu et al. (2017) have noted that teaching and learning represent the most documented themes in tourism education scholarship in the period 2005–2014. The work of Johanson and Haug (2008) and Lashley and Barron (2006) in particular has shed light on not only the presence of different modes of learning (reflective, pragmatist, theorist, etc.) in different student cohorts, but also the importance of moulding what we teach to student learning preferences.

With this in mind, it is appropriate to turn our attention to ecotourism education specifically. Bluntly, we wish to ask: does the standard tourism student really care about being educated on the machinations of an industry sector for which most of them have some level of personal experience (Cini, Van der Merwe, & Saayman, 2015), but which offers limited career prospects in their immediate future? Acknowledging the lack of practical employment opportunities afforded by ecotourism is crucial for the current discussion. If we assume that students come to university with a job to be done focused on career advancement in the tourism industry, our job as educators is to critically consider the role that a knowledge of ecotourism should have in their achieving that goal. Christensen, Dillon et al. (2016) have suggested that a series of questions may be posed in order to understand the nature of the job to be done. Questions include (Christensen, Dillon et al. 2016, pp. 32–33) the following:

- 'What progress is that person trying to achieve?'
- 'What are the circumstances of the struggle [to get the job done]?'
- 'What obstacles are getting in the way of the person making that progress?'
- 'Are consumers making do with imperfect solutions through some kind of compensating behaviour?'
- 'How would they define what quality means for a better solution, and what trade-offs are they prepared to make?'

Hypothetically, it would be possible to answer these questions for a student in our tourism education context. If we did, the responses would potentially look something like this:

- 'What progress is that person trying to achieve?' *I want to understand the inner workings of the global tourism industry and be equipped to progress to being a trainee manager in a sector of the industry of my choosing.*
- 'What are the circumstances of the struggle [to get the job done]?' *I see a range of universities offering similar tourism degree offerings, and I'm finding it difficult to find a niche for myself.*
- 'What obstacles are getting in the way of the person making that progress'? *I'm focused on getting my degree ASAP whilst ensuring that I leave university with as much practical experience as possible – some of the electives, though, that I'm forced to take in areas like sustainability seem like a distraction from my business education* (see Reid, Petocz, & Taylor, 2009).
- 'Are consumers making do with imperfect solutions through some kind of compensating behaviour?' *I'm studying in a degree that I cannot see leading to a future career that I'm likely to enjoy or that is likely to give me the security that I need* (see Richardson, 2009).
- 'How would they define what quality means for a better solution, and what trade-offs are they prepared to make?' *I want a degree that will give me a head start on career advancement, but also the flexibility to chart my own future career direction.*

In theory, the study of ecotourism should provide an important avenue for addressing the aforementioned job to be done – 'to understand the inner workings of the global tourism industry and be equipped to progress to being a trainee manager in a sector of the industry of my choosing'. Ecotourism is, after all, an interdisciplinary concept with the potential to act as a mechanism for students to explore a range of ethical, scientific and business management issues. To date, there has been limited literature that has directly examined student perceptions of ecotourism (exceptions include Cini, Leone, & Passafaro, 2012; Cini & Passafaro, 2017; Cini, Van der Merwe, & Saayman, 2015). In one study of 613 undergraduate tourism students from five universities that form part of the International Competence Network of Tourism Research and Education (ICNT), it was established that students often possess a shallow conceptualisation of what is or isn't ecotourism. Many tourism students in the study equated ecotourism with nature-based tourism, whilst largely ignoring other key tenets, including preservation and conservation of the cultural environment and local community participation.

The presence of a shallow understanding of ecotourism should not be surprising if one takes into account the results of a recent study of Generation Y and the tourism curriculum space (Benckendorff & Moscardo, 2014). Drawing on multiple secondary data sets, Beckendorff and Moscardo (2014) observed how undergraduate students placed a lower level of importance on attaining a multidisciplinary understanding of tourism. In contrast, there was a prioritisation given by the sampled students to the development of practical and entrepreneurial and management skills – "there was also a feeling that Australian institutions may be over servicing in the areas of sustainability, impacts and ethics" (p. 429). What is interesting for the present discussion is that while students were offering these and other perspectives on aspects of their degree program, they were also indicating a desire for jobs that would provide dynamic environments, opportunities to lead, challenges and social interaction. To be successful in a job with these characteristics requires the development of future-oriented skills. It is not enough to be able to manage in complex environments; one must also develop the ability to manage in wicked environments.

Luckily the student gaze is an essentially malleable construct (Wilkes, 2008). Like the tourist gaze, the student gaze is a socially constructed phenomenon – the tourist "gazes on the world through a particular filter of ideas, skills, desires and expectations ... gazing is a performance that orders, shapes, and classifies, rather than reflects the world" (Urry & Larsen, 2011, p. 2). The key for ensuring positive outcomes for students is preparation. Academics must equip graduates with the ability to respond to the changing circumstances that will inevitably befall them throughout their careers. We must consider carefully the gaze we wish a student to have, whilst always being mindful of the alignment of this gaze with the student's current job to be done. The study of ecotourism and sustainability is a threshold in many students' educational journey. As with all thresholds, passing through it can be tough. We must embrace in the context of our institutional realities the self-evident fact that "good education takes time and effort, personalised guidance, trust and work. An educated mind is built with imagination and work" (Popenici, 2013 in Dredge, Airey, & Gross, 2015, p. 543). By working with students and preparing them for the possibility that education may radically alter their gaze, we will hopefully inspire them to live up to Roosevelt's challenge.

Looking into the future: transitioning ecotourism to the 22nd century

The title of the present volume, *Ecotourism: Transitioning to the 22nd Century*, was chosen specifically to imply that the path of ecotourism development in the future is not set. Honey (2008) noted at the end of the 20th century that ecotourism remained the path less travelled in comparison to mass tourism; travellers, she noted, still have a choice of which road to take in the future. Wearing and Neil (2009) concluded their second edition of the work *Ecotourism: Impacts and Possibilities* by observing the threats and opportunities of ecotourism in the area of climate change. In recent years, commentary on the interaction of tourism with climate change has proliferated (see for example, Becken, 2004; Hall, Scott, & Gössling, 2011; Scott, 2003; Scott, 2011; Scott & Becken, 2010; Weaver, 2011). As we move into the future, we argue that instead of fixating solely on inward-looking investigations of the impacts of ecotourism on the climate and vice versa, we must instead focus more on the development of future leaders with the skills to critically assess and lead debate over climate science and other evolving forces in the ecotourism environment.

Austin (2012, p. 58) recently observed that "the primary responsibility for those that teach within higher education is to prepare students for an uncertain and changing world". A recent exchange on climate change in the journal *Tourism Management* (Hall et al., 2014; Hall et al., 2015; Shani & Arad, 2014a; Shani & Arad, 2014b) to us perfectly exhibited the wickedness (or socially constructed nature) of the world in which tourism and tourism education find themselves. We will not at the present time offer any comments on what we deem to be the veracity of information contained within the various articles that make up the exchange and how these relate to our own personal perspectives on the climate change and tourism issue. What we will do, however, is express a regret that discussions over the interplay of climate science and tourism have been broken down by a series of leading academics into a simple debate over the reputability of evidence, and the right (or not) of academics to be sceptical of climate science. While everyone reading this chapter will doubtless have their own views on both these matters, what is to us a more fundamental question is: can we ever hope to lead in a pluralistic world if we draw battle lines on wicked problems?

Dredge et al. (2015) have observed that tourism and hospitality education "provides a lens on our social world, a lens through which processes of change can be identified, understood and critically analysed". Given that no policy-based or industry-based change to the human condition will ever be to everyone's satisfaction, it becomes inevitable that educators must always look to cultivate values such as those proposed by the Tourism Education Futures Initiative: values of mutuality, stewardship, knowledge, ethics and professionalism (Sheldon, Fesenmaier, & Tribe, 2011). Each of these values is, in different ways, encapsulated in the various chapters in the present book, as well as in much of the existing literature on ecotourism (e.g., Fennell, 2008b; Nepal, 2002; Ross & Wall, 1999; Weaver & Lawton, 2007). They also underpin what Metcalf and Benn (2013) define as the fundamental task of sustainability leadership – to ascertain and execute a link between the inward-looking sustainability of the organisation and the wider system in which that organisation is situated. The environmentalist Fabien Cousteau recently noted at the World Travel and Tourism Council's (2016 Global Summit in Dallas that he "looks forward to the day when sustainable tourism is called just tourism". We applaud these sentiments, notwithstanding the challenges it may cause, if realised, for the ongoing employment of sustainability-focused academics such as ourselves. At the same time, though, we wonder if it is achievable or advisable. Would it perhaps not be better to hope for a day when we can say that our legacy has been to instil in leaders of tomorrow a morality that allows them to control their minds and act for the betterment of society?

Further reading

Jamal, Borges and Stronza's paper critically evaluates some of the inequities that currently exist in ecotourism, with a focus on cultural aspects such as human–ecological relationships. The authors argue that some elements of ecotourism have come to reflect the very values it seeks to transcend, such as commodification and instrumentality. Cobbinah, Amenuvor, Black and Peprah provide an examination of the inequities in the distribution of tourism benefits from ecotourism at a destination.

Jamal, T., Borges, M., & Stronza, A. (2006) The institutionalisation of ecotourism: Certification, cultural equity and praxis. *Journal of Ecotourism*, 5(3), 145–175.

Cobbinah, P. B., Amenuvor, D., Black, R., & Peprah, C. (2017). Ecotourism in the Kakum Conservation Area, Ghana: Local politics, practice and outcome. *Journal of Outdoor Recreation and Tourism*, 20, 34–44.

This chapter by Craig-Smith attempts to predict what may happen in the South Pacific as a result of global warming and its impact on the different tourism types in the area, including urban tourism, ecotourism, winter-based tourism, ocean-based tourism and small island tourism. The Mkiramweni, DeLacy, Jiang, and Chiwanga case study identifies climate-related shocks and stressors and implied effects on ecotourism, while also assessing ecotourism stakeholders' awareness and perceptions on climate change in the area.

Craig-Smith, S. J. (2004). Global warming and tourism in Oceania. In C. Cooper & C. M. Hall (Eds.), *Oceania: A Tourism Handbook* (pp. 353–361). Clevedon: Channel View Publications.

Mkiramweni, N. P., DeLacy, T., Jiang, M., & Chiwanga, F. E. (2016). Climate change risks on protected areas ecotourism: Shocks and stressors perspectives in Ngorongoro Conservation Area, Tanzania. *Journal of Ecotourism*, 15(2), 139–157.

This special edition of the journal investigates the creative contribution and partnerships that NGOs are playing in sustainable tourism operations around the world.

Journal of Sustainable Tourism 2005, 13(5).

Question

As we move into the future, how will we evaluate ecotourism impact on the climate and vice versa?

References

Austin, A. E. (2012). Challenges and visions for higher education in a complex world: Commentary on Barnett and Barrie. *Higher Education Research & Development, 31*(1), 57–64.

Becken, S. (2004). How tourists and tourism experts perceive climate change and carbon-offsetting schemes. *Journal of Sustainable Tourism, 12*(4), 332–345.

Benckendorff, P. & Moscardo, G. (2014). Generation Y and the curriculum space. In D. Dredge, D. Airey, & M. Gross (Eds.), *The Routledge Handbook of Tourism and Hospitality Education* (pp. 422–439). London: Routledge.

Blamey, R. K. (2001). Principles of ecotourism. *The Encyclopedia of Ecotourism, 2001,* 5–22.

Caton, K. (2015). On the practical value of a liberal education. *The Routledge Handbook of Tourism and Hospitality Education,* 43–54.

Ceballos-Lascuráin, H. (1987). The future of ecotourism. *Mexico Journal, 1*(17), 13–19.

Christensen, C., Dillon, K., Hall, T., & Duncan, D. (2016). *Competing against Luck: The Story of Innovation and Customer Choice.* New York: Harper Business.

Christensen, C., Hall, T., Dillon, K., & Duncan, D. (2016). Know your customers' "jobs to be done". *Harvard Business Review, 9,* 54–62.

Christensen, C. M., Anthony, S. D., Berstell, G., & Nitterhouse, D. (2007). Finding the right job for your product. *MIT Sloan Management Review, 48*(3), 38–47.

Cini, F., Leone, L., & Passafaro, P. (2012). Promoting ecotourism among young people: A segmentation strategy. *Environment and Behavior, 44*(1), 87–106.

Cini, F. & Passafaro, P. (2017). Youth and ecotourism: A qualitative exploration. *Tourism and Hospitality Research,* doi:10.1177/1467358417704887.

Cini, F., Van der Merwe, P., & Saayman, M. (2015). Tourism students' knowledge and tenets towards ecotourism. *Journal of Teaching in Travel & Tourism, 15*(1), 74–91.

Coles, T., Hall, C. M., & Duval, D. T. (2006). Tourism and post-disciplinary enquiry. *Current Issues in Tourism, 9*(4–5), 293–319.

Coles, T., Hall, C. M., & Duval, D. T. (2016). Tourism and postdisciplinarity: Back to the future? *Tourism Analysis, 21*(4), 373–387.

Crompton, J. (2007). On undergraduate "benevolent coercion" and graduate collegiality. In D. Dustin & T. Goodale (Eds.), *Making a Difference in Academic Life* (pp. 225–235). State College: Venture Publishing.

Dredge, D., Airey, D., & Gross, M. (2015). *Creating the Future: Tourism, Hospitality and Events Education in a Post-Industrial, Post-Disciplinary World.* In D. Dredge, D. Airey, & M. Gross (Eds.), *The Routledge Handbook of Tourism and Hospitality Education* (pp. 535–550). London: Routledge.

Dredge, D., Benckendorff, P., Day, M., Gross, M. J., Walo, M., Weeks, P., & Whitelaw, P. (2012). The philosophic practitioner and the curriculum space. *Annals of Tourism Research, 39*(4), 2154–2176.

Fennell, D. (2008a). *Ecotourism.* London: Routledge.

Fennell, D. (2008b). Ecotourism and the myth of indigenous stewardship. *Journal of Sustainable Tourism, 16*(2), 129–149.

Fennell, D. (2013). Ecotourism. In A. Holden & D. Fennell (Eds.), *The Routledge Handbook of Tourism and the Environment* (Vol. 323–333). London: Routledge.

Fidgeon, P. R. (2010). Tourism education and curriculum design: A time for consolidation and review? *Tourism Management, 31*(6), 699–723.

Hall, C. M., Amelung, B., Cohen, S., Eijgelaar, E., Gössling, S., Higham, J., … Scott, D. (2014). No time for smokescreen skepticism: A rejoinder to Shani and Arad. *Tourism Management, 47,* 341–347.

Hall, C. M., Amelung, B., Cohen, S., Eijgelaar, E., Gössling, S., Higham, J., ... Scott, D. (2015). Denying bogus skepticism in climate change and tourism research. *Tourism Management, 47,* 352–356.

Hall, C. M., Scott, D., & Gössling, S. (2011). Forests, climate change and tourism. *Journal of Heritage Tourism, 6*(4), 353–363.

Honey, M. (2008). *Ecotourism and Sustainable Development: Who Owns Paradise?* Washington, D.C.: Island Press.

Hsu, C. H., Hsu, C. H., Xiao, H., Xiao, H., Chen, N., & Chen, N. (2017). Hospitality and tourism education research from 2005 to 2014: "Is the past a prologue to the future?". *International Journal of Contemporary Hospitality Management, 29*(1), 141–160.

Inui, Y., Wheeler, D., & Lankford, S. (2006). Rethinking tourism education: What should schools teach. *Journal of Hospitality, Leisure, Sport and Tourism Education, 5*(2), 25–35.

Johanson, L. & Haug, B. (2008). Students' preferred learning styles and the importance of curriculum content: A study of Norwegian tourism and hospitality students. *Journal of Hospitality & Tourism Education, 20*(2), 24–33.

Kiper, T. (2013). *Role of Ecotourism in Sustainable Development.* Retrieved from tream/handle/1969.3/28978/InTech-Role_of_ecotourism_in_sustainable_development_[1].pdf?sequence=1.

Lashley, C. & Barron, P. (2006). The learning style preferences of hospitality and tourism students: Observations from an international and cross-cultural study. *International Journal of Hospitality Management, 25*(4), 552–569.

Lawton, L. (2001). Protected Areas. In D. Weaver (Ed.), *The Encyclopaedia of Ecotourism* (pp. 287–302). Oxford: CABI.

Leiper, N. (1981). Towards a cohesive curriculum tourism: The case for a distinct discipline. *Annals of Tourism Research, 8*(1), 69–84.

Leiper, N. (2000). An emerging discipline. *Annals of Tourism Research, 27*(3), 805–809.

McKercher, B. & Prideaux, B. (2014). Academic myths of tourism. *Annals of Tourism Research, 46,* 16–28.

Metcalf, L. & Benn, S. (2013). Leadership for sustainability: An evolution of leadership ability. *Journal of Business Ethics, 112*(3), 369–384.

Mkiramweni, N. P., DeLacy, T., Jiang, M., & Chiwanga, F. E. (2016). Climate change risks on protected areas ecotourism: Shocks and stressors perspectives in Ngorongoro Conservation Area, Tanzania. *Journal of Ecotourism, 15*(2), 139–157. doi:10.1080/1472 4049.2016.1153645.

Morgan, M. (2004). From production line to drama school: Higher education for the future of tourism. *International Journal of Contemporary Hospitality Management, 16*(2), 91–99.

Moscardo, G. (2008). Sustainable tourism innovation: Challenging basic assumptions. *Tourism and Hospitality Research, 8*(1), 4–13.

National Park Service. (1906). *American Antiquities Act of 1906.* Retrieved from www.nps.gov/history/local-law/anti1906.htm.

Nepal, S. K. (2002). Mountain ecotourism and sustainable development: Ecology, economics, and ethics. *Mountain Research and Development, 22*(2), 104–109.

Prebežac, D., Schott, C., & Sheldon, P. (2016). *The Tourism Education Futures Initiative: Activating Change in Tourism Education.* London: Routledge.

Reid, A., Petocz, P., & Taylor, P. (2009). Business students' conceptions of sustainability. *Sustainability, 1*(3), 662–673.

Richardson, S. (2009). Undergraduates' perceptions of tourism and hospitality as a career choice. *International Journal of Hospitality Management, 28*(3), 382–388.

Ross, S. & Wall, G. (1999). Ecotourism: Towards congruence between theory and practice. *Tourism Management, 20*(1), 123–132.

Runte, A. (1997). *National Parks: The American Experience.* Lincoln: University of Nebraska Press.

Scott, D. (2003). *Climate Change and Tourism in the Mountain Regions of North America.* Paper presented at the First International Conference on Climate Change and Tourism, Djerba, Tunisia, 9–11 April 2003. Retrieved from www.researchgate.net/profile/Daniel_Scott9/publication/267198542_Climate_Change_and_Tourism_in_the_Mountain_Regions_of_North_America/links/54b674ae0cf24eb34f6d1ee1/Climate-Change-and-Tourism-in-the-Mountain-Regions-of-North-America.pdf.

Scott, D. (2011). Why sustainable tourism must address climate change. *Journal of Sustainable Tourism, 19*(1), 17–34.

Scott, D. & Becken, S. (2010). Adapting to climate change and climate policy: Progress, problems and potentials. *Journal of Sustainable Tourism, 18*(3), 283–295.

Scott, N. (2015). A portrait of Chris Cooper. *Anatolia, 26*(1), 122–128.

Shani, A. & Arad, B. (2014a). Climate change and tourism: Time for environmental skepticism. *Tourism Management, 44*, 82–85.

Shani, A. & Arad, B. (2014b). There is always time for rational skepticism: Reply to Hall *Tourism Management, 47*, 348–351.

Sheldon, P. J., Fesenmaier, D. R., & Tribe, J. (2011). The tourism education futures initiative (TEFI): Activating change in tourism education. *Journal of Teaching in Travel & Tourism, 11*(1), 2–23.

Sigala, M. & Baum, T. (2003). Trends and issues in tourism and hospitality higher education: Visioning the future. *Tourism and Hospitality Research, 4*(4), 367–376.

Tribe, J. (1997). The indiscipline of tourism. *Annals of Tourism Research, 24*(3), 638–657.

Tribe, J. (1999). *The Philosophic Practitioner: Tourism, Knowledge and the Curriculum.* Doctoral Thesis: Institute of Education, University of London.

Tribe, J. (2000). Indisciplined and unsubstantiated. *Annals of Tourism Research, 27*(3), 809–813.

Tribe, J. (2015). The curriculum: A philosophic practice. In D. Dredge, D. Airey, & M. Gross (Eds.), *The Routledge Handbook of Tourism and Hospitality Education* (pp. 55–73). London: Routledge.

Urry, J. & Larsen, J. (2011). *The Tourist Gaze 3.0.* London: Sage.

Wearing, S. & Neil, J. (2009). *Ecotourism: Impacts, Potentials and Possibilities?* Amsterdam: Butterworth-Heinemann.

Weaver, D. (2011). Can sustainable tourism survive climate change? *Journal of Sustainable Tourism, 19*(1), 5–15.

Weaver, D. B. & Lawton, L. J. (2007). Twenty years on: The state of contemporary ecotourism research. *Tourism Management, 28*(5), 1168–1179.

Wilkes, C. D. (2008). The Student Gaze. Retrieved from http://commons.pacificu.edu/cgi/viewcontent.cgi?article=1005&context=casfac.

Wood, M. E. (2017). *Sustainable Tourism on a Finite Planet: Environmental, Business and Policy Solutions.* Oxfordshire: Taylor & Francis.

Glossary

Agenda 21 A product of the United Nations Rio Earth Summit in 1992; a non-binding resolution providing a blueprint for the development of local sustainability solutions by governments and non-governmental organisations.

Agro-ecotourism A form of ecotourism that aims to create synergies between nature-based tourism and agriculture.

Alternative tourism The common feature of 'alternative tourism' is the suggestion of an attitude diametrically opposed to what is characteristically viewed as mass tourism. Alternative tourism is often presented as existing in fundamental opposition by attempting to minimize the perceived negative environmental and sociocultural impacts of people at leisure in the promotion of radically different approaches to tourism. Examples include ecotourism, green tourism, nature-oriented tourism, soft tourism, pro-poor tourism and defensive tourism.

Anthropocentric Focuses on the human and the instrumental value of nature, regards humans as the central fact of the universe and therefore interprets everything in terms of humans and their values.

Areas of high conservation value Areas important at a regional or national level for the conservation of native fauna, flora, natural features or systems or sites deemed to be of cultural significance.

Baseline study Assessment of the present situation in order to measure changes in that environment over time.

Best practice Involves seeking excellence, keeping in touch with innovations, avoiding waste and focusing on outcomes that are in the community interest. It involves managing change and continual improvement, and in this way it encompasses all levels of an organization.

Biocentric Focused on living things (different species and genetic variability) as the central point to the development of value systems, as opposed to anthropocentrism, which focuses on the human and the instrumental value of nature. See also **Ecocentric**.

Biodiversity The variety of different species and genetic variability among individuals within each species.

Glossary

Biological diversity The variety of all life forms; the different plants, animals and microorganisms, the genes they contain and the ecosystems they form. It is usually considered at three levels: genetic diversity, species diversity and ecosystem diversity.

Bioregion A territory defined by a combination of biological, social and geographic criteria rather than by geopolitical considerations; generally, a system of related, interconnected ecosystems.

Built environment A reference to buildings, dwellings, structures, utilities, roads and services that enable people to live, work and play, circulate and communicate and fulfil a wide range of functions. The built environment of a place reveals its historical and spatial development, its past and present and something of its social structure and conflicts.

Carbon offset Any trading system designed to offset carbon emissions from one activity (such as burning fossil fuels in manufacturing, driving or flying) with another (such as installing more efficient technologies, planting carbon-reducing plants or establishing contracts with others not to partake in carbon-releasing activities) (Dictionary of Sustainable Management, 2012).

Carrying capacity The level of visitor use an area can accommodate with high levels of satisfaction for visitors and few impacts on resources. Carrying capacity estimates are determined by many factors, such as environmental, social and managerial.

Climate change Refers to significant long-term changes in average weather patterns for a particular region. Changes in climate are effected by myriad factors, including solar radiation, the earth's orbit, ocean currents, tectonic plates and volcanoes. In recent years, the term 'climate change' has been used in conjunction with 'global warming', which scientists now agree is most likely caused by human influences attributed to the increase in CO_2 gases into the atmosphere. See also **Global warming**.

Code of conduct Guidelines for appropriate social, cultural and environmentally responsible behaviour. Codes of conduct are in no way binding on the industry or the individual.

Commodification The production of commodities for exchange via the market, as opposed to direct use by the producer. One form of commodified leisure today can be seen in specific forms of tourism, where travel to distant and different places is marketed as 'paradise gained'. Tourism becomes a 'freely chosen' leisure activity to be consumed.

Community See **Local community**.

Community-based tourism (CBT) CBT is generally considered a privately offered set of hospitality services (and features) extended to visitors by individuals, families or a local community. A key objective of CBT is to establish direct personal and cultural exchange between host and guest in a balanced manner that enables a mutual understanding, solidarity and equality for those involved.

Conservation The protection, maintenance, management, sustainable use, restoration and enhancement of the natural environment (ANZECC Task Force on Biological Diversity, 1993). The management of human use of the biosphere so that it may yield the greatest sustainable benefit to present generations, while maintaining its potential to meet the needs and aspirations of future generations (Australia's Biodiversity Conservation Strategy 2010–2030).

Conservationists People who believe that resources should be used, managed and protected so that they will not be degraded and unnecessarily wasted and will be available to present and future generations. See also **Environmentalists**.

Constant attractions Attributes that are widespread or have an intangible quality about them (e.g., good weather, safety, etc.).

Creative thinking The act of redefining an issue by looking at it from a new perspective.

Decentralization A conscious policy of locating or relocating some parts or the whole of an organization to outlying regions, away from metropolitan areas with concomitant developments of infrastructure, coupled with extensions of existing residential areas or the establishment of new towns. The policy may aim at the strengthening of specified regional administrative centers.

Deep ecology The belief that the earth's resources should be sustained and protected, not just for human beings but also for other species. People who believe in this philosophy tend to have a life-centered approach rather than a human-centered approach to managing and sustaining the earth's resources by working with nature, not wasting resources unnecessarily and not interfering with nonhuman species to meet the needs of humans.

Demarketing The term is used to emphasize that marketing may be used to decrease as well as increase the number of satisfied customers. It is used to decrease numbers so that an increase in clientele satisfaction can be achieved through preserving a higher-quality experience.

Development The modification of the biosphere and the application of human, financial, living and non-living resources to satisfy human needs and improve the quality of human life (World Conservation Strategy). Inevitably, development involves modification of the biosphere, and some aspects of development may detract from the quality of life locally, regionally, nationally or globally.

Ecocentric Focused on the environment as the central point to the development of value systems, as opposed to anthropocentrism, which focuses on the human and the instrumental value of nature. See also **Biocentric**.

Ecologically sustainable development Using, conserving and enhancing the community's resources so that ecological processes, on which life depends, are maintained and the total quality of life, now and in the future, can be increased (Resource and Conservation Assessment Council, ND).

Glossary

Ecologically sustainable tourism An activity that fosters environmental and cultural understanding, appreciation and conservation.

Ecosystem A dynamic complex of plant, animal, fungal and microorganism communities and the associated non-living environment interacting as an ecological unit.

Ecotourism There is no general definition currently in circulation, but any conception of ecotourism must involve travel to relatively undisturbed or uncontaminated natural areas with the objective of studying, admiring and enjoying the natural environment of that area. An ecotourist has the opportunity of immersing themselves in nature in a way that most people cannot enjoy in their routine, urban existences. As there is no strict consensus on a specific definition of ecotourism, it has been suggested that it also involves responsible travel that conserves natural environments and sustains the wellbeing of local people.

Endangered species Fauna and flora likely to become extinct due to direct exploitation by humans, intrusion into highly specialized habitats, threats from other species, interruption of the food chain, pollution or a combination of such factors.

Endemic tourism Broadly defined as tourism that recognizes that each individual locality or community has its special character, and that particular character or identity may well constitute its major attractiveness to tourists.

Environment Defined by Attfield (2003 in Holden, 2008, p. 26) as either one's surroundings, objective systems of nature (e.g., reefs, mountains) or one's perceived surroundings "that lend a sense of belonging and home".

Environmental economics A recognized field of specialization in economic science. Environmental economics examines the costs and benefits of pollution control and protection of the environment.

Environmental education A concept ranging from media coverage of environmental issues to formal environmental education, its aims ranging from raising awareness to formal training.

Environmental impact assessment (EIA) A method of analysis that attempts to predict the likely repercussions of a proposed major development upon the social and physical environment of the surrounding area.

Environmentalists People who are primarily concerned with preventing pollution and degradation of the air, water and soil. See also **Conservationists**.

Ethics What we believe to be right or wrong behaviour.

Ethic of Nature Holds that nonhuman entities are of equal value with the human species. It is broadly intrinsic and ecocentric.

Ethic of Use This is the normative or dominant mode of how human beings relate to nature: nature is viewed predominantly as a set of resources which humanity is free to employ for its own distinct ends. It is an instrumental and anthropocentric view.

Global warming Refers to the increase in temperature of the earth's lower atmosphere and oceans in the twentieth and twenty-first centuries. In recent years, scientists all over the world have noticed a steady and slight increase in temperatures of 0.6 degrees Celsius since 1900. The Intergovernmental Panel on Climate Change indicates that observed increases in globally averaged temperatures since the mid-twentieth century are very likely due to man-made greenhouse gas concentrations. Scientists are predicting that if greenhouse-causing gases are not reduced, then average worldwide temperatures could increase by 5°C by 2100. Increases in global temperatures will cause sea levels to rise and there will be an increase in severe weather events, such as droughts, floods and storms. This will dramatically affect agricultural yields, lead to glacier retreats and species extinction and increase the range of diseases such as malaria (Porteous, 2000). See also **Climate change**.

Greenwashing A term that merges the concepts of green (environmentally sound) and whitewashing (to conceal or gloss over wrongdoing). Greenwashing is any form of marketing or public relations that links a corporate, political, religious or nonprofit organization to a positive association with environmental issues for an unsustainable product, service or practice. In some cases, an organization may truly offer a green product, service or practice. However, through marketing and public relations, one is wrongly led to believe that this green value system is ubiquitous throughout the entire organization.

Infrastructure The buildings or permanent installations associated with a site. Infrastructure for ecotourism is often developed in protected areas and usually involves a scaled-down or minimal approach to physical development and change. Infrastructure such as boardwalks and viewing platforms can be used by resource managers to provide for visitor access to ecotourism destinations, while at the same time assisting the management of environmental impacts and the physical protection of natural resources.

Institutional planning Planning by institutional agencies and public bodies not central to the planning process, yet having significant implications for environmental planning. One of the functions of the central planning agency is to accommodate and coordinate proposals to enable the objectives of other agencies to be reconciled with overall planning objectives.

Integrated planning Planning process which takes into account the social and cultural priorities of host communities to shape tourism into a form appropriate for each locality.

Intergenerational equity Refers to a concept that the present generation should ensure that the health, diversity and productivity of the environment are maintained or enhanced for the benefit of future generations.

Glossary

Internalization of environmental costs Internalization of environmental costs involves the creation of economic environments so that social and private views of economic efficiency coincide. It is concerned with structures, reporting mechanisms and tools to achieve this end.

Interpretation An educational activity which aims to reveal meanings and relationships through the use of original objects, first-hand experience and illustrative media, rather than simply by communicating factual information.

Intrinsic value Value that exists in its own right, for its own sake.

Land-use zoning Land-use zoning divides sections of land into areas based on their sensitivity and conservation values.

Limits of Acceptable Change (LAC) A model used to help establish the maximum 'damage' level for a resource that society is prepared to accept as custodian of resources for both present and future generations and to define the maximum level of use consistent with that damage level.

Local community The concept of local community concerns a particularly constituted set of social relationships based on something that the individuals have in common – usually a common sense of identity (e.g., Marshall, 1994, pp. 73–76).

Management plan The process of the coordination and preparation of a document and the realization of a set of goals within a protected area or local community or organization that leads to some common directions.

Market demand How much of an economic good consumers are willing to buy at a particular price.

Market supply How much of an economic good producers are willing and able to produce and sell at a particular price in a given period.

Mass tourism Mass tourism is generally seen as being an overarching term for tourism that is undertaken by the majority of travellers. Developing as a global phenomenon after the Second World War, mass tourism is often described as being accessible to the growing global middle class. It is a broad tourism form often seen as the antithesis of **alternative tourism**, and is often aligned with high visitor numbers, economic leakage and packaged experiences.

Microsocial Macro- and microsocial are used in the context of sociology. The former generally examines the wider structures, interdependent social institutions, global and historical processes of social life, while the latter is more concerned with action, interaction and the construction of meaning. It is important, however, not to generalize too greatly, as the relationship between social system and social actor is not always clearly distinguished (e.g., Marshall, 1994, p. 298).

Millennium Development Goals An aspirational series of goals for humanity framed by the United Nations after the 2000 Millennium Summit. In 2016, the goals were superseded by the 17 goals articulated under the *2030 Agenda for Sustainable Development*. For further information see www.un.org/millenniumgoals/.

Motivations The factors that determine a human's reasons for doing something; in the context of travel, the reasons for someone to travel to a destination.

Multiple use Principle of managing public land, such as a national forest, so it is used for a variety of purposes, such as timbering, mining, recreation, grazing, wildlife preservation and soil and water conservation.

Natural Existing in or formed by nature; non-urban. Also incorporates cultural aspects.

Performance standards Standards employed in environmental planning that specify desired results and do not in themselves specify the methods by which performance criteria should be met.

Philosophy The system of principles concerning all the conditions in which humans live and that influence their behaviour and development.

Precautionary principle Where there are threats of serious or irreversible environmental damage, lack of full scientific certainty should not be used as a reason for postponing measures to prevent environmental degradation. In the application of the precautionary principle, decisions should be guided by careful evaluation to avoid serious or irreversible damage to the environment and by an assessment of the risk – weighted consequences of various options.

Productivist A conviction that growth and economic productivity is the purpose of human endeavour.

Pro-poor tourism A form of alternative tourism that attempts to reduce poverty by using tourism in poor communities to generate local employment and profits. Pro-poor tourism is not a specific product or sector of tourism, but an approach to the industry. Its strategies aim to unlock opportunities for the poor, whether for economic gain, other livelihood benefits, or participation in decision making (Ashley, Boyd, & Goodwin, 2000).

Protected areas Defined in Article 2 of the International Convention on Biological Diversity as a geographically defined area that is designated or regulated and managed to achieve specific conservation. Protected area system characteristics are adequacy – the ability of the reserve to maintain the ecological viability and integrity of populations, species and communities; comprehensiveness – the degree to which the full range of ecological communities and their biological diversity are incorporated within reserves; and representativeness – the extent to which areas selected for inclusion in the national reserve system are capable of reflecting the known biological diversity and ecological patterns and processes of the ecological community or ecosystem concerned.

Recreation opportunity spectrum (ROS) The basic assumption of ROS is that a quality recreational experience is assured by providing a diverse range of recreational opportunities, catering to various tastes and user group preferences. The ROS

Glossary

focuses on the setting in which recreation occurs. A recreation opportunity setting is the combination of physical, biological, social and managerial conditions that give value to a place. ROS has been described as a framework for presenting carrying capacities and managing recreational impacts. The ROS provides a systematic framework for looking at the actual distribution of opportunities and a procedure for assessing possible management actions.

Social impact assessment (SIA) An assessment of the impact on people and society of major development projects; social impact assessment is often a weak point in environmental impact assessments. Social impacts are defined as those changes in social relations between members of a community, society or institution, resulting from external change.

Stewardship An approach to the care of nature through its dominance by humans relying on predominantly economic value systems and the pre-eminence of technology (backed up by enormous advances in scientific understanding).

Strategic planning A dynamic and issue-oriented process to help an individual or organization to take control of significant and desirable potential futures. Strategic planning is the process of deciding what the future of the operation should be, and what strategies should be followed in order to make that future happen.

Sustainable Able to be carried out without damaging the long-term health and integrity of natural and cultural environments.

Sustainability A contested concept that has been variously framed on the basis of a balance between ecological, economic and social influences on human activity.

Sustainable design Environmentally and culturally sensitive building design, where construction methods and materials have minimal impact on the environment.

Sustainable development Defined by the World Commission on Environment and Development (WCED) in 1987 as "development that meets the needs of the present without compromising the ability of future generations to meet their own needs". Environmental protection and management is central to sustainable development.

Sustainable yield The use of living resources at levels of harvesting and in ways that allow those resources to supply products and services indefinitely.

SWOT analysis SWOT is an assessment of a project or organization's strengths and weaknesses and an analysis of the opportunities and threats that exist in the market place.

Technocentrism A belief system that supports the idea that the creation of new products and processes will be able to improve our chances of survival, our comfort and our quality of life before the depletion or destruction of renewable resources.

Tourism Optimization Management Model (TOMM) This model builds on the LAC system to incorporate a stronger political dimension, and it seeks to monitor and manage tourism in a way that seeks optimum sustainable performance, rather than maximum levels or carrying capacities. TOMM involves identifying strategic imperatives (such as policies and emerging issues); identifying community values, product characteristics, growth patterns, market trends and opportunities; positioning and branding and alternative scenarios for tourism in a region. It also seeks optimum conditions, indicators, acceptable ranges, monitoring techniques, benchmarks, annual performance and predicted performance. Having done this, it can examine poor performance and explore cause/effect relationships.

Tourism industry The collection of all collaborating firms and organizations that perform specific activities directed at satisfying leisure, pleasure and recreational needs.

Tourists All visitors traveling for whatever purpose, involving at least an overnight stay, at a minimum 40 kilometers from their usual place of residence.

User pays The principle that management and maintenance costs for individual products or services should be borne (either partially or fully) by those using them.

Utilitarian A focus on the usefulness of nature in terms of human values rather than in terms of beauty or spirituality; practicality of nature's use by humans for material gain.

Visitor activity management process (VAMP) The visitor activity management process relates to interpretation and visitor services. This framework involves the development of activity profiles that connect activities with the social and demographic characteristics of the participants, the activity setting requirements and trends affecting the activity. The VAMP framework is designed to operate in parallel with the natural resource management process.

Visitor impact management (VIM) The visitor impact management process involves a combination of legislation and policy review and scientific problem identification (both social and natural). The principles of VIM are to identify unacceptable changes occurring as a result of visitor use and to develop management strategies to keep visitor impacts within acceptable levels, while integrating visitor impact management into existing agency planning, design and management processes. It attempts to do this based on the best scientific understanding and situational information available. Both LAC and VIM frameworks rely on indicators and standards as a means of defining impacts deemed unacceptable and place carrying capacities into a broader managerial context. VIM, however, makes reference to planning and policy and includes identifying the probable causes of impacts, whereas LAC places more emphasis on defining opportunity classes.

Volunteer tourism Volunteer tourism emphasizes positive interactions between tourists and local communities based on travellers visiting a destination and taking part in some form of project that makes a positive difference to social, economic and/or environmental conditions. Projects are commonly based on nature, people or the restoration of buildings and artifacts.

Glossary

Wilderness Land that, together with its plant and animal communities, is in a state that has not been substantially modified by, and is remote from the influences of, European settlement; or, land that is capable of being restored to such a state, and is of sufficient size to make its maintenance in such a state feasible. A wilderness area is a large, substantially unmodified natural area (or area that is capable of being restored to such a state). Such areas are managed to protect or enhance this relatively natural state, and also to provide opportunities for self-reliant recreation in a relatively unmodified natural environment.

Zone of opportunity A geographic area that ideally encompasses an endemic core resource as well as particular resources or attractions.

A guide to ecotourism agencies and other sustainable tourism resources

Top 50 ecotourism websites: www.qunar.travel/top-50-ecotourism-websites.html

Best responsible travel and ecotourism websites: www.transitionsabroad.com/list ings/travel/responsible/ecowebsites.shtml

List of ecotourism locations: http://traveltips.usatoday.com/list-ecotourism-locations-16302.html

Centre on Ecotourism and Sustainable Development: www.ecotourismcesd.org

Climate Care: www.climatecare.org

Dictionary of Sustainable Management: www.sustainabilitydictionary.com

Ecotourism Association of Australia (EAA): www.ecotourism.org.au

Ecotourism Laos: www.ecotourismlaos.com

Ethical Escape: www.ethicalescape.com

Friends of the Earth: www.foe.co.uk

Galapagos Conservation Trust: www.gct.org

Global Volunteers Network: www.volunteer.org.nz

Himalayan Trust UK: www.himalayantrust.co.uk

International Centre for Responsible Tourism: www.theinternationalcentrefor responsibletourism.org

International Ecotourism Association (IEA): www.ecotourism.org

International Porter Protection Group: www.ippg.net

Interpretation Australia Association: www.interpretationaustralia.asn.au

International Union for Conservation of Nature (IUCN): www.iucn.org

Journal of Ecotourism and Journal of Sustainable Tourism: http://taylorandfrancis. com/journals/

National Geographic Center for Sustainable Destinations: www.nationalgeographic. com/travel/sustainable

People and Planet: www.peopleandplanet.net

Pro-Poor Tourism: www.propoortourism.org.uk

Sustainable Arctic Tourism: www.arctictourism.net

Sustainable Tourism Net: www.sustainabletourism.net

References

ANZECC Task Force on Biological Diversity. (1993). *Australia's First National Report to the Convention on Biological Diversity*. Retrieved from Canberra: www.environment.gov.au/system/files/resources/35065e5c-46cd-4103-a7dd-4478c456ea87/files/first-national-report.pdf.

Ashley, C., Boyd, C., & Goodwin, H. (2000). Pro-poor tourism: Putting poverty at the heart of the tourism agenda. *Natural Resource Perspectives, 51*(March 2000), 1–6.

Dictionary of Sustainable Management. (2012). *Ecological Marketing*. Retrieved from https://sustainabilitydictionary.com.

Holden, A. (2008). *Environment and Tourism*. London: Routledge.

International Union for Conservation of Nature and Natural Resources. (1980). *World conservation strategy [kit]: Living resource conservation for sustainable development*. Retrieved from Gland, Switzerland: https://portals.iucn.org/library/sites/library/files/documents/WCS-004.pdf.

Marshall, G. (1994). *The Concise Oxford Dictionary of Sociology*. Oxford: Oxford University Press.

Porteous, A. (Ed.) (2000) *Dictionary of Environmental Science and Technology* (3rd ed.). New York: Wiley Blackwell.

Resource and Conservation Assessment Council. (ND). Eden NSW Forest Agreement (pp. 1–131). Sydney: Resource and Conservation Division, Department of Urban Affairs and Planning.

World Commission on Environment and Development. (1987). *Our Common Future*. Oxford: Oxford University Press.

Index

Note: Information in figures is indicated by page numbers in *italics*. Information in tables is indicated by page numbers in **bold**.

Aboriginal Subsistence Whaling 7
accreditation 86–87
advertising 45
aesthetic justification 16
Agenda 21 82
agro-ecotourism 111
alternative tourism 2
Amboseli National Park (Kenya) 51
anthropocentrism 16, 19, 44–45
Antiquities Act (US) 146
appropriate use 50, 53
athletic justification 16
Australia 16, 25, 26–27, 29–33, 34–37, 46, 50, 63, 124–125, 127, 146
Australian Great Barrier Reef 112
authenticity 108, 138
awards for excellence 85

Baker, Gerard 99
Belize 48–49
biodiversity justification 16
biological justification 16
bio-piracy 105
Bower, David 94
brochures 45
buen vivir 109

capitalism: ecotourism as sustainable and situational 4–6; and slow tourism 123; sustainability of 5; tourism as 5
capitalist realism 47–50
Caracas Action Plan 44
carrying capacity 28, 55, 56–57
Carson, Rachel 17
cathedral argument 16
CBET *see* community-based ecotourism (CBET)
certification 86–87, 130
China 128

Chinese view 14
civic environmentalism 7
Cockscomb Basin Wildlife Sanctuary (Belize) 48–49
codes of conduct 85–86
commodification 43–44, 48
community(ies): authenticity and 108; defined 106; development and 107–108; host, challenge for 105–111
community-based ecotourism (CBET) 15, 105, 111–115
competition, positional 112–113
concession 68
conservation 15, 16, 19–20; symbiosis with 82; utilitarianism in 44–45
consumption 1–2
Coolidge, Calvin 98
Cooper, Chris 147
Cousteau, Fabien 152–153
Cuba 111
customer orientation 82

demarketing 125, 128, 130
development 107–108
donations 69

ecocentrism 17, 18; values-based perspective on 18–20
eco-certification 130
ecotourism: community-based 15; defined 137; future of 152–153; paradox of 1–2; philosophical foundations of 14–15; protected areas and 50–53; as situational capitalism 4–6; smart 127–128; as sustainable capitalism 4–6
ecotourism opportunity spectrum (EOS) 58
eco-volunteering 125–126
Ecuador 15

Index

education: curriculum in 148–151; environmental 14; as focus in ecotourism 147; interpretation and 95; natural resource management and 66–68; purpose of 147; role of 95; student gaze in 151

Elaboration Likelihood Model 96

employment 110–111

empowerment 106, 124

environmental education 14

environmentalism, civic 7

environmental movement 17

EOS see ecotourism opportunity spectrum (EOS)

ethic of nature 16

ethic of use 15–16

ethics 14–15

exclusivity 113

expenditures, leakage of 51

expertise 83

5R model **129**, 129–130

Fogg Dam Conservation Reserve 16

future 152–153

Generation X 127

Generation Y 151

geographic information system (GIS) 104

geographies of space 127

geographies of tourism 104

Giddens, Anthony 4

GIS see geographic information system (GIS)

Glacier National Park (US) 114

globalization 43

Gold Coast 124–125

Grand Canyon National Park (United States) 62

Great Barrier Reef 112

greenwashing 86, 130

guidebooks 45

gymnasium argument 16

habitat/species management **47**

Hirsch, Fred 112

Holiday Makers, The (Krippendorf) 123

host communities, challenge for 105–111

Houay Kaeng (Laos) 114–115

Huaorani Ecolodge 15

Hunstein Range (Papua New Guinea) 107

Hutchings, James Mason 137

Iceland 6

indigenous people 106–107

indigenous whaling 7

Indonesia 109

information technology (IT) 108–109

institution, defined 31–32

International Union of the Conservation of Nature (IUCN) 3, 43, 46

interpretation: defined 94; defining endgame of 94–96; marketing and 132; principles 94–95; provocation in 93–94, 95, 96–99; revelation and 94; sustainability and 132

IT see information technology (IT)

IUCN see International Union of the Conservation of Nature (IUCN)

Japan 6

justifications, for preservation and conservation of nature 16

Kakadu National Park (Australia) 146

Kangaroo Island 63

Kenya 51

knowledge: marketing and 124; professionalisation and 83

laboratory argument 16

LAC see limits of acceptable change (LAC)

Lamon, Robert 137

Langford, Nathaniel 97

Laos 109, 114–115

last-chance tourism (LCT) 43, 69, 113–114

laws: quality assurance and 84

LCT see last-chance tourism (LCT)

leakage, of tourist expenditures 51

Lefebvre, Henri 2, 6

Leidig, Charlie 138

licensing 84

limits of acceptable change (LAC) 55, 56, 58, 59–60

MacCannell, Dean 4

Madagascar 107

managed resource protected area **47**

marine tourism 2

marketing: business acumen and 125; defined 125; delivery, tree model of *126*, 126–127; demarketing 125, 128, 130; of ecotourism in tourism marketing tradition 123–129, *126*; environment 124; knowledge and 124; mix 126; and motivations of ecotourists 124–125; nature and 45; niche 125–126; place in 131; price in 130; product in 130; segmentation and 127–128; semiotics and 131; social 128–129; sustainability and 123–124, **129**, 129–132; and tourism management 123–124

mass media 45

mass tourism 15, 33, 54, 94, 106, 124, 152

Mather, Stephen 97
McCarthy, E. Jerome 126
McDonaldisation 105
media 45
Merriman, Tim 97–98
Millennium Development Goals 82
Mission 66 (US National Park Service) 94
monument, natural **47**
motivations, of ecotourists 124–125
Mount Rushmore National Memorial (US) 98–99, 109
Muir, John 97, 137, 138, 139, 140–141, 146
multiple use 43
Myanmar 26

nationalism 98–99
national parks 46, **47**, 94, 96–99, 109
National Parks and Wildlife Act (Australia) 50
Native Americans 98–99, 109, 114
natural monument **47**
natural reserve, strict **47**
natural resource management 45–46; carrying capacity and 56–57; education and 66–68; limits of acceptable change and 59–60; recreation opportunity spectrum and 57–58; tourism optimization management model and 61–62; trail system design and 65–66; use limitation and 62–65; user fees and 68–69; visitor activity management process and 60–61; visitor impact management and 60; zoning in 65; *see also* user fees
nature, ethic of 16
neoliberalism 2, 43–44
Nepal 51
nonrepresentational geographies of space 127
Norway 6

ocean tourism 2
orientation, customer 82
Osborn, Henry 140
Osmond, Margy 128
overtourism 43, 44, 57

paideia 147
Papua New Guinea 107
paradox, of ecotourism 1–2
Pardee, George C. 138
philosophical foundations 14–15
Pinkley, Frank 97
place 4, 6, 104–105, 131
planning, enactment of policy through 33–37
policy: defined 27; enactment of, through planning 33–37; making process *28*, 28–29

politics 25
positional competition 112–113
positivism 4–5, 83
price, in marketing 130
product, in marketing 130
Production of Space, The (Lefebvre) 3
professional, as term 82–83
professional body 83
professionalisation 82–84
promotion, in marketing 131
pro-poor tourism 14, 110
protected areas 43–45; appropriate use dilemma with 50, 53; capitalist realism and 47–50; categories of 46, **47**; defined 46; ecotourism and 50–53; function and purpose of 45; recreation and 46; sustainable management techniques with 53–56; *see also* natural resource management
protected landscape **47**
provocation: in interpretation 93–94, 96–99

quality assurance: accreditation in 86–87; awards in 85; certification in 86–87; codes of conduct in 85–86; instruments 84–87; legislation and 84; measures 84–87
Quebec Declaration on Ecotourism 26

realism: capitalist 47–50; in sustainable tourism marketing **129**
recreation opportunity spectrum (ROS) 55, 56, 57–58
redistribution 64
regionalism, in sustainable tourism marketing **129**
relationships, in sustainable tourism marketing **129**
research, in sustainable tourism marketing **129**
responsibility, in sustainable tourism marketing **129**
revelation: interpretation and 94
Roosevelt, Theodore 137–141, 146
ROS *see* recreation opportunity spectrum (ROS)
Royal Botanic Gardens (Sydney, Australia) 25, 29–33, 34–37, 128
Royal National Park (Australia) 46
royalties 69
Rushmore, Charles E. 109

sales 69
Schweinsberg, Stephen 8
scientific justification 16
security 81
See America First campaign 114

Index

semiotics 131
Sierra Club 94
Silent Spring (Carson) 17
silo argument 16
Sioux Native American Tribe 98–99, 109
situational capitalism 4–6
Skomer Island (Wales) 62
slow tourism 123
smart ecotourism 127–128
social elements 14–15
Social Limits to Growth (Hirsch) 112
social marketing 128–129
Solow, Robert 18
Southern New Hampshire University 149
space 3, 127
spiritual justification 16
stakeholder groups 31
stakeholder networks 3
standards 84
strict natural reserve **47**
student gaze 151
sustainability: business acumen and 125;
   of capitalism 5; interpretation and 132;
   marketing and 123–124, **129**, 129–132;
   philosophical foundations of 14–15; protected
   areas and 53–56; UN consensus resolution on
   122; values and 8; values-based perspective
   on 18–20; as wicked problem 18
Sustainable Tourism on a Finite Planet:
   Environmental, Business and Policy Solutions
   (Wood) 147

Tanzania 51
Tasmania 26–27
taxation 69
technology 108–109
Terai Arc Landscape 51
Theory of Planned Behaviour 96
Tilden, Freeman 94
time space compression 104–105
TOMM *see* tourism optimization management
   model (TOMM)
tour guides 83–84
tourism optimization management model
   (TOMM) 56, 61–62, 63
Tourist, The: A New Theory of the Leisure Class
   (MacCannell) 4

tourist expenditures, leakage of 51
Tourist Gaze, The (Urry and Larsen) 111–112
Tower, John 126
trail system design 65–66
training: professionalism and 82
tree model of marketing delivery *126*, 126–127
trust 81
Tuan, Yi-Fu 4–5

Uluru 127
use, ethic of 15–16
use limitation 62–65
user fees 68–69
US National Park Service 94, 96–99, 109
utilitarianism 7, 16–18, 44–46, 49, 146

values: exchanging 15–18; sustainability and 8
values-based perspective 18–20
VAMP *see* visitor activity management process
   (VAMP)
Venezuela 44
VIM *see* visitor impact management (VIM)
visitor activity management process (VAMP) 55,
   56, 60–61
visitor impact management (VIM) 55, 56, 60
volunteer tourism 104, 124, 125–126

Wales 62
WCED *see* World Commission on Environment
   and Development (WCED)
Wearing, Stephen 7, 8
Western view 14
whale tourism 6–8
whale watching 3–4
whaling 6–7
Wheeler, Benjamin Ide 138
wilderness area **47**
World Commission on Environment and
   Development (WCED) 25, 26
world heritage areas 27

Yellowstone National Park (US) 97, 114
Yosemite National Park (US) 97, 137–140, 146

zoning 28, 35, 36–37, 65